LOYALTY ON THE FRONTIER

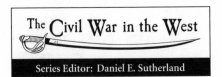

The Civil War in the West

Series Editor: Daniel E. Sutherland

LOYALTY ON THE FRONTIER

OR

SKETCHES OF UNION MEN
OF THE
SOUTH-WEST

WITH INCIDENTS AND ADVENTURES IN
REBELLION ON THE BORDER

BY A. W. BISHOP
LIEUTENANT COLONEL, FIRST CAVALRY VOLUNTEERS

Edited by Kim Allen Scott

The University of Arkansas Press
Fayetteville
2003

07   06   05   04   03   5   4   3   2   1

Designed by Ellen Beeler

⊛ THE PAPER USED IN THIS PUBLICATION MEETS THE MINIMUM REQUIREMENTS
OF THE AMERICAN NATIONAL STANDARD FOR PERMANENCE OF PAPER FOR
PRINTED LIBRARY MATERIALS Z39.48-1984.

Library of Congress Cataloging-in-Publication Data

Bishop, Albert Webb.
  Loyalty on the frontier; or, Sketches of Union men of the South-west :
  with incidents and adventures in rebellion on the border / by A.W.
  Bishop ; edited by Kim Allen Scott.
    p. cm. — (Civil War in the West)
  Originally published: St. Louis : R. P. Studley and Co., 1863.
  Includes bibliographical references (p.) and index.
    ISBN 1-55728-757-0 (cloth : alk. paper)
    1. Arkansas—History—Civil War, 1861–1865. 2. Bishop, Albert Webb.
  3. United States. Army. Arkansas Cavalry Regiment, 1st (1862–1865)
  4. Unionists (United States Civil War)—Arkansas—Biography. 5. Guerrillas
  —Arkansas—Biography. 6. Arkansas—Biography. 7. Arkansas—History
  —Civil War, 1861–1865—Personal narratives. 8. Arkansas—History—
  Civil War, 1861–1865—Underground movements. 9. United States—
  History—Civil War, 1861–1865—Personal narratives. 10. United States
  —History—Civil War, 1861–1865—Underground movements. I. Title:
  Loyalty on the frontier. II. Title: Sketches of Union men of the South-west.
  III. Scott, Kim Allen, 1954– IV. Title. V. Series.
  E496 .B61 2003
  973.7'467'0922—dc22

                                                            2003018577

Contents

LOYALTY ON THE FRONTIER; OR, SKETCHES OF
UNION MEN OF THE SOUTH-WEST WITH INCIDENTS
AND ADVENTURES IN REBELLION ON THE BORDER

Series Editor's Preface

The Civil War in the West has a single goal: To promote historical writing about the war in the western states and territories. It focuses most particularly on the Trans-Mississippi theater, which consisted of Missouri, Arkansas, Texas, most of Louisiana (west of the Mississippi River), Indian Territory (modern-day Oklahoma), and Arizona Territory (two-fifths of modern-day Arizona and New Mexico), but it also encompasses adjacent states, such as Kansas, Tennessee, and Mississippi, that directly influenced the Trans-Mississippi war. It is a wide swath, to be sure, but one too often ignored by historians and, consequently, too little understood and appreciated.

Topically, the series embraces all aspects of the wartime story. Military history in its many guises, from the strategies of generals to the daily lives of common soldiers, forms an important part of that story, but so too do the numerous and complex political, economic, social, and diplomatic dimensions of the war. The series also provides a variety of perspectives on these topics. Most importantly, it offers the best in modern scholarship, with thoughtful, challenging monographs. Secondly, it presents new editions of important books that have gone out of print. And thirdly, it premieres expertly edited correspondence, diaries, reminiscences, and other writings by witnesses to the war.

It is a formidable undertaking, but the hope is that The Civil War in the West, by focusing on some of the least familiar dimensions of the conflict, will significantly broaden our understanding of that dramatic story.

At the time Albert W. Bishop wrote *Loyalty of the Frontier*, between November 1862 and July 1863, he was the lieutenant colonel of the First Arkansas Cavalry (U.S.). His regiment had been posted at Fayetteville with orders to maintain Union control of northwest Arkansas. Bishop not only fulfilled his military mission but also became acquainted with the history of the war in that region. From his perspective, it was a heroic tale about the triumph of Unionism in a Confederate state and a story, he believed, that could elicit sympathy for the South's Unionists and inspire patriotic citizens everywhere. Bishop's book became one of the earliest eyewitness accounts of the plight of Southern Unionists on the Trans-Mississippi "frontier." At the same time, it describes the activities of Bishop's regiment, his tenure as provost marshal in Fayetteville, and the course of the war in Arkansas up to the summer of 1863.

Published originally in 1863, *Loyalty on the Frontier* provides a perspective on the war that remained largely obscure until recent years. As historians become increasingly aware of the fissures in Confederate society, they gain a better understanding of those Southerners who resisted secession and the Confederate government. In no part of the western Confederacy was such resistance more apparent than in northwest Arkansas. William Baxter's *Pea Ridge and Prairie Grove,* issued as part of this series in 2000, relates part of the Unionist story; by expanding on the Unionist theme, Bishop's book serves as an ideal compliment to Baxter.

The innate value of this classic and increasingly rare work has been enhanced by the skillful editorial work of Kim Allen Scott. A special collections librarian and history instructor at Montana State University, Scott has published widely on the Civil War in Arkansas. His insightful introduction to this first modern edition of Bishop's book contains a biographical sketch of Bishop, an evaluation of his work, and commentary on the place of his narrative in the broader context of the war. Additionally, Scott's reference notes identify people and explain events not fully described by the author, and he has prepared a detailed index, which the original edition lacks. Taken together, Bishop and Scott have provided a valuable research tool and an important perspective on a little-known, yet extremely revealing, corner of the war.

Daniel E. Sutherland
Series Editor

Acknowledgments

The editing of a text like *Loyalty on the Frontier* is, for the most part, a lonesome task while sitting at the word processor, but the gathering of information preceding that solitary work is full of enjoyable inter-action with helpful people in various libraries and archives across the country. Without their generous assistance, many details of Albert Bishop's life would have remained uncovered. I would specifically like to thank Patricia Virgil and Linda M. Kennedy of the Buffalo and Erie County Historical Society Library; Jake Schuhle, archivist for the State University of New York College at Cortland; Mary Ann Kane, the director of the Cortland County Historical Society; Andrea Cantrell, Anne Prichard, and Ethel Simpson of the Special Collections Division of the University of Arkansas Libraries, Fayetteville; and the staffs at the Richard C. Butler Center for Arkansas Studies at Little Rock, the Arkansas History Commission in Little Rock, and the Searcy County Library in Marshall, Arkansas.

I would especially like to thank Daniel Sutherland, who suggested I undertake this project, and my friend Paul Dolle of Rogers, Arkansas, for his generous sharing of research material he has collected on Albert Webb Bishop. Finally, I would like to thank my wife, Jayne, whose love and encouragement has sustained me through so many projects over the years. I could not have done it without her.

Editor's Introduction

Published first-person reminiscences of life in Civil War Arkansas are probably much like those written by participants in other southern states. The agony of the battlefield, the sufferings of the innocents, and the incredible devastation brought by the conflict has been told from the vantage point of soldiers and civilians from every state in the Confederacy, and the pathos of their commonality with those from Arkansas is easily recognized. While some historians have argued there is a difference between those works that saw print while the war raged and those that appeared years afterward, other researchers have stressed the difference between published works and the more visceral expressions found in diaries and private letters.1 This is certainly true for Arkansas war reports. Unlike those sent to individuals, letters obviously composed for distribution that appeared in the *Arkansas Gazette* and other newspapers generally have some sort of axe to grind, either a commendation of comrades for heroic deeds, a condemnation of leaders for their shortcomings, or a damnation of enemies whose vileness caused the war in the first place. The books that came from the field, lengthy treatises that are candid in their arguments of exactly who was to blame for the awful events that were presently unfolding, share the same characteristics of the published letters. Despite the obvious political slant of these works, there is an overwhelming honesty of feeling in these immediate voices from the past.

When one considers these voices in the context of the actual type of warfare that visited Arkansas in 1861–65, what strikes the modern reader is a disturbing similarity to the upheavals displayed by the mass media at the opening of the twenty-first century. Indeed, those stories that include the exploits of guerrillas and partisan fighters in Arkansas, Missouri, and Kansas during the Civil War are only made all the more powerful when one considers the perpetrators of this terror were, for the most part, of the same ethnic and racial groups as their victims. The savagery of Osama bin Laden's vendetta against the United States can be partially explained by the cultural divide between the Middle East and the West, but any rationalization of the intensity of terrorism fails when one considers the bombing of the Oklahoma City federal building by Timothy McVeigh; the sack of Lawrence, Kansas, by William Quantrell; or even the butchering of settlers along Pottawattomie Creek by John Brown.

In his personal version of Arkansas's struggle, Albert Webb Bishop had both the time and the inclination to indulge his views on the cause, the meaning, and the consequences of the Civil War even while the outcome was still by no means certain. Writing in the winter of 1862 and spring of 1863 while primarily assigned to desk duty, Bishop carefully described only three classes of people in northwest Arkansas: heroes, villains, and victims. He confronted daily the scourge of guerrilla warfare, either through the stories related to him by eyewitnesses or by occasional direct observation, and he wrote with an honest, unrelenting passion to cast the blame for it all. Bishop's background as an attorney made him an especially articulate spokesman for this last task, making his story as much a legal treatise on Arkansas's journey to secession as it is a series of adventure stories regarding those caught up in the maelstrom of warfare.

Born on January 8, 1832, in Alden, New York, Albert Webb Bishop was the second of six children born to Calvin and Emily Webb Bishop. Calvin, a grocery wholesaler, moved his family to Buffalo in 1844, became a successful merchant, and provided a comfortable living for his family, taking part in local politics as time allowed and serving briefly as an alderman of the Third Ward for his adopted city. Tragedy struck the Bishop household in 1846 when Albert's older brother, Henry Bryant Bishop, died in a fire that destroyed the warehouse of Walbridge and Company on Buffalo's Main Street. Shortly afterward, the Bishops sent Albert away to school, first to the Cortlandville Academy near Calvin's hometown of Homer, New York, and finally to Yale University, where Albert graduated in 1853.

Instead of returning to Buffalo, Bishop began the study of law with his uncle, Horatio Ballard, in Cortland. At that time a vacancy occurred in the principal's position at the Cortlandville Academy, and the directors of the school offered Bishop the job. Even though he amply demonstrated a talent for school administration, Bishop found the study of law much more attractive than the profession of a teacher, and he resigned after one year. In 1856 he moved to back to Buffalo but returned to Cortland for an important matter the next year. Bishop married Maria L. Woodward of Cortland on September 15,

1857, and the couple established their home in Buffalo while he worked in turn for the firms of Wadsworth and Cameron, Bowen and Rodgers, an office that later would employ another young lawyer, Grover Cleveland. While establishing his career as a promising attorney, Bishop also gained a reputation as an energetic citizen, even finding time to play on the local baseball team.

In 1858 he formed a partnership with Augustus B. Fitch and, like his father Calvin had done, became heavily involved in politics. The new Republican Party had made great progress in New York State, and Bishop enthusiastically embraced the movement, eventually becoming the president of both the Young Men's Republican Club and the "Wide Awakes," a fraternal order of men dedicated to advancing the candidacy of Abraham Lincoln. On January 3, 1860, Bishop's personal life seemed to ascend as rapidly as his professional career when his wife gave birth to a daughter, Maria, who they nicknamed "Mina."

Again tragedy struck Bishop's life, for just a few days after Mina's birth, Maria died, leaving him with an infant to care for and a restlessness that would drive him from his hometown. An opportunity came that summer to give a speech for the Republican Party in Wisconsin, and after an initial visit, Bishop decided to relocate to La Crosse, taking along his widowed mother to care for Mina. On the night of July 28, 1860, the Buffalo Young Men's Republican Club and "Wide Awakes" formed a torchlight parade to march him to the train station, presenting him with a formal resolution thanking Bishop for his "uniform courtesy, the dignity of his bearing, the promptness and intelligence of his rulings, and the energy and efficiency in which he discharged the several duties devolved on him in both organizations."[2]

In La Crosse, Bishop campaigned hard for Lincoln, worked for a local law firm, and enlisted in a militia artillery battery that had been formed in anticipation of the coming strife with the Southern states. After the election of Abraham Lincoln and the outbreak of war, this unit was formally inducted into the state's volunteer forces as the First Independent Battery, Wisconsin Light Artillery, and Bishop received a commission as a second lieutenant on September 3, 1861. At this time he sent his widowed mother and his daughter back to Cortland, New York, where they lived with Mrs. Bishop's sister, Olive Webb Edgecomb. As a result, Mina was brought up without ever really knowing her father and would always consider her Cortland relatives as her immediate family.[3]

A little over a month later, shortly after the battery moved to Camp Utley at Racine, Wisconsin, Bishop resigned his commission to accept the captaincy of Company B, Second Wisconsin Volunteer Cavalry, then in training at Milwaukee. The first assignment of the Second Wisconsin was to Benton Barracks, St. Louis, until May 15, 1862; then to Jefferson City; and finally to Springfield, Missouri, where they garrisoned the town until mid-June.

Although Bishop had seen no combat during his first nine months in uniform, he quickly learned about the dirty side of war that summer through stories from Unionist refugees who gathered in Springfield. Many Arkansas citizens who had remained loyal to the Union had fled north when conditions at home became intolerable under Confederate rule. Tales of forced conscription, house burnings, torture, and murder at the hands of the irregular troops who infested the Ozark Mountain region came to Bishop from every knot of men, women, and children who staggered into the safety of the Union lines. Many of the men, able-bodied and invalid alike, burned with a desire for revenge against their tormentors and asked to join the Federal army—so many, in fact, that one of Bishop's colleagues, M. LaRue Harrison, came up with a plan to form them into a unique regiment quite separate from those presently serving in the District of Southwest Missouri.

Harrison was born in 1829 and, like Bishop, a native New Yorker. He obtained a college education in Michigan and in 1855 became a civil engineer working with the Chicago, Burlington, and Quincy Railroad. When the war broke out, he enlisted in the Thirty-Sixth Illinois Infantry and was promoted to captain on July 10, 1862. While working on the defenses of Springfield, Missouri, that summer, he saw the opportunity to advance in rank by organizing Arkansas refugees and successfully convinced his superiors to authorize the formation of an Arkansas cavalry regiment and to make himself its colonel.[4]

The First Arkansas Cavalry (U.S.) was formally mustered in at Springfield on August 7, 1862. Initially attached to the District of Southwest Missouri, in October 1862 the regiment was assigned to the Army of the Frontier until December, when the Confederates tried to retake the northwest corner of Arkansas during the Prairie Grove campagin. But the First Arkansas never really fought together as a unit, never trained as a unit, and to use Bishop's own words, was "ordered first by one general and then another—the innocent shuttlecock between distant battledoors"—before its true utility became apparent. The loyal mountaineers from Arkansas found their purpose in counterinsurgency warfare, and by using the First Arkansas as scouts and guerrilla hunters, Union commanders found an effective weapon against the Rebels.

Bishop's role in the regiment during his first year's service was primarily as an executive officer, while the scattered companies of the First Arkansas moved about the region ferreting out guerrilla camps and performing scouting patrols. His duties expanded when the army assigned him to be a provost marshal, requiring him to act as judge and jury for those civilians arriving at his post who wished to prove their loyalty or renounce their former Southern allegiances. While engaged in these activities at Elk Horn Tavern, Arkansas, site of the March 1862 battle, Bishop found ample time to write and began to record some of the anecdotes he heard from the people who had come within Union lines, many of whom enlisted in the new regiment. Here too Bishop had the time to make the acquaintance of Isaac Murphy, the Arkansas Secession Convention delegate from Madison County who refused to give that body a unanimous vote to join the Confederacy. From Murphy, Bishop learned much about the political forces that had led Arkansas to war, and he found ample cause to place partial blame for the state's defection on Judge David Walker, a prominent Fayetteville attorney who, as president of the convention, had initially tried to keep the state from seceding only to later bow to the pressure of those who wanted a different outcome.

Following the battle of Prairie Grove on December 7, 1862, the First Arkansas Cavalry moved its base to nearby Fayetteville, where they remained for the first four months of 1863. While there, Bishop saw his first fight of the war when a Rebel force under the command of Brig. Gen. William L. Cabell attacked the town on the morning of April 18, 1863. Bishop acquitted himself well under fire, earning special praise from Colonel Harrison for his bravery while leading the left wing of the defending forces. When the Union army abandoned Fayetteville a few days later, Bishop, along with his disenchanted comrades, accompanied hundreds of refugees north to the relative safety of Springfield. He bitterly resented the order to evacuate Arkansas and wrote passionately of the "imbecility" of the decision.

At this point in his career, Bishop was again put on detached service as the chief inspector for the cavalry of the District of Southwest Missouri, and while in St. Louis on that duty, he finished his manuscript,

Loyalty on the Frontier, and submitted it for publication by the R. P. Studley firm. In January 1864 he again rejoined his regiment, which had returned to Fayetteville, and began a period of active campaigning, personally leading scouting patrols until a childhood injury to his groin made riding an agonizing torture. Fortunately, he received a temporary respite on March 25, 1864, when ordered to command the Union garrison at Fort Smith, Arkansas, but he then became so sick with chronic diarrhea that he was forced to go to Little Rock to seek treatment in June.[5]

In the long run, the medical removal to Little Rock proved fortunate for Bishop because he was able to visit with his old friend Isaac Murphy, who had been elected as governor of the Unionist government for Arkansas. Murphy had been charged by the Lincoln administration to enforce the state's civil authority, but his administration was entirely dependent on the fickle cooperation of Maj. Gen. Frederick Steele, the commander of military forces in Arkansas. In Bishop, Murphy recognized a valuable ally, and he offered the colonel the position of state adjutant general. Bishop assumed his new duties at Little Rock on October 1, 1864. His official resignation from the First Arkansas Cavalry was approved in the following spring.[6]

Bishop's charge as adjutant general of Arkansas included the creation of militia units to help protect the loyal civilians of northwestern Arkansas. Part of this effort resulted in the creation of post colonies, essentially fortified communal farms where refugees could eke out a precarious living while guarding against raids by bushwhackers. When peace finally came in April 1865, Bishop still had the responsibility for administering the military forces necessary to pacify the countryside.

Always a gifted orator, Bishop spent as much time on promoting the presidential reconstruction plan to the people of Arkansas as he did on administrative duties. He had harangued the citizens of Fayetteville in February 1863, when the Union army needed loyal Arkansas men, and he returned to the town to deliver a Fourth of July speech in 1865 to affirm the exclusive right of those victorious volunteers to rule the state.[7] "The loyal people of a rebellious state, be their number great or small, are the appropriate custodians of political power," he argued:

> *They are the state,* and around them should gather the elements
> of social and material growth, as one by one they spring up from
> the battlefields and crop out of confusion. Nor should these

states be retained in a condition of pupilage until their old citizens, who followed the false fires of secession, shall return and submit to the new order of things. The sacrifices, the constancy, the heroism of the Union men of the south are entitled to encouragement not only, but reward. They are the germ of a new development, a new power, and one which to grow well must grow by accretion.[8]

In the spring of 1865, Governor Murphy managed to get the Arkansas legislature to pass the Thirteenth Amendment to the U.S. Constitution, which prohibited slavery, as required by the presidential plan for recognizing the civil government of former Confederate states, but the next year, when Arkansas voters replaced the Unionists in the legislature with former secessionists, they rejected the Fourteenth Amendment guaranteeing equal rights for all citizens. Murphy, Bishop, and other Republican members of the executive branch stood by helplessly as the Conservative-controlled legislature went on to pass a series of restrictive black codes and allocated state money for pensions to be paid to ex-Confederate soldiers. Bishop became particularly irritated when the Conservatives refused to print, at public expense, his official report detailing the volunteer forces from Arkansas that had served the Union. "This newly created legislature proceeded without delay to endeavor to embarrass what was left of the government of the Union men of the State," he fumed in an essay he published twenty-eight years later. "To this report the legislature paid no attention except to shelve it, but to the writer, the case was different. In the Senate, on the first day of the session, and directly after the opening prayer, a bill was introduced to repeal the law that gave him the pay of his grade, and to reduce his compensation to $200 a year." Although the bill did not pass, Bishop knew the report would never see print in Arkansas and so took his manuscript directly to Washington, D.C., where the Radical Republican–controlled Senate ordered, by a unanimous vote, its publication by the Government Printing Office.[9]

Congress reacted angrily to the reluctance of all former Confederate states to enfranchise freedmen within their jurisdiction and passed the Reconstruction Act of 1867, which effectively abolished the legislature in Arkansas and put the state temporarily under direct military rule. With a disciplined force of regular soldiers now occupying the state, Bishop resigned his position as adjutant general on July 1, 1867, and obtained an appointment as register in bankruptcy for the Second Congressional District of Arkansas. He found plenty of work, considering the wretched state of Arkansas's postwar economy, and surprisingly enough, he formed a partnership with Freeman W. Compton, a former Confederate supreme-court justice, for the private practice of law. Compton had been ousted from the newly established Arkansas Supreme Court by the military authorities in 1868. He also had a daughter, Kate, who Bishop began courting. On June 19, 1871, the couple was married in Little Rock at a Presbyterian ceremony officiated by the Reverend Thomas R. Welch.[10]

The Reconstruction Act of 1867 enforced the "iron-clad" oath on the Arkansas electorate, a requirement that disfranchised most ex-Confederates and allowed for massive registration of freedmen to swell the ranks of loyal Republican voters. The result of this jockeying for voting rights allowed the Radical Republicans to dominate the legislature again, draft a new constitution, and elect Powell Clayton, a former Kansas cavalry officer, as governor in 1868. But Bishop stayed out of public office as he quietly profited from the patronage of the Clayton administration and prospered from his bankruptcy work. What active role he did play in state politics came when the legislature authorized the establishment of the Arkansas Industrial University and Bishop accepted an appointment as treasurer of the board of trustees. A beautiful hillside in Fayetteville became the site of the new campus, and in June 1872 Bishop returned to the town where he had seen his first combat to deliver the commencement oration. Black voters had become very important to the Republican Party, and unlike Bishop's 1863 assertion of the "absurd notion of negro equality," he now boasted that the question of race had been settled at the new school and that "all are privileged to attend, and with equal facilities to struggle after that preeminence, which is the reward alone of industry and capacity." In reality, though, the only black man with the determination to attend the school had been forced to stay in an outbuilding near campus and individually instructed there during off hours by Noah P. Gates, the institution's president, who wished to avoid controversy.[11]

Bishop continued to take an active role on the board of trustees and in 1873 was sent to Yale and other schools in the East to recruit a new president to replace Gates. Successful in soliciting the president of the Iowa State Agricultural College, A. S. Welch, to come to Fayetteville, Bishop returned to Arkansas and resumed his practice in Little Rock. But after Welch made a brief visit to deliver the commencement speech in June, he wrote to the board refusing the position, and the trustees then offered the position to Bishop himself. As staunch Republican, Union army veteran, and Yale graduate, he seemed the logical choice for the job. On July 11, 1874, Bishop was duly inaugurated in Fayetteville with full ceremony. His speech was reported to be "an eloquent, dignified, scholarly effort. Gen. Bishop is alive to the subject of education, full of energy, and will fill the office of president of the Arkansas Industrial University with credit."[12]

But that credit proved difficult to demonstrate. Bishop spent little time actively administering the school, allowing Professor Gates to handle the day-to-day matters while the general made frequent trips to Little Rock. He would have preferred to actively tour and speak of the glorious future for higher education in Arkansas, but Bishop knew the realities of the state's economy would make a mockery of such efforts. When the voters elected Augustus H. Garland as the first Democratic governor since the war and Democrats once more dominated the legislature, Bishop saw his moral and financial support evaporate. His salary was reduced from $4,000 a year to $2,700, and he became discouraged and bitter. When a relatively harmless letter appeared in an obscure Iowa religious monthly suggesting a faculty member at the university had been released because he was a Union man, Bishop replied stridently with a letter he titled "A Slanderer" in which he proudly pointed to his own northern birth and service to the Union. More trouble came the next month when the Democratically controlled legislature focused unwelcome attention on Bishop's handling of a student disciplinary matter. Some boys at the college had committed acts of vandalism during the fall term, and when President Bishop interrogated one of the suspects, he refused to identify his guilty classmates. Bishop promptly expelled the boy, but the president had not reckoned on the student's political connections. So much agitation resulted from the dismissal of Walter S. Amis that the legislature passed a joint resolution to impanel an investigation committee.[13]

One apocryphal story concerning Bishop's tenure as president helps explain the reasons behind his severity in punishing Amis. Apparently some students out after curfew removed a few planks from a footbridge leading into town, and when Bishop attempted to pursue them, he fell through the hole into the stream below. If this incident were true, it is no wonder he found Amis's refusal to inform on his classmates such an outrage. Bishop eventually found the presidency such a burden that he resigned on June 17, 1875. His closing remarks to the students accused some as being "types of a class who, since school rooms were known, . . . have apparently lived but to personify annoyance and illustrate original sin."[14]

But Bishop had yet to leave the public arena of Arkansas. The Democrats may have taken control of the statehouse and governor's mansion, but Bishop felt his high-profile exposure as the AIU president could catapult him into an even higher office. Ever since the bitter split in the Republican Party over the 1874 dispute between Joseph Brooks and Elisha Baxter for the governor's office, the Democratic Party had dominated Arkansas politics by electing candidates who became known as "Redeemers." The Redeemers, many of whom were recently refranchised ex-Confederates, took advantage of the Republican factionalism by courting the black vote and pointing out the seemingly endless corruption of the GOP during their hold on the state.

Under Bishop's leadership, a section of the Republican Party staged their own nomination convention, calling themselves the "New Dealers." This action predictably angered "Regular" Republicans, and after the New Dealers nominated Bishop for governor and W. L. Copeland, "a prominent member of the colored race," for secretary of state, the Regulars held another convention in August and nominated Joseph Brooks as their gubernatorial candidate. For a time it appeared there would be a three-way race for the governor's office: Bishop and Brooks squaring off against William R. Miller, the Democratic candidate. But cooler heads in the party leadership prevailed, and with some deal making, which included replacing Copeland with John H. Johnson, the Regulars agreed to unite with the New Dealers, and Brooks went back to his old job of managing the Little Rock Post Office.[15]

The campaign during the late summer of 1876 proved particularly hard for Bishop, for scandals in the administration of Pres. Ulysses S. Grant kept reminding Arkansas voters of the excesses of Republican rule in their state. When Bishop tried to give a speech at Conway, his usual oratorical skill failed, and he appeared defensive to the crowd as he delivered an address "mainly devoted to apologies for the sins of his party and insisting he should not be held responsible for them." According to the newspaper correspondent who heard the Democratic rebuttal, Bishop got "the most complete skinning ever received by man," and he claimed that the next morning the general looked like a wet chicken.[16]

Things went no better for Bishop in his other campaign appearances. John H. Johnson proved to be a horrible stump speaker, and when he shared the podium with Bishop, their efforts seemed all the more pandering to black voters. William R. Miller proved particularly adept at linking "Grant and his party of criminals" to Bishop's candidacy. Particularly damning were the figures Miller could recite that showed the state's public debt almost doubled during the period 1868–72, the first four years of Radical Republican rule. Bishop would bitterly denounce the charges, but he found disputing them a hard sell to most crowds. To no one's great surprise, Miller throughly trounced Bishop on election day, and the general returned to his private law practice. Although he stayed active in the Republican Party, he never again sought office, and his last recorded public address in Arkansas consisted of a literary review for the Little Rock Young Men's Christian Association.[17]

Bishop fell on hard times after the election of 1876 and, finding he simply could not make a living in Little Rock anymore, returned to Buffalo at the end of 1879. On his way back to his hometown, Bishop stopped in Washington, D.C., and with some bitterness reflected on his seventeen years in Arkansas to a reporter from the *National Republican.* Intemperately he suggested that he had been "literally starved out" of Arkansas and that Republicans had routinely been defrauded at the ballot box, and the newspaper presented his complaints as editorial fact. In reporting the interview, the *Arkansas Gazette* savagely attacked Bishop, claiming that his ill-fated bid for governor had

> wrecked the last remains of his fortune; he then went into the practice of law, and not being able to successfully compete with the older and better lawyers with whom he was brought into contact, simply failed. . . . Being cut off from political preferment, and not being able to make a living at the practice of law, he determined, as a last resort, to leave the state and as a device for covering and hiding his own faults and the real cause of his failures and disasters, he meanly and ungratefully saddles them upon the alleged persecutions of a people whom he has no cause to remember otherwise than kindly.[18]

Bishop replied to the blistering editorial from Buffalo, denying to have said he had been ostracized in Arkansas but admitting he had complained that "a republican in the south lives at a disadvantage, which for years he cannot expect to see overcome."[19]

The strain on Bishop's married life can only be imagined, but certainly his wife Kate, "intimately connected with some of the best and oldest families, and a recognized belle," could not have been pleased with the editorial flogging of her husband, especially when the *Arkansas Gazette* added, "in making this charge Gen. Bishop insults his own family and puts a stigma upon his own household." It is not clear if Kate went with her husband to Buffalo or if she remained behind in Little Rock, but on May 3, 1886, the chancery court of Pulaski County, Arkansas, granted her a decree of divorce.[20] Bishop did his best to obscure the failure of his second marriage, and his success can be gauged by the fact that not a single obituary of the general appearing in the several Buffalo newspapers after his death even hints at Kate's existence.

Bishop's final years in New York were spent in the practice of law with no remarkable degree of success. He never recouped any of the money he had made in Arkansas, and by 1890 he was reduced to living as a border in a Buffalo rooming house. His daughter, Mina, lived with him for a time, but her teaching career took her back to Cortland, where she became a professor at the Cortland Normal School and eventually head of the School of Practice. Bishop remained alone, quitting the practice of law in 1891 when he became deaf and trying desperately to get a pension for his service-related disabilities.[21] He lived off the pittance that the government awarded him and attended meetings at the Chapin Post of the Grand Army of the Republic. He never took any active public role in Buffalo during the last decade of his life, but an incident occurred in 1894 that shook the old general from his lethargy and once more inspired him to pick up his pen.

After Congress ratified the Fifteenth Amendment, prohibiting discrimination of voters on the basis of race, in 1870, various Southern states had worked to circumvent the law in order to gradually disfranchise blacks. Anticipating this move on the part of the states, Congress also passed the Enforcement Act of 1870, which put teeth into the amendment by imposing criminal penalties for anyone interfering with rights guaranteed by the Fourteenth and Fifteenth Amendments. Yet during the following decade, the U.S. Supreme Court had upheld some challenges to the Enforcement Act as they applied to private individuals, and in 1894 the act itself was repealed by Congress. Bishop's reaction to the latter shows how far he had come in considering the potential of black citizenship since writing *Loyalty on the Frontier.*

Bishop believed that an 1890 volume of essays entitled *Why the Solid South; or, Reconstruction and Its Results* was partly responsible for the repeal of the Enforcement Act, for he claimed that the book had become "a special source of inspiration to those men who are endeavoring to emasculate the Fifteenth Amendment," and he set out to refute the work point by point. Hilary A. Herbert, Grover Cleveland's secretary of the navy, had edited *Why the Solid South* as an appeal to Northern businessmen to show "the consequences which once followed an interference in the domestic affairs of certain states by those who either did not understand the situation or were reckless of the results."[22] Calling on prominent Southern politicians to discuss the effects of Reconstruction in each state, Herbert chose Arkansas governor William M. Fishback, a Union-army veteran and Democrat, to evaluate the state's experience. Fishback's essay particularly galled Bishop since it accused the administration of Isaac Murphy of financial mismanagement and tarred Bishop's reputation with the same brush. Even though his reduced circumstances had forced him into subsisting on a meager disability pension, Bishop wrote a lengthy rebuttal entitled *What Is the Situation Now? A Review of Political Affairs in the Southern States* and took it to the printing firm of Matthews-Northrup to have it published at his own expense. The pamphlet, which likely sold no more than a few dozen copies, meticulously refuted all of the allegations made by Fishback regarding the Republican role in Reconstruction Arkansas.[23] As a testimonial of his lifelong loyalty to the Republican Party and the Union cause in the Civil War, *What Is the Situation Now* would stand as Bishop's final public statement on his role during the conflict and his defense of his participation in postwar Arkansas.

Bishop's final years were spent in isolation and poverty. His daughter lived in Cortland and could not visit as often as he would have liked. When he moved to a new boarding house on 259 Hudson Street on November 19, 1901, he wrote to her in anticipation of a Thanksgiving Day visit. She never came, and in the early morning hours of the twenty-ninth, as Bishop sat quietly in his room reading the evening paper, his heart failed. A few hours later the mail arrived, and George W. Dixon, the proprietor of the boardinghouse, brought up a letter to Bishop's room. When no answer came to his knock, Dixon opened the door and discovered the old general had expired; Bishop would never read the letter from his daughter apologizing for missing the holiday. The memorial and executive committees of the

Chapin Post handled the funeral arrangements, and aside from those old veterans, the only mourner who accompanied the general's body to the cemetery was Mina, who finally did arrive at Buffalo to be with her father one last time.[24]

Evaluating Albert W. Bishop's role during the Civil War and Reconstruction is made difficult by the fact that he left no personal papers. All that exist are a handful of letters he wrote during his postwar Little Rock law practice, now held by the University of Arkansas Libraries, and two folders of correspondence he collected from the files of Arkansas Confederate governors Henry M. Rector and Harris Flanagin. Bishop kept these papers for the remainder of his life, citing some of them in his 1894 pamphlet, and they are currently held by the Buffalo-Erie County Historical Society in Buffalo, New York. But Bishop's wartime book gives the most complete portrait of the man, his views of what Arkansas's Civil War experience meant, and his intentions once the guns fell silent.

Loyalty on the Frontier is more than a Civil War reminiscence: it is both a legal treatise on the politics of Arkansas secession and an articulate account documenting two facets of the Union army's four-pronged effort to meet the exigencies of guerrilla warfare in the state and restore civil government during the conflict. This strategy incorporated the establishment of "a provost marshal enforcement system, expanded use of riverine assets . . . , recruitment of Arkansas Unionists for counterguerrilla operations, and the development of fortified farm colonies"; all four developed over the course of the war as the Federals tried to halt the depredations of bushwhackers.[25] In *Loyalty on the Frontier,* Bishop describes his participation as both a provost marshal and a recruiter of loyal Arkansans, and his book hints at his vision for the state's postwar reconstruction by those who stood by Union during the struggle.

Provost marshals became organized under a statewide command after the capture of Little Rock by the Union army in September 1863, but their duties had already been established by local Federal forces in occupied territory. Charged with administering loyalty oaths and arresting disloyal and suspicious persons, provost marshals like Bishop acted as "judge, jury and sheriff" as they administered the law in the absence of civil authority. Bishop's limited humor shows brightest when describing these duties and the people with whom he had to deal, making his record all the more enjoyable for historians interested in this phase of pacification. Here too he describes the cunning necessary to ferret out secessionists who acted as spies and informants, a valuable testimony on the techniques used by Federal forces.

Regarding the recruitment of Arkansas Unionists into an effective counterguerrilla force, Bishop indulges in his most hyperbolic writing, relating tales of derring-do that would make a dime novelist proud. Many of the incidents he describes of the "Union Men" cannot be corroborated by any other source, and the details of their adventures are to be taken by modern readers with more than a few grains of salt. For example, the filibustering exploits related in the chapter on DeWitt C. Hopkins are demonstrably faulty, and the details of Hopkins's early adventures in Central America and Mexico are almost too incredible for belief. Even without these antebellum stories, Bishop's tale of Hopkins's activities as a spy would have to be suspect, from his daring escape from the Confederate officer's mess at Fort Smith to his avoiding a sentence of execution based on a legal technicality discovered by Albert Pike. In the other biographical chapters, Bishop mentions incidents that (if they were true) tantalize the reader with a sense of the vagaries of history and the role chance may have played in the sequence of events. The dramatic story of Thomas Wilhite's pursuit of the lightly guarded carriage conveying Confederate general Thomas C. Hindman to Hogeye suggests how differently events would have unfolded had Wilhite's bullets found their mark.

But in addition to providing testimony to the practical workings of the provost marshal system and the recruitment of Unionists, Bishop's major purpose in writing this book mirrors his training as a lawyer. The personalities and events that led to the secession of Arkansas are analyzed at the level of a legal brief, and as he does in the other portions of the book, Bishop determines to name the guilty and the innocent. His main villain, and the man on whom Bishop places the most blame for Arkansas's agony, is Judge David Walker. Walker's guilt in leading the state astray could not be condoned, argues Bishop, for the judge's former public position as a Unionist betrayed his constituents during the constitutional crisis of 1861.

Walker was born in Kentucky on February 19, 1806, and came to Fayetteville, Arkansas, in October 1830. He had a keen mind and a reputation for fairness, and he held a number of public offices prior to the war, including prosecuting attorney of the Third Judicial District, representative in the 1835 territorial legislature, and a delegate to the

1836 Arkansas Constitutional Convention. In a state ruled by a Democratic clique known as the "Dynasty," Walker stood out as a leading member of the Whig Party, gaining the trust of the relatively slaveless constituency he represented in northwest Arkansas even while becoming one of the largest slaveowners in Washington County. In 1848 he was elected to the Arkansas Supreme Court, but he tried to retire from public life in 1855.[26]

The political differences of people living in the cotton-growing and mountainous regions of Arkansas centered on slavery and the socioeconomic system that depended on the institution. But as long as the one-party system dominated by the Dynasty controlled the state, "those differences could be suppressed." On the eve of the Civil War, that control broke down when a revolt among Democratic Party members led by Thomas C. Hindman actually managed to elect a governor who had not been the Dynasty's choice.[27] By the time Arkansas voters needed to elect delegates to a convention to consider secession, the regional differences, and not the Dynasty's leadership, told in the numbers of Conditional Unionists elected. David Walker, as the most prominent of all those who opposed immediate secession, became president of the convention and managed to forestall Arkansas's defection for another two months.

Bishop describes Walker's actions in reconvening the convention after Fort Sumter as nothing short of premeditated treason. But he finds in Isaac Murphy, who cast the lone vote against secession, a suitable hero to counterbalance the vileness of Walker. This oversimplification of a very complex series of events makes Loyalty on the Frontier more of an indictment than a reminiscence, and its passion is emphasized when one considers Bishop's insistence, even as late as the spring of 1863, that secessionists had been frightened by the "absurd notion of negro equality." By that time the Federal war aims had grown beyond mere restoration of the Union to include emancipation, which if admitted would have made Southern determination to secede in the very least understandable. Bishop wanted to make sure his readers would understand exactly who was wrong and who was right in starting this "causeless war" and to publicly announce who would be fit for political office in Arkansas once hostilities ended.

Several words of explanation must preface the edited version of Loyalty on the Frontier. First and foremost is the utter impossibility of identifying each and every person mentioned by Bishop in his book. Since he wrote with a lawyer's shrewd eye toward making the disloyal known regardless of what their major or minor roles in the Arkansas rebellion may have been, so many obscure names appear that they cannot be identified at all—or at most as only an entry in a census schedule. In this sense Bishop wrote precisely in the opposite fashion of William Baxter, a civilian who lived in Fayetteville during the early months of 1863 when the Wisconsin colonel arrived in town. Baxter's *Pea Ridge and Prairie Grove,* published in 1864, is filled with veiled references to local civilian and military personalities and shows a marked reluctance to positively identify anyone other than a few key players. But the two men's motivation for writing differed greatly. Baxter had left Arkansas for good when he sent his book to the publisher, while Bishop had intentions to remain in the state and participate in its political reconstruction.

The problem with identifying all of Bishop's villains and heroes is probably the most evident in the chapters on John W. Morris and Paris G. Strickland, which are ironically the shortest of any in the book. For example, Bishop attempts to reconstruct Strickland's persecution by the Confederate authorities in such meticulous detail that the names of even those peripherally involved are given. Since Strickland did not join the First Arkansas Cavalry, there is no evidence that he even survived the war, much less returned home to Searcy County. In the presentation of that chapter, I have bowed to the previous research of James M. Johnston, whose unpublished study "Searcy County, Arkansas, During the Civil War," has attempted to identify the people mentioned by Bishop. In other chapters I have limited my annotations to those individuals for whom I could find substantial information or positively identify.

Bishop's spelling has also been preserved in the following text, but in the case of personal names, I have presented the correct spelling in the notes. His use of the hyphen in "south-west" or "north-west" is inconsistent in the original edition, but I have followed his lead in this whenever appropriate. In some of the "sketches," the actions of the participants simply cannot be corroborated in any other contemporary source, including the *War of the Rebellion: The Official Records of the Union and Confederate Armies.* In such cases I have pointed out the lack of supporting documentation, not as a suggestion that the events are fictional but merely to remind readers that Bishop and his informants are history's sole witnesses for their veracity.

LOYALTY ON THE FRONTIER

OR

SKETCHES OF UNION MEN
OF THE
SOUTH-WEST

WITH INCIDENTS AND ADVENTURES IN
REBELLION ON THE BORDER

By A. W. Bishop
Lieutenant Colonel, First Cavalry Volunteers

St. Louis
E. P. Studley and Co., Printers,
South-West Cor. Main and Olive Sts.
1863

PREFACE

WHILE ON DUTY at Elkhorn Tavern, Arkansas, in November, 1862, the preparation of the following pages was begun. We had no particular object in view, certainly no thought of authorship, but as facts accumulated, they suggested a project and a plan, and as our leisure would admit, we wrote away.

At Pea Ridge, our conveniences were limited, The only house at the Post was the old Elkhorn Tavern—two apartments and a "lean-to" that served as a kitchen. Into this last we retreated, whenever we could, even for half an hour at a time, and taking position at one end of a table, while our contraband[1] cook kneaded away at the other, endeavored to bring our thoughts into line. Our sanctum let in the light from above very freely, so much so that in rainy weather we were compelled to suspend operations altogether. At such a time, we would go into the camps or send for particular men, gathering thus the experiences that we have attempted to relate.

Ordered to Prairie Grove a few days after the battle, we endeavored to prosecute our plan there, and to some extent succeeded. Coming finally to Fayetteville, we took up our quarters at a private house. Having access now to a choice library, to which we are indebted for an occasional quotation, and to "Webster's Unabridged," to settle our orthography, we continued the sketches.

The President's proclamation of January, 1, 1863, declared Arkansas in rebellion. So far as a proclamation and a knot of rebel politicians who revolve around Little Rock, can make her rebellious, she is. Practically, western Arkansas, even to the Louisiana line, and many counties in the eastern portion of the State, are not. The masses are loyal, and had the battle of Prairie Grove been fought three months earlier, the people of the western section of the State could have availed themselves of the proclamation of September 22, 1862, and might now be represented in the national legislature.[2]

They nevertheless dare the rebel authorities at Little Rock, and are now rallying south of the Arkansas River, in the Magazine Mountains and elsewhere, as six months ago they fought Hindman's men on the White River Hills.[3]

It is distressing beyond expression to witness the destitution and know of the sufferings of hundreds of the Union men of the south-west. As we write, we are just from an interview with a man and his wife, both past middle age, who have walked the entire way from Bastrop county, Texas, a distance of three hundred and thirty miles, to Fayetteville, and are here on the day typical of national grandeur, *with their lives alone.*

The Government knows but little of the sufferings of the loyal men of the Border. It is no easy thing to adhere to the Union in a seceded State, and when insult, outrage and beggary are the conse-quence, the unfortunate sufferer becomes the object of our warmest sympathy, and if help cometh not quickly, if hope is so long deferred that the heart sickens, we must not be surprised when the steadfast waver and the doubting rebel against the "Constitution and the laws."

It is therefore an object of serious concern, that army move-ments in a seceded State often look so little towards the re-creation of a healthy public sentiment, and that army officers should some-times be inclined to treat those with whom they have an ancestry in common, as the inhabitants of a conquered province. Many are brave enough in the field, but if so fortunate as to leave it victors, occasionally find themselves in the predicament of the man who caught the elephant.

Winning battles and holding territory will not alone bring American citizens back to their allegiance. The commonalty of the South must be informed why we fight, for on that point they have been fearfully misled. Remove the scales from their eyes, and they will do as certain Texan regiments have recently done, disband and go home, swearing never again to take up arms in defense of that miser-able pretension, the Southern Confederacy.[4] Many slaveholders also are at heart loyal, and are aiding in various ways the cause of the Government. Naturally enough they have sought to preserve their property, whether human or otherwise, and it is very much to be lamented that in the conduct of the war, such license should exist as is occasionally permitted the soldiery. Exasperation at the needless destruction of property begets the feeling, first, of indifference, then of hostility, and many loyal men are reluctant to put trust in a Government—generous, and they know it—the officers in whose army, through ignorance or design, have little or no regard for private rights. Still, the loyalty of the South-west continues to "crop out." It endures the severest hardships, submits to the most trying privations; and if in the following pages their faint reflex is made to appear, as also that of the incidents and adventures that give to war its charm, we may not have written in vain.

FAYETTEVILLE, ARK.,
March 4, 1863.

INTRODUCTION

IN NO SECTION of the country has the Great Rebellion created such intense personal hate, or separated more widely friends and relations, than in the South-West. Early in the war the indications of a divided sentiment were apparent, and there were needed but a few cracks of the rifle—an occasional shot from the "brush"—to fan the flame of political discussion into the consuming fire of partisan strife. The "peculiar institution" came in, of course, for its share of obloquy and commendation. Advocates of secession—the lights of street corners and cross roads—found no subject so fertile of conversions among hard working farmers, as the absurd notion of negro equality. It was the burden of discourse not only, but of conversation, and was well calculated to alienate the poorer classes, who, though owning but few slaves themselves, or generally none at all, were yet born on Southern soil, and possessed that aversion of the negro, which, whatever else it might concede, could not brook for a moment the thought of his social or political equality.[1]

The poison spread, and soon infused itself into the minds of hundreds of peaceable citizens, transforming them into bands of armed and headstrong men, ready at a moment's notice to fire the house, plunder the property, and take the life of an inoffending neighbor, if suspected, even, of sympathy with the "Lincoln Government." Nobody, in fact, could be so bad as a "Fed." "He's no better nor a nigger," said one; "He's a nigger thief," said another; "He wants to put niggers into office over us," would chime in a third; and so on through a long diatribe of senseless and vindictive calumnies. Personal abuse was followed up by the shot gun, and a few weeks sufficed to fill the Border with roving bands of reckless men, fighting for a phantom. It was nothing else. The Federal Government still stood as from its beginning. The Army of the Union fought for, not under cover of, the Constitution, and was called into being upon the spur of a great emergency—the imperiling of a nation's life. A Republican President had been elected, but his Republicanism could stand the test of scrutiny. There was nothing unconstitutional or extreme in its composition. Declaring in his inaugural address, that he had neither the power nor the desire to interfere with slavery in the States, he would assuredly have respected the compromises of the Constitution, had an impartial people given his administration a fair trial.[2]

But the madness of insanity seemed to possess the pro-slavery element in our civil polity. It had ceased to hold the balance of power, and that fact becoming annoyingly apparent, nothing would satisfy the yearnings of its ambitious leaders but separation—secession—peaceable, if possible; but in any event, secession. The memory of the past—the prosperity of the present—the hope of the future—were nothing. A lamentable confusion of terms, and a mistaken impression of the character of Northern sentiment, made every opponent an Abolitionist. The success of the Republican party in the general election of 1860, was considered the victory of William Lloyd Garrison[3] and Wendell Phillips,[4] disguised as it might be, and no argument could pierce the stubbornness of this conclusion. Sensible men knew it to be erroneous. But no matter. The Union must be broken up. The equilibrium of the sections had been lost, and separate existence must now follow. The idea of a hopeless minority was unendurable. Slavery, the fruitful source of Southern woe, could not brook restraint. Power had nursed and must uphold it, and if the Federal Union could not give it scope, disruption must ensue.

It is idle to say that the Northern people have desired, or now desire, to infringe upon the rights of the South, much less to subjugate her.

It was an easy thing for South Carolina to pass the ordinance of secession, and for her misguided sisters to catch the contagion of her example. A very few men in representative positions can vote a State out of the Union, but when the martial power necessary *to keep it there* is to be summoned forth, motives must be presented before men will fight bravely and hopefully.

In the Border States these motives were wanting, yet men must be had. Effective secession implied them, and neither the slaveholders of the South, nor the system upon which the new Government was to be based, could create the necessary stimulus to enlistments.

The poorer classes, small farmers and day laborers, with here and there a wealthy land-holder, who had the independence to do and hire his own labor, must be "whipped in."

Numbers make armies, and that plan which would the quickest create prejudices and arouse animosity, stood the best chance for adoption. Men were told that the grand object of the war on the part of the Federal Government was to lift the negro to a state of equality with the whites, freeing him from bondage, and giving him the right to exercise the elective franchise and hold office; statements whose falsity was only equaled by the lamentable credulity given to them. But the means brought about the end, and the fires of secession raged all the more fiercely from the fanaticism of its dupes.

There was here and there, however, an oasis in this desert of public opinion, now and then a surging of the popular wave, that betokened a living and abiding faith in the Government. Not every man could be made to believe that the present war was one of aggression and subjugation. Many discovered its true object, the perpetuation of the Union as it was when the war broke out, and under the protection of which they had gathered what of substance they possessed.

Poverty and rebellion were not always nursed by the same firelight. The old frontiersman, sitting musingly in his chimney corner, on the slope of a mountain spur, could not see wherein the election of Abraham Lincoln had injured him. The slow course of an uncertain mail, or the garrulous tongue of a neighbor, had told him what "Old Abe" said on the steps of the Capitol, and he was simple enough, as many thought, to believe in him.

He had prospered in his way, and though poor, it is true, could hunt without fear, and eat his corn bread and bacon in quiet. His more ambitious neighbor in the valley below could not discover any power in secession to render his crops more abundant than they had been.

The fear of negro equality had never disturbed him, and he was very certain that the Government of the United States had thus far permitted him to be the architect of his own fortunes. His sturdy common sense told him that a Revolution "was the very last resource of the thinking and the good," and he could neither see, hear nor read of those signs of material decay that always forebode the downfall of a nation.

Thus thought the Union men of the Border, and though far removed from the great heart of American political life, they nevertheless felt its pulsations, and gave a prompt response to the enthusiasm of their brethren in the East. And now came the veritable "tug of war."

Sterling Price,[5] with the executive co-operation of Claiborne F. Jackson[6] to justify him, and possessing also, in no small degree, the confidence of the people of south-western Missouri, had raised an army of State Guards, ostensibly, but rebels at heart, who, after a few months of hypocrisy, became well ordered, if not disciplined, foes of the Government.

The mass was heterogenous: one portion was rebel from principle —if the expression can be pardoned—another from policy, and a third from ignorance.

Those, however, who had the least to gain by rebellion, were its most malignant supporters. War answered their purposes as well as peace—better, in fact—for with them it meant license, rapine and murder.

Thus sprung into existence numerous guerrilla bands, that have rendered the people of the South-west familiar with the names of Bledsoe, McFarland, Joslin and Livingston,[7] giving a local notoriety to men who, but for their crimes, would not be known beyond the ravines or bushes wherein they skulked.

In the earlier stages of the rebellion, particularly after the battle of Wilson's Creek, and during the occupancy of Springfield by General Price in the winter of 1861, they were wont to call themselves "Price's men," and depredated upon the surrounding country with a degree of malignity for which history does not often find a parallel. Gradually their operations extended into Arkansas, and before the battle at Pea Ridge, the citizens of Benton, Washington, Carroll, Madison and Crawford counties, had frequent occasion to realize that the utterance of loyal sentiments was what insurance brokers would call "extra hazardous."

After that engagement their condition was but little improved. The Federal army, it is true, left the field victorious, and pushed on through the State.

Rebellion was partially stunned in the valleys of the White and Arkansas rivers, and men who before had preserved a discreet silence, now defined their position and prepared to meet the consequences.

These were not slow in coming. Organized treason was still powerful, and daily becoming more oppressive. Militia or "township meetings," as they were called, were frequently held, for the purpose of creating or organizing companies or detachments; and whenever the people failed to turn out freely, personal notice was given.

Individuals suspected of Union proclivities came especially under the ban of this surveillance, and any tardiness to enroll was the signal for abuse and insult. But evidently this condition of things could not long prevail.

A State at war with others cannot know neutrality within itself. To succeed, her people must be a unit, and naturally enough, the leaders of secession in Arkansas sought to make the unit as perfect as possible. Still the elements would not mingle.

The crucible broke when the fires of ultraism were applied to it. Love of country and attachment to the new Confederacy could not be compounded.

They were as oil and water, and neither swords nor statutes could make them mingle. A conscript act was passed, and now men must either enroll or flee,—and quiet, orderly, peaceable citizens, were compelled to accept the latter alternative.

The army had passed on to Batesville, and thence rapidly to the Mississippi. It went as speedily as it came, and the Union men who had hovered upon its border, or filed into the ranks, marked by their conduct and betrayed by their sympathy, were left without organization or protection.

To remain longer at home was worse than to leave wives and children, (temporarily, as they thought,) and thus began the hegira of the South-west. About this time Federal forces were again accumulating at Springfield, and thither hunted, but not disheartened, the Unionists of Arkansas bent their steps. To them it was the North star of hope— the Mecca of faith. No obstacles daunted, no dangers appalled them. Lying in the woods by day, at early nightfall they resumed their toilsome journey, carefully shunning highways, and trusting to the instinct of self-preservation, and the inconstant guidance of the stars, for ultimate safety.

Nor did their dangers and fears desert them when they had crossed the Missouri line. A comparatively new peril now beset them. A grand stamping ground of "bushwhackers" had to be crossed, and woe to the luckless wight who endeavored to pass through the miserable village of Keitsville.[*8]

It is hardly necessary to add, that Keitsville was frequently avoided. Its surrounding hills, however, were traversed in a manner that bid defiance to all laws of engineering, and specimens of its lawless population were occasionally "hoist by their own petard."

---

*Keitsville, Barry county, Mo., has been noted since the origin of our national troubles as a rendezvous for marauders of the worst description. One "Joe Peevie," living a short distance west of the village, seemed to be the leader of the gang, and no atrocities were too inhuman for them to commit.

Lieut. ——— Miller, of the First Missouri Cavalry, was brutally murdered near there in the spring of the present year, and since that event a number of men, citizens and soldiers, have been fired upon from the bushes, and not afterwards heard of.

The village has paid dearly for the rebel proclivities of its inhabitants. There is scarcely a house left standing in it. Fire has completed what rebellion began, and all that Keitsville can bequeath to posterity, save the enduring loyalty of Thomas Keit, its founder, is a *hard name*.]

In the spring of 1862, the refugees began to appear at Cassville, Mo., many with their families, and what little stock and furniture they had succeeded in "getting out."

Their love for the Union was strong, and their alacrity to enlist could not be surpassed. The idea having been prosecuted of enlisting them into the United States service, not many months thereafter a regiment stood up to swear lasting vengeance upon the men who had so cruelly robbed and persecuted them, and theirs were no idle threats.

The god of war was never more firmly seated than when he received their vows, and all the sacrifices to be laid at his feet by them have not yet passed the "portals of the gates of death."

There is a retributive future for those men, who, in the spring and summer of 1862, from Fort Smith to Little Rock, and from the Arkansas river to the Missouri line, hunted their old friends and neighbors like wild beasts of the forest, simply because they were true to the Union as their fathers made it.

Oaths of allegiance taken at the eleventh hour will not be coats of mail for them.

The future will take its complexion from the past, until individual hate is sated, personal injuries are atoned for, and he who took up the sword shall have perished by it.

Moralists teach a different doctrine, but for ages, personal safety, lawful war and public justice, have been exceptions to the New Testament exhortation of turning the other cheek when one has been smitten.

Such, in brief, is the experience of the Union men of the South-West, many of whom are officers and soldiers of the First Arkansas Cavalry.

From the enlistment of its first man to the mustering of the twelfth company, the camp of the regiment was a continuous story of wrongs and outrages, and old men and boys, women and children, were subsisted by the Government, whilst husbands and brothers were preparing for the avenging strife. Singly and in groups they came to Springfield. Weary and sore, they stood up to be "sworn in," many infirm of limb, but firm of purpose, and thus arose the regiment.

Others have sought to serve their Government in civil capacity. One in particular has immortalized his name and patriotism in standing firmly by the Union in the legislative halls of the State of Arkansas, when none of his compeers were bold or true enough to follow his example.

With him we commence our sketches.

ELK HORN TAVERN, ARK.,
November, 1862.

ISAAC MURPHY.

THE CAUSELESS WAR now convulsing the American nation has developed few more noble instances of stern, unyielding devotion to principle, than is presented by the subject of this sketch. Emigrating from Tennessee to Washington county, Arkansas, in 1834, he early became identified with the growth of his adopted state, and has ever since proved true to the convictions of early manhood.

A democrat in principle, he has dared to ignore party lines when honesty and ability were at issue, preferring competency in the whig party to inefficiency in his own. A lawyer by profession, he early learned to think for himself, and during the troublesome scenes of his later life, was buoyed up by the consciousness that he was taking counsel of his judgment, while his friends and neighbors were swayed by prejudice or overawed by power.

Settling at Fayetteville, where in the spring of 1836 he was admitted to the bar, he early took rank as a man of influence and sagacity, and in August, 1846, was elected as a representative in the lower house of the State Legislature. In August, 1848, he was re-elected, and served until the spring of 1849, when he went to California.

During his legislative career he was attentive to his duties, was ever watchful of the interests of the State and his own section, and lost no opportunity to foil the plans of corruptionists—men always found hovering around a capital—State buzzards who feed and fatten upon the dissolution of everything that makes a people prosperous or a nation great.

Arkansas, at this time, was literally in the hands of a few men. The Johnson family, known throughout the State, was at the height of its power. The father,[1] for many years United States District Judge of the District of Arkansas, had died some time previously, bequeathing to his heirs a handsome fortune, and to the State three ambitious sons, and a generous, high-minded son-in-law, Ambrose H. Sevier.[2] That the State, however, was benefitted by a portion of the bequest, has not become apparent. The son-in-law, after serving with honor in the United States Senate, was sent to Mexico to bear amendments to the proposed treaty of peace between that power and the United

States. Returning to Little Rock during the session of the Legislature of 1848, and at which a United States senator was to be chosen, he found party politics, or party dissensions rather, running high, and Solon Borland a candidate against him.[3]

It then lacked but a few days of the time appointed for the election. Feeble in health, he gave his cause but little personal attention, trusting mainly for success to the Johnson brothers—his allies in politics as well as by affiliation—but the coalition against him was too strong.

Democrats, disaffected with the Johnson family, and whigs, whose individual proclivities overrode fealty to party, struck hands with each other, and Solon Borland was elected by a majority of one, himself a democrat of the straightest sect. Upon Mr. Sevier the blow fell with a crushing weight. His supporters knew *him* to be a statesman, and *he* knew that his opponent was not.

Mortification mingled with disappointment, and he immediately left Little Rock for his plantation near Pine Bluff, on the Arkansas river. A few says later, his body lay at the levee of the State Capital, and until his death was mentioned to the member from his county by the subject of this sketch, it was not known to the Legislature. A profound sensation followed—marks of respect of no ordinary character were shown to the memory of the deceased, and thus sank beneath the sod, one of the true friends of Arkansas, who, though bound by ties of family to scheming, designing men, was yet superior to the low cunning and sly artifice, that for years practically gave them control of the finances of the state.[4]

Robert Johnson,[5] first a Congressman, and, when the State seceded, a member of the United States Senate; Richard Johnson,[6] for many years editor and proprietor of the Little Rock *Democrat,* doubtless the most influential paper in the State; and James Johnson,[7] a younger brother and a lesser light, recently a Colonel in the rebel army, now deceased, were the trio, whose baneful influence, as popularly accredited, impoverished the State at home, and impaired its credit abroad. This, at least is true: the family were all powerful at Little Rock when the State bank and its branches were created; when the Real Estate Bank was established; when a seminary fund—72 sections of land—and an internal improvement fund—500,000 acres—were placed under the control of the State, to be disposed of for her best interests.

Robert Johnson and collateral branches of the family were especially active in the management of the banks and the disposition of the funds; and, in the latter case, what was intended as a great State benefaction became the means and appliances of strengthening the power of individuals. The banks broke, and the funds were squandered; but the Johnson family maintained its state. That specious argument, which told the people that the proceeds of the seminary fund should be distributed throughout the counties for common school purposes, met with favor for a time.

Large sums of money were paid to county treasurers, but they were loaned to private individuals. No better evidence, in fact, of the mis-management of this fund can be asked for than the lamentable ignorance of a large proportion of the population of the State. A school-house at a crossing of roads is a rare sight in many localities; and there have been wider departures from fact, than the story that "they send out the hounds, on the White river hills, to catch the children on a Sunday morning, to put clean clothes on." In politics, also, this family was all-powerful. They had their "strikers" and "tools" in every county in the State, and it was almost impossible to secure an office, high or low, or a morsel of patronage, small or great, without their intervention in some shape. To Washington, even, this influence extended, and Federal appointees from Arkansas had first to reflect the views and prejudices of the Johnson brothers. With the schemes of these men, Isaac Murphy was never in sympathy. While a legislator, he worked indefatigably for the development of the best interests of the State; framed resolutions and bills, and presented and enforced them, but often without result. Some stultifying or plausible amendment would be proposed. Delay would follow deliberation, and measures calculated beyond question to build up a great State, fell still-born where they were conceived.

Mr. Murphy's ill-health was the cause of his going to California. For years he had been troubled in this respect, and a change of climate with relief from all harassing mental labor, was thought to be the best prescription.

Availing himself of an opportunity to journey with a number of his acquaintances, who were about to seek the new land of gold for its own sake, he started overland in April, 1849, and reached the Sacramento river in August of that year.

He remained in California until the Spring of 1854. His health improving while there, the prevailing infection seized him, and he was soon among the miners as one of them. As in the case, however, of many others, prospecting found a law-suit, and he left the State embarrassed by the expenditures of a bootless litigation. Returning to Arkansas, he settled in Huntsville, Madison county, and was elected to the State Senate from Madison and Benton counties in August, 1856. His Senatorial career was not marked by any events of special interest not identified with the general history of the times. A Democrat, as has already been observed, his course proved him loyal to every genuine political project, and a warm adherent to the interests of the South.

After the expiration of his term, he returned to Huntsville and remained quietly at home practicing his profession, until was begun the ominous Presidential campaign of 1860. He saw the storm coming, and prepared to breast it. A democrat of the Douglas school, he was zealous in the advocacy of its peculiar theories. In his own State, a division in party sentiment occurred, and he found himself numerically upon the weaker side. But circumstances did not affect his position, although sufficiently hostile to deter most men from effort. The Charleston Convention had adjourned. Its members separating to their several States, began plying anew the rod of secession, and in Arkansas it was wielded by Thomas C. Hindman,[8] Robert and Richard Johnson, and Henry M. Rector,[9] late Governor of the State. Secession, should Lincoln be elected, was boldly advocated, and these men, with others, canvassed the State for Breckenridge and Lane, yet notwithstanding, it was difficult to make honest yeomanry believe that they really intended to take the State out of the Union in case of a defeat at the polls. They claimed, in fact, to be Union men, but there was a fearful "if" in their patriotism.

While these events were passing, the other wing of the democratic party was not idle. Active measures were taken to get up a Douglas electoral ticket. Hon. Albert Rust,[10] then member of Congress, was especially zealous and his efforts were heartily co-operated in by Mr. Murphy. The result, however, was inauspicious. The "Junto" at Little Rock was too powerful, and honest men were compelled to look to *defeat* for encouragement. Election day came and went. The Legislature convened and passed an act to call a State Convention to take into consideration the policy of seceding from the Union. Delegates to the Convention were to be elected on the 18th of February, 1861. The time was very brief, and most people were taken by surprise. They had not anticipated this movement. Supposing that the contest of the November previous would pass away like its predecessor, they neither busied themselves with devising treasonable schemes nor in plotting rebellion.

The Knights of the Golden Circle, or rather, Knaves of the Godless Communion, were busily at work during the fall campaign, and to their zeal is mainly attributable the treasonable complexion of the Legislature.[11] Its passage of the act referred to, was a lasting disgrace to the State, and happy the man who could meet interrogation with an honest "Thou can'st not say I did it."

On the 11th of February Mr. Murphy was requested by citizens of Huntsville to announce himself as a candidate for a seat in the Convention. At first he declined to do so, but urged, consented to the use of his name. There were but a few days for effort, and popular excitement was running high. A secession candidate was in the field against him, and that night the labor of the "stump" began. Daily thereafter until the election was held, he addressed his fellow-citizens in different parts of the county, and with what effect is best shown by the fact that he received all the votes cast—several thousand in number—but 144. In other sections of the State similar evidences of attachment to the Union were manifested. North-western Arkansas, by the almost unanimous action of its citizens demonstrated its devotion to the "old flag." The whole country, in fact, north of the Arkansas river, was alive with unionism, and there was needed but the Promethean spark of competent leadership to fire a train of causes that would consume secession with all its woes. Even cotton planting counties south of the river returned Union delegates, and the approaching convention promised to be a blessing in disguise. No one, however, anticipated thorough harmony. The times and men were both "out of joint," and rash acts were expected. The Convention met at Little Rock, and delegates at once assumed that they had all the power the people could give them, untrammeled by the Constitution or other organic law. No oath was administered upon taking their seats, and license was thus given, as it were, to reckless action.

An ordinance of secession was brought before the Convention, but voted down by a majority of five. The traitorous members of the Convention, failing to accomplish their purposes, an ordinance was passed to refer the question of secession to the people of the State, at an election to be held on the first Monday of August then next ensuing. The Convention then adjourned to convene again, upon the call of its president, Judge David Walker, of Washington county, with the implied understanding, however, that the Convention was not to reassemble until after the August election, an implication strengthened by the fact, that the members of the Convention were appointed returning officers of the vote then to be cast.

Before the Convention rose, the minority threatened frequently to leave it—to take up arms and force the State out of the Union by Military power, but nothing was done, and the Convention adjourned in a body. Shortly afterwards the bombardment of Fort Sumter took place, and the occurrence was sized upon as a pretext for renewed agitation. Extraordinary efforts were made to urge the people into a favorable mood for secession. The gallant conduct of Major Anderson was stigmatized as an attempt at coercion. Unscrupulous politicians hissed out their venom against the North, and no appliances were left untouched which were thought to be calculated to exasperate the people, and arouse hatred of the Union. The excited state of public feeling had its effect upon the members of the Convention. With Judge Walker, as President, rested the discretionary power of calling it together, and it was for him to say whether or not public events required him to do so. He was the sole judge of the propriety of its reassembling. In his hand was held, at that time, the destiny of the State. He could have averted secession by declining to call the Convention, and it is doing too much injustice to his intelligence to say that he was not conscious of his power. He felt it, and though enjoying the reputation of being an honorable, high-minded man, took the initiative in a series of acts, that in a brief period of time, dragged the State from its high pedestal to leave it a prey to the contending passions of revengeful men.[12]

He called the Convention for the sixth day of May. Immediately attempts were made to instruct the delegates. Every conceivable pressure was brought to bear upon them. Nearly all the slaveholding states had seceded, and the *virus* was creeping toward Little Rock. It required no ordinary *stamina* now to enable public men to maintain their consistency. The fury of unthinking hate—the rashness of impulsive action, and above all, the evil influences of State example, were rapidly tainting public opinion. Quiet secessionists became bold and uncompromising, and Union men of the February preceding, expressed the intention of remaining such, *if the State did not secede.*

The Convention was to sit on Monday. The Saturday previous delegates and citizens began to swarm promiscuously into Little Rock. There was but one subject of interest, one topic of conversation, and on Monday morning the steps of all were bent in the same direction. Yet there was no cheerfulness in the excitement that swayed the city.

Delegates greeted each other sullenly, and although now a large majority seemed determined to vote for secession, at all hazards, men felt that they were walking on volcanic ground. The hours grew apace, and the dawn of that eventful day broke in upon as headstrong an assemblage of men as were ever gathered within corporate limits.

It is an old saying, "Whom the gods would destroy, they first make mad," and a few hours later the Arkansian capital verified it. At 10 o'clock A.M. the Convention was called to order. The spacious hall of the House of Representatives was filled to repletion. Every nook and corner was occupied. The aisles were full—the galleries crowded —men jostled ladies, and ladies each other. Boys perched upon window sills, and nestled by the chairs of members. Even the sun-light seemed to catch the spirit of the hour, as it streamed through the windows and shot its rays angrily through the room.

The usual formalities were observed. The clerks of the old session were made clerks of the new. For a moment there was a death-like, but ominous silence. A member then arose, presented an ordinance of secession, and asked that the ayes and noes be taken without debate. No one offered to speak. That intensely excited throng could not brook the ordeal of discussion. Nearly all the delegates were in their seats, and the voting began. It was mainly in the affirmative, and those who so voted were applauded to the echo. Here and there, was an occasional "no," and the utterance of this now doubly significant monosyllable, became the signal for hisses and execration.

For a few moments order and decorum were entirely disregarded, and the President was hardly equal to the task of restoring them. At length, the last to vote, he rose. All eyes were instantly centered upon him, and the hall became suddenly still as a charnel house. He commenced to speak; he manner was excited, and his utterance somewhat confused. In eloquent language he alluded to the assumed coercion of the South in the attack on Fort Sumter; told how grand a thought it would be to contemplate the South as unanimous in her action—visited his anathemas upon the Abolition North, as he saw fit to term it, and then addressing himself to those delegates who had voted "no," urged them to change their votes that the action of the Convention might go forth to the world as unanimous. Turning to the subject of this sketch, who sat not far from him, he complimented him upon his firmness of purpose and integrity of character, but at the same time casuistically urging him to betray the principles that he had nurtured for a life-time. He had nothing to say in defense of the old constitution—

the government that had enriched him came in for no share of his panegyric. Memory was swallowed up by hope—reason by vanity, and the strange handwriting on the wall did not more clearly foreshadow the fate of Belshazzar, than David Walker told his own in the single word "aye," as he resumed his seat! Again the crowd applauded to the echo—cheer rang out after cheer, and doubtless many an observer envied the proud recipient of all this homage.

But pause a moment. David Walker had been an earnest advocate of the cause of the Union. In early life, emigrating to Arkansas, he had amassed property, and acquired reputation. He had been a judge of the Supreme Court of the State, holding the scales of justice evenly and with a steady hand. He was widely known, was large hearted and generous, but possessed an overweening love of applause. Washington county sent him as a delegate to the Convention, a Union man. At Fayetteville, during the canvass, he had stated that he would suffer his right arm to be cut off, sooner than vote for an ordinance of secession. But alas! the vanity of human resolution. Circumstances and his own inherent weakness mastered him, and from the moment of his casting the fatal vote, reputation and confidence forsook him, and though he has since taken the oath of allegiance to the government at which he aimed so powerful a blow, his old *status* cannot be restored. Though rich in houses and land, he is poor in the esteem of former friends. *He is dead while he yet liveth.*

To return to the hall. As the President sat down, four of the members, who had voted "no" rose one after another, and asked leave to change their votes.[13] As before, the crowd were uproarious in their applause, and now, Isaac Murphy, alone in the negative, was expected to swing easily into the popular current. His name was called by the chair. For a moment there was another death-like stillness. "Murphy," "Murphy," was now shouted from the lobby, the gallery, and at last from the floor of the Convention rose the noisy call. He stood up. Calmly and clearly he spoke of his Southern life. "My principles are all Southern," said he; "if necessary, I would lay down my life for the benefit of the Southern States, but I would rather lose a thousand lives than aid in bringing about the untold evils that would assuredly follow in the train of secession. Again I say, to the passage of this ordinance, 'No!'"

He resumed his seat. Storms of hisses instantly burst forth. "Traitor!" "Traitor!" "Shoot him!" "Hang him!" madly resounded through the Hall, but no personal violence was attempted. The business of the Convention moved on. There was a gradual subsidence of the wild excitement that had so recently reigned; and not until the convention adjourned for the day, did Mr. Murphy leave the hall. He had not anticipated doing so alive. He knew when he entered it, that a dread ordeal was approaching; that he was to be tried by fire; but relying on God and a clear conscience, had fully determined to be true to himself, *and History will be true to him.* He was boarding at the time with a daughter, and to the house of her husband he repaired.[14]

It is somewhat singular, in view of the irascible disposition of Southern men, that he was not molested *en route.* Apparently nothing but his age and uprightness saved him from insult, and possibly death. He reached the house in safety, but, during the balance of the session, his friends would not permit him to go into the streets after dusk. The convention adjourning, he returned to Huntsville. Passing up the Arkansas river to Ozark, he found himself in company with members of the Convention, and a large number of rebel officers and soldiers. Unexpectedly to him, he was not drawn into conversation in relation to his recent course, and he was treated on all occasions with the utmost respect.

On the journey from Ozark to Huntsville he was often met by Union men, and congratulated upon his firmness. Arriving at home he was similarly greeted; still, the secession element was there. He was not out of danger. Twice or thrice mob violence was threatened against him, but nothing was done. At length, a public notice, intended especially for him, was nailed to the court house door, commanding all Union men to leave the town in ten days. It was pulled down, however; and of this, also, nothing came. A series of questions, bearing upon the political issues of the day, and which he was requested to answer, was then sent to him. He refused to do so, except at a public meeting of the citizens of the town. Such a meeting was accordingly called, and largely attended. After the usual preliminaries were observed, he commenced addressing the people, but was speedily interrupted in an ungentlemanly and insulting manner, by a portion of the secession rabble of the place. He persisted, however, answering all questions of point, and turning the laugh upon his enemies; but the confusion increased, and at length the assemblage, to use an expression more truthful than elegant, broke up in a row. Yet this occurrence was a triumph for the Union men.

Mr. Murphy was now permitted for a time to live in peace. At length, private threats were made; not to him directly, but in such a manner that they reached his family. Assassination was hinted at; and now, acting upon the advice of genuine friendship, he secretly left his home, accompanied by Dr. J. M. Johnson and Frank Johnson, his brother, both citizens of Huntsville.[15] They were followed, but, evading pursuit, overtook the rear of General Curtis' army near Keitsville, Mo. This was in April, 1862. From that time until the September following, they remained with the Army of the South-west, when Mr. Murphy came to Springfield, Mo., in the hope that army movements would be of such a character as to permit him to re-visit his home and family. He accompanied the Army of the Frontier on its march into Arkansas, saw it "go up the hill and then down again," accomplishing no object commensurable with the time, money and labor expended, and when it returned to Missouri, he remained at Elk Horn Tavern, waiting for another and more effectual advance. There he now is, practically expatiated, a prisoner of hope, an honest man.

ELK HORN TAVERN, ARK.,
November, 1862

JOHN I. WORTHINGTON.

THE MISFORTUNES OF early life are often the guaranty of subsequent success. A boy, whom the force of circumstances has prematurely thrown upon the world, and who possesses the latent spark of intrepid action, will, before majority, either kindle his funeral pile, or pave the way to an honorable and useful career.

Adversity is no trifler—it makes or it unmakes, and he upon whom is forced the hard lot of night without shelter, and hunger without food, will either become the sworn enemy of his race, or nobly fight the battle of life, despite care and anxiety, pain and poverty. Thus is it that out of darkness cometh light, and that those occurrences which at the time were considered so unfortunate, often mark the birth of a new and more vigorous life. For a boy, nothing is more to be deplored than the loss of a father and abnegation of home. The fact of the first, and the willfulness of the second event, render his case one of peculiar solicitude, and if the world takes no interest in him, heaven help the morals of those with whom he comes in contact.

In this perilous position fortune placed John I. Worthington. His energy helped him out of it. Born in Somerset county, Pennsylvania, on the 14th day of June, 1826; at four years of age a fearful accident left him fatherless. Possessed of ardent impulses and a firm will, a child's quarrel, had with another boy, when eleven years of age, and for which his mother punished him, thoroughly roused his anger, and he ran away. Like all boys who thus take the bits within their teeth, he did that which was apparently a descent from bad to worse, and hired out as a canal driver to a Captain Pickworth, living in Johnstown, Cambria county, and who was then running a line boat on the western division of the Pennsylvania canal.

In this instance, however, the fact was otherwise. His employer was kind and watchful, and the boy's morals did not undergo the usual transformation of the calling. Shortly after arriving at Johnstown, his mother ascertaining his whereabouts, sought to induce him to return home. But he was obstinate, and though not wanting in filial affection—always in after life contributing whatever he could to the comfort of his mother—he was fully determined to have his own way in this matter. At sixteen he was promoted from the *tow-path* to the *cabin,* and as captain of the boat for four years succeeding, managed its affairs with skill and economy.

The Mexican war arising, he enlisted on the 17th of December, 1846, as a private in Company B, Second Regiment Pennsylvania Volunteers. The company was commanded by John W. Geary, afterwards well known as Governor of Kansas; the regiment by William Roberts, wounded at Cerro Gordo, and dying at San Augustine three months later, from the effects of the injury. On the 3d of January, 1847, the regiment left Pittsburg for the seat of war. Arriving at Vera Cruz on the 10th of March, it was engaged in the memorable siege of that city. After its capitulation, the command moved inland, and participated in the battle of Cerro Gordo. It was then stationed at Jalapa, and remained there until the 19th of June. Marching thence for Puebla to join the main army, and guarding with other troops an immense train, at Lahoya their advance was resisted by three thousand guerrillas under Zenobia. A severe and desperate battle was fought from hand to hand, and tree to tree, as guerrillas can alone be successfully contended with, and they were routed.

On the 8th of July the regiment reached Puebla. Puebla is eighty miles from the city of Mexico, and the main army under General Scott was concentrating there for its march on the doomed city. August 8th, 1847, the column moved—the Second Pennsylvania constituting a portion of General Shields' brigade, in General Quitman's division. On the 19th and 20th days of that month, was fought the battle of Contreras. In this engagement the regiment was held as a reserve, drawn up in line of battle, but not ordered under fire. Six miles nearer the city, the fortifications at Cherubusco, on the Acapulco road, hastily thrown up, but still formidable, confronted the victorious army. A bloody and obstinate battle ensued, in which the Second Pennsylvania lost one-third of its men in killed and wounded.

The enemy, completely routed, fled in great confusion to the city, hotly pursued by infantry, cavalry and artillery. The 20th of August was a dark day for Mexico. Her grand army had been signally defeated, and Santa Anna asked for an armistice for the purpose of effecting a treaty of peace. It was entered into, and according to its conditions, twenty-four hours' notice of its termination were to be given before it could be broken. An unprovoked attack upon a commissary train in the city, by a swell mob, on the 6th day of September, and for which General Scott asked, but was denied redress, was the occasion of its dissolution.

The army was lying at Tacubaya, San Angelo and San Augustine, points within supporting distance of each other, and but a few miles from the city. A rapid movement was made upon it, resisted first at Molino-del-Rey, then at Chapultepec. On the morning of the 13th instant the storming column advanced, led by General Quitman. In this movement the Second Pennsylvania participated, and during its progress young Worthington was wounded in the arm, but not so severely as to cause him to leave the field. Later in the day a spirited attack was made by the same General's division at the Garita-de-Belen; and at two o'clock in the afternoon the position was carried. It was of the first importance, and our gallant forces determined to hold it at all hazards. They did so during the day, but with a loss to the division, numbering at the time only eight hundred, of three hundred and ninety-seven, killed and wounded.

On the following morning the city was surrounded, and one of the most brilliant campaigns in modern warfare seemed to be drawing to a successful close. It was, indeed, near its termination; but there was yet work to be done. Santa Anna, with a refinement of malignity that harmonized well with his other traits of character, had, on the night of the thirteenth instant, released all the convicts in the city prisons, and taken other measures to arouse the worst passions of the lower classes. The surrender, in form, of the city, was no barrier to their opposition. From street to street, they resisted the progress of the American forces; and three days of determined hand-to-hand fighting were necessary, before order could be restored.

The Mexican war was then practically ended. Winter quarters were sought; the Second Pennsylvania, however, remaining in the city until the 19th of October. From that time until the 30th of May, 1848, when peace was declared, it was quartered at San Angelo, seven miles from the city. In all the engagements mentioned, with the exception of Molino-del-Rey and Contreras, our hero fought. After the taking of Vera Cruz, he was made Corporal. At Puebla he was elected orderly sergeant, and on the 19th of October, 1847, was promoted to the first lieutenancy of his company. Immediately after peace was declared he returned to Cambria, Pennsylvania, arriving there August 19th 1848. The company was received with military honors, a flag was presented to it, and upon Mr. Worthington was imposed the duty of responding to the presentation speech. He did so in a manner creditable alike to the occasion and himself. On the 24th day of the same month, he was married to Miss Mary White, of Cambria. Shortly afterwards he purchased a canal-boat and a stock of goods, and pursued the vocation of a trader, moving up and down the canal, where formerly he had toiled and prospered, until the 11th of May, 1849, when his wife died.

Upon a young man there can scarcely fall a severer blow. The agonizing loneliness of his situation, when the dread reality becomes a conscious fact, is fearful to experience. When no eye but that of Omnipresence can penetrate his seclusion, he moans out his uncontrollable anguish. Hope is swallowed up in foreboding, fruition in disappointment; and the world, that till now was so joyous and full of promise, is draped in profoundest gloom, if not despair. Life seems bereft of its ambition, domesticity of its charm, and all the inducements to labor, "stale, flat, and unprofitable." But the grief of a man is his servant, not his master. Idle despondency is the sure sign of great weakness. "What cannot be cured must be endured," is a saying trite but true; and young Worthington, accepting its philosophy, struggled up against his affliction, and prepared anew to fight the battle of life. Changing alike his habitation and his calling, be occupied the position of conductor on the Pennsylvania Central Railroad, and remained in its employ until the succeeding Spring. Going then to Mississippi, he hired out as an overseer to one John W. Henderson, taking charge of a large plantation nine miles below Vicksburg.

In this position he remained until the Autumn of 1852, when he applied himself to school-teaching, taking a private school at Richmond, Madison Parish, La. There he remained until July, 1853, when he abandoned the stool of the pedagogue, and returned to Johnstown, Pa. Residing there until January, 1854, the restless spirit of adventure and gain combined seized him, and he started for California. Selecting an overland route, and having an eye to a speculation *in transitu,* he proceeded to Napoleon, Arkansas, and there took passage on the steamboat Caroline for Jacksonport, on White river. In the valley of this stream, and on the adjacent uplands, he had intended to purchase a drove of cattle for transportation across the plains and sale in the new El-Dorado. On the 26th of March the steamboat was burned to the water's edge.[1]

This disaster occurred at mid-day, and in spite of every exertion, so rapidly did the devouring flames do their work, between thirty and forty lives were lost. Young Worthington barely escaped with his own, and when the full extent of his losses became known, he found himself on shore, the possessor of a pair each of socks and pants, and $3.25 in money. Taking passage on the "Julia Dean," which opportunely arrived at the place of the catastrophe, he proceeded thirty miles up the river to Jacksonport, and there set foot again on *terra firma*. His means were now still nearer exhaustion, and it was necessary that something should be done at once to replenish them.

The California project was temporarily abandoned and immediate employment sought upon any terms. A warehouse opened its inviting door, and our friend worked in it for thirty days. Starting then on foot for the over-land route to California, and intending to pass through Bentonville, for the purpose of ascertaining where the nearest train might be overtaken, a few days found him at Carrollton, the county seat of Carroll county,[2] with three "bits" in his pocket, not enough to ensure supper and lodging and his honor at the same time. He therefore hurried on a few miles, urged alike by poverty and prudence, and sought entertainment at a substantial farm house. While there he learned there was a vacant school to be had in the neighborhood; that it had been made vacant, in fact, the same day, by the suicide of its teacher, one Alfred Louthers. Prepossessing his host, who was one of the Justices of the District, the school was offered to him and he took it, taught three months at twenty dollars a month, boarding himself, and was then re-employed for a like period. Meantime, he had formed the acquaintance of, and married a Miss Nancy Irvin, the daughter of a highly respectable farmer.

His roving inclinations were now somewhat subdued, and land in Carroll county being very cheap, he purchased eighty acres and went to farming, and for a year worked early and late, and it was not his fault that the earth did not yield freely of her bounty. The elements were against him. A drought, long continued and exhaustive, prematurely parched his corn, and he had the poor satisfaction of gathering two and a half bushels per acre. His thoughts now centering on his former occupation of school teaching, and not knowing but that his second year's experience as a farmer might be a repetition of the first, he bartered his land and improvements for a pony and started for Cassville, Mo., in search of a school.

The day of his arrival, one Lee, a notorious character in the South-west, was undergoing the usual preliminary examination on a charge of murder, and knowing the Sheriff of the county, and taking an interest in the proceedings, Mr. Worthington quietly ventured the opinion that Lee was guilty and could be convicted. The only attorneys in the place had been employed by the prisoner, and they were not without their sharpness. The Justice before whom the examination was had, was one Joel Grammar, still living in Cassville. He was also deputy clerk of the circuit court, thus assuming to hold contemporaneously, two offices in the gift of the State. This a constitutional provision prohibited, but the Justice's ignorance was his bliss, and the examination went on. It lasted ten days, and at its close one of the attorneys moved that the case be dismissed for want of jurisdiction, insisting, also, that though the proceedings could go no farther, the acts of the Justice were those of a magistrate *de facto,* and were conclusive so far as the prisoner was concerned. The motion was granted, but the prisoner was still held in custody by the sheriff. At this juncture Mr. Worthington was retained by the friends of the deceased, one Risley, and he lost no time in directing the sheriff to keep Lee imprisoned, suggesting farther, that if he failed to do so he would be held responsible on his bond. It was a bold move for a stranger and a novice, but the schoolmaster was emphatically "abroad." His farming experience flitted unpleasantly across his mental vision. He felt that something must be done at once to keep soul and body together, and in early life he had studied law a trifle, reading Blackstone, and Lewis on Statutory Criminal Law, when captain of a canal boat. Possessed of an unusually retentive memory, and never having stupefied it by liquor or narcotics, what he had read now came to his aid, and he was bold enough to apply it. His shrewdness told him, moreover, that if he played the game and won, he might pass for a promising lawyer, if not indeed an old and successful practitioner. There was no time to lose, and he immediately sent a message after one Mr. McCluer, a justice living seven miles from the town, with instructions to return with him at once.

The order was promptly obeyed, and at daylight on the following morning a warrant for the re-arrest of Lee was in the hands of the sheriff. The "bird" had not "flown," and a second examination now began. It lasted three days, conducted on the part of the prosecution by Mr. Worthington, and resulted in Lee's commitment on the charge of murder in the first degree.[3] Eighteen months later he was tried at Springfield, Mo., convicted, and sentenced to be hung; but intermediate his sentence and the day of execution, he showed his partiality for life by escaping. As usual, nobody was to blame, and again Justice was cheated of her victim.

His success before Justice McCluer so encouraged our friend that he determined to adopt the legal profession at once. He had made a favorable impression, and he knew it; yet his common sense told him that he was not a lawyer. Business poured in upon him, and he took it, for to stop was as "perilous as go on." He opened an office, and by dint of unceasing labor, soon acquired what before he had assumed.

The spring term of the circuit court for Barry county having lapsed, on account of the illness of the judge, he labored on without the benefit of a regular admission to practice until the July term following, when he was formally enrolled among the "*Fratres Legibus.*" Cases at issue in courts of record had already been entrusted to him, and he had set about their preparation for trial with all the assiduity of an experienced attorney. Clients had given him their unexpected confidence, and fully determining to know no such word as *fail,* he had worked day and night at his pleadings and briefs. Looseness in practice, and the moderate talent of the bench, were in his favor, and he soon availed himself of the advantage his industry gave him. He went into court boldly, stated his propositions clearly, and never failed to present an authority, if one was to be had. Immediately after the close of the term, feeling satisfied that the new town of Granby, in the adjoining county of Newton, offered greater professional inducements, he removed there with his family, now consisting of a wife and child.

Granby, at this time, was to south-western Missouri what six years earlier California became to the United States, with this difference only, that the attraction was leaden, not auriferous. Its population, numbering between two and three thousand souls, was thrown in promiscuously, and naturally *threw out* an inordinate amount of litigation. The town arose in this wise: In 1855, one Robert Brock, from Wisconsin, purchased a tract of land in Newton county, and supposing it to contain lead, immediately went to prospecting, not only on it but on lands adjoining. Unluckily for him, he discovered the coveted deposit—not on his own possessions, but on what proved to be land belonging to the Pacific Railroad Company. In ignorance of its ownership, he kept his secret, and at once applied for a patent. Finding that the railroad had one, he suddenly became large-hearted, and made his discovery public. This occurred in the winter of 1855–6. The veins of the mine were unusually rich, the mineral containing a very large per centum of pure ore, and being easily and conveniently worked. The announcement was electric; and

the lands belonging to a "soulless" corporation, the whole community yearned after the body.

As usual, the worst spirits—foul as the witches of Macbeth—
"squatted" first, and in an almost incredibly brief period of time a
town arose. It was the gamblers' paradise. The "double-six"[4] of the
night charmed away the twelve hours toil of daylight. The pistol and
the knife gathered in what the pick and the crusher accumulated; and
when Mr. Worthington entered the town, it contained as complete an
assortment of knaves, of high and low degree, as could be found outside of prison walls. There was some leaven, however, in this lump of
humanity. A few honest men—tradesmen and laborers—had located
in Granby, and their number was steadily on the increase. They were
powerless to maintain a high standard of order and morality, and they
therefore contented themselves with getting along as best they could.
For a certain kind of practice, a lawyer could not have selected a better theatre.

It would not be just to Mr. Worthington to say that he sought his
future home for its then existing vileness; yet it must be admitted, that
a shrewd lawyer, in selecting a residence, will go where money and
business excitement beckon, without making very particular inquiry
into the morals of the place. The practice was, in a large part criminal, and Mr. Worthington took cases that brought fees; though he was
never in sympathy with the corrupt element of the town, and wished
heartily to see the place purged of it. Justice was administered, or
assumed to be, with the least possible regard for appearances. The
officers of the law had generally one additional calling, aside from
those that imply knavery, and this not unfrequently the keeping of a
south-western "grocery." Courts, especially justices', were held wherever chairs could be induced to approach each other, and tables had
regard enough for the majesty of the law to *stand on their legs*. After
wrangling in the court-room, where justice failed, perhaps, to maintain her balance, attorneys, constables, jurors, clients, and witnesses
would adjourn to one of these groceries, and there the goddess would
lose her balance entirely.

But even such occasions for an interchange of feeling, false or
genuine, as the case might be, were not so often sought as a more convenient intimacy with the pleasure-giving contents of the "groceries."
The bottle was frequently brought into the court-room, placed in state
before his "Honor," and *not out of reach of the lawyers;* and when
the stream of justice began to run thick with doubts, objections, and

quarrelsome citations, "forty-rod" whiskey was poured into it, and all became smooth again. With a law-book under his arm, and a knife and pistol in his belt, Mr. Worthington was wont to pass through the streets of Granby. He invariably carried weapons. The arrest of hardened offenders raised mobs, and an examination for commitment was the signal for rescue. He, however, prosecuted or defended—threatened life for life—was known to possess unflinching bravery, and was not molested. His practice grew large and lucrative, and he soon acquired the reputation of being one of the shrewdest and most successful lawyers in south-western Missouri. By the Spring of 1857, the presence of the gambling, counterfeiting, and horse-stealing fraternity had become intolerable, and the respectable citizens of Granby employed Mr. Worthington to prosecute the ringleaders, and, if possible, purge the town. He procured the indictment of five, including one Berry Dodson, a constable. Eighty or ninety took fright and ran away, and the remainder were wise enough to hide their diminished heads in silence, and assume the outward appearance at least, of respectability. The usual incidents of an attorney's life then attended Mr. Worthington, until war loomed up threateningly in the political horizon.

On the last Monday of December, 1860, the Missouri State Legislature convened at Jefferson City, with a working majority of secessionists, or at least of tender-footed conditional Union men. A bill was speedily introduced calling for a convention to take into consideration the condition of the country. The bill was referred to the Committee on Federal Relations, and reported back with a recommendation that it pass. On its second reading it was amended by the insertion of a clause that whatever the action of the convention might be, it should be submitted to a vote of the people of the State. February 18th, 1861, contemporaneously with a similar event in Arkansas, the election was held for delegates to the convention. The district in which Mr. Worthington resided polled a large Union vote, and the State was carried by Union men.[5]

It is not our purpose to enter, in this connection, the field of general history. Let it suffice to say that the State did not secede. While the convention was in session, prominent rebels were untiringly at work, educating the masses for the ready adoption and hearty support of secession. Attempts were also made to organize the able-bodied men under an odious military bill of the previous winter. Resistance sprang up at once, and in Granby Mr. Worthington rallied the loyal men. Once a week they appeared on drill and at all times were ready to obey the call of any emergency that might be sprung upon them. Occasionally our friend appeared in public debate. At Bolivar, Polk county, in March, 1861, he boldly took issue with Hon. Waldo P. Johnson,[6] giving the lie, to use plain language, to his unfounded calumnies, and to the assertion that northern men would not fight, declared himself one, and repeated the declaration that the statements of his antagonist were false, and he knew them to be so, and awaited the issue. None came—the meeting adjourned, and secession in Polk county received a serious check. He also met, in public discussion, the late rebel General Rains,[7] and found no difficulty in "driving him to the wall."

On the retreat of General Price from Boonville in June, 1861, the military of South-western Missouri, not yet efficiently organized, and to a considerable extent indecisive, especially in the vicinity of a large armed force, scattered. Mr. Worthington's company proving, in part, to be men in buckram,[8] he abandoned the militia and hastening to Springfield, offered his services as a scout and guide to General (then Colonel) Sigel.[9] Rendering him essential aid in ascertaining the movements of General Price and those with whom he was co-operating, he started two days before the battle at Carthage for Lamar, Barton county, to ascertain the strength and movements of a force under Generals Parsons[10] and Rains, understood to be moving south to form a junction with Price. To cut off this force was Colonel Sigel's great object.

One Nathan Bray, with whom Mr. Worthington was well acquainted, then lived at Lamar, and for reasons not necessary to allude to here, kept himself well advised of rebel movements in the South-west. This our friend knew, and determined, if possible, to see him. Arraying himself in orthodox "butternut," he made his way easily to Lamar, and entered the town. He was well acquainted in the county, and not having heard of any troops at or in the immediate vicinity of Lamar, anticipated no danger. But rebel uniforms are hard to describe; and alas for human calculations! our friend, on entering the town, saw the streets thronged with citizens apparently, but who nevertheless seemed to take an especial interest in him, and he soon found himself in "durance vile." Thus ended his scouting for the present. Sigel, however, fought Parsons and Rains, with Governor Jackson thrown in, at Carthage, and had he not received intelligence of the near approach of Generals Price and McCulloch, with a greatly superior force—

in fact they were then but twenty-two miles away—the result of the day's contest might have been very different. As it was—but no matter—we are not essaying history. Our friend was at once ordered into close confinement as a spy, and so held until after the battle of Carthage. The rebels, notwithstanding their success, moved in a southerly direction, taking Mr. Worthington with them. From this point until he was again master of his movements, we insert his own narrative:

"We reached Cow-skin Prairie on the ninth of July, four days after the battle of Carthage. Here an *ex parte* examination was held in my case, by General Price, and it was decided that I should be retained as a prisoner during the war. I was then turned over to the custody of Lieutenant Still,[11] Provost Marshal of Parson's division. Something now had to be done. The rebels of Rains' division resided in south-western Missouri, and were my inveterate enemies. To Parsons and his men I was an utter stranger. Knowing that an animosity had sprung up between Generals Parsons and Rains, which had communicated itself to their men, I determined to avail myself of this to the utmost. The evidence against me came entirely from Rains' division. I sought an interview with Parsons, and boldly told him that my confinement, and the charges that led to it, were malicious; that the men who gave evidence against me were my personal enemies; that many of them were deeply indebted to me, and desired my death—hoping that thus their debts would be cancelled—while others were my political enemies. I also stoutly affirmed that I had always been a State Rights democrat and a Southern man.

"About the time that I had this interview, we were joined by Pierce's brigade, from Arkansas.[12] To most of the officers of the Fifth Regiment of that brigade I had been well known as a State's Rights democrat, and this circumstance confirmed what I had insisted upon before General Parsons. Among others, a Lieutenant Jones,[13] of Carroll county, Arkansas, whom I had known some years before—by the way, an unprincipled and unpopular specimen of Secessiondom—undertook for fifty dollars to procure my release. Going to General Parsons, he told him that I had been a rebel from the beginning and used all his influence with the Arkansas officers in my favor. I was soon allowed the liberty of the camp, and this gave me still further opportunity to gain the confidence of the rebel officers. In this I made such progress, that on the 8th day of August I was released from custody, but ordered to remain within the lines until after the approaching battle of Oak Hill (Wilson's Creek). This occurred on the 10th of that month. I was that morning with Lieutenant Jones, in the camp of the Fifth Arkansas, and was eating breakfast when the fight began.[14]

"The attack was made in that part of the general camp by Col. Sigel. In the confusion I was overlooked, and made my way to him, and acted with him as a guide until about noon, when I was wounded in the neck by a musket-ball. The Federal forces soon after gave way, and I was left on the field. During the evening I was picked up and taken to a hospital. In answer to inquiries from rebels, I stated that I had been wounded by the Federals in the first attack on the camp; that I had endeavored to follow the rebel army until I sank with loss of blood. This tale, strengthened by Jones' representations, transformed me in rebel eyes from a Black Republican to a Southern hero. I was treated with the most marked attention, and on the 23rd of August was sent out of camp with a commission from General Price, as a Captain in the Missouri State Guard."

Thus ended an experience within the rebel lines, as singular as in its issue fortunate. Mr. Worthington's conduct was certainly very bold; but "nothing risked, nothing had," and he determined to pursue a systematic course of deception, until he should accomplish his purposes, or, in other words, escape. The old Jesuitical maxim came to his aid, and not inquiring very critically into its morality, he employed any means that his circumstances rendered available in bringing about the desired end. The Missouri State Guard was practically to him a nonentity. The captaincy therein, so trustingly tendered by a duped General, was not considered worth any active effort. The commission given served very well as a pass beyond the rebel lines, but the outside world once gained, it became *functus officio*.

Mr. Worthington now returned home, and his wound being very troublesome and painful, he was confined to the house until the first of November. Convalescing about that time, though he had very little strength in his wounded arm and shoulder, the rebel sympathizers in his vicinity became clamorous for his entry upon active service. They began also to regard him with suspicion, apprehending he was deceiving those whose cause he had assumed to espouse. They were right; but Mr. Worthington was not yet ready to attempt his ultimate escape from the meshes that circumstances had woven around him. He was still corresponding with and enjoying the protection of General Parsons. He treated their threats therefore with contempt, and quietly resolved to remain at home until his physical condition would admit of his joining the United States army. Its appearance was then confidently expected by the Union men of the South-west. General Frémont came to Springfield with a grand army. Price was then at Pineville with disheartened and demoralized troops, and had a vigorous advance been made upon him, with the powerful force that Frémont controlled, he could, at least, have been driven from the State. An advance was, in fact, made by Sigel's Division to Crane Creek, thirty miles below Springfield, and events looked promising. But something had gone wrong and Frémont was removed.[15]

General Hunter on assuming command, fell back, and dividing his army, moved one to Sedalia and the other to Rolla.[16] There may have been ample justification for this policy, but the people of South-western Missouri have not yet discovered it. Subsequent events have shown that Hunter could have driven everything before him, even to the Arkansas river, and it is an ineffaceable stain upon the national escutcheon, that General Price should have been permitted to take up his winter quarters in Springfield. The retrograde movement commencing, the Union men of the South-western counties of the State became alarmed for their own safety. The near approach of the Federal army had inspirited them, but their hope failed, and those who could, escaped northward. There was no other alternative. To remain, involved service in the rebel army or death, and neither alternative was sufficiently inviting to make them forgetful of their first duty to themselves.

The retirement of the Federal army was the signal for rebel boldness. Price's men took heart and retraced their steps. Mr. Worthington now considered himself in danger, and immediately made provision for his family during the winter. He gave out in conversation with both Union men and rebels, that he was intending to join the Confederate army and assume command of a company in Riley's regiment of Missouri State Guards. About the same time he wrote to General Parsons, stating his intention, as soon as his arrangements should be completed, and expressing a wish to command a company in the regiment referred to. The letter was entrusted to one Ryan, a genuine rebel, who returning brought an order from Parsons assigning Mr. Worthington to the desired command. Suspicion was now allayed, and the current of his life flowed smoothly until New Year's day, 1862, when a band of guerillas, led by ———— Wilburn and ———— Cole arrested him. They alleged that he was intending to join the Federal forces at the first favorable opportunity, and true to the instincts of their natures, plundered his home. It afterwards appeared that he had been reported by a little girl, who had overheard him tell his wife that he was going to Fort Scott, then held by Kansas troops. Wilburn was one of the "grocery" keepers of Granby, and to his establishment the mob was marched. Liquor had added to their hate, and a glance at his captors convinced Worthington that but little mercy was to be expected. He therefore asked none. A rope was brought to "stretch his neck," as they considerately informed him, and for three hours he was alternately threatened and promised. They charged him with knowing where the Federal forces were, especially the "Kansas men," but they brow-beated to no purpose.

By this time the news of his arrest had spread through the town, and been conveyed to one Captain Whitney, then commanding a rebel Home Guard company. He was a personal friend of Worthington, and now interested himself in his behalf. Marching up a squad of men, he demanded his release, and after some little altercation it was agreed that he should be delivered to Captain Whitney. The Captain then liberated him, with orders to report in the morning, when he would be furnished with an escort to Springfield, where the rebel army was then encamped. The same evening Mr. Worthington informed his wife that he should go at once either to Rolla or Fort Scott, determining his course after he had had an interview with Capt. Gullett of Lawrence county. That night he started and traveling until day-break, reached the house of his friend, and there learned that the Hunter and Lane expedition was about to move southward from Fort Scott. This intelligence shaped his course, and proceeding on foot, he arrived at Fort Scott on the 7th day of January. Here again we take up Mr. Worthington's narrative.

"On arriving, I immediately went to Col. Judson,[17] commanding the Sixth Kansas Cavalry, and enlisted as a private in company 'A' of the regiment. On the following day I was appointed second duty sergeant of the company, and detailed to recruit for the regiment at Fort Scott. At this time guerrillas were overrunning south-western Missouri, driving Union men from their homes, and committing numberless outrages upon persons and property. Singly and in small parties a large number came to Fort Scott. They were my neighbors and friends, and enlisted to such an extent that in a few days a full company was mustered. Being well acquainted with the country in south-western Missouri, I was shortly after my enlistment entrusted with the management of the scouts, in addition to my duties as a recruiting sergeant. On the first day of February I was appointed, by Col. Judson, regimental commissary sergeant, but as rations were drawn and issued tri-monthly only, this service did not materially interfere with my other duties.

"The Union men of Missouri continued to be closely watched by the rebels to prevent their joining the Federal forces, and one of our most arduous duties was scouting into the State to bring them out. About the 3d of February, I left Fort Scott with seven men, dressed in 'butternut,' for Newton county, Missouri, eighty-five miles distant. We represented ourselves as rebel scouts in the employ of Colonel Stan Waitie,[18] whose regiment was in the Indian country. South-west Missouri was at the time full of straggling bands of rebel soldiers, the country being in their possession, and General Price occupying Springfield. At Indian Creek, ten miles south of Neosho, which place was reached the fourth day after leaving the Fort, we commenced operations by attacking and dispersing a party of twelve guerrillas, under one Doctor Cummings, killing three men and taking seven horses. We then moved rapidly six miles north, to Granby, and surprised and captured nine soldiers belonging to the army at Springfield, took their horses and arms, and paroled them.

"We now gave out that we were part of a combined movement, under Colonel Jennison;[19] that all the roads were occupied by our troops, and that we intended taking in all the home guards and straggling soldiers in the country. We then moved on very rapidly from point to point, through the country, arming and taking with us all the Union men we could persuade to leave. The rebels, believing we were in the brush in great force, made no attempt to concentrate, and the result was, that in three days we had been reinforced by twenty loyal men, whom we had mounted and armed; had paroled thirteen prisoners and retained thirty-seven; taken forty-three horses, besides those rode by the prisoners and recruits, and eighteen mules; and as we were now so much encumbered, and expecting that a scout would be sent from Springfield, we commenced a rapid retreat towards Fort Scott. On the 9th of February we reached Langley Farm, six miles from Carthage, where we encountered a rebel captain named Potts, with sixty men. I immediately drew up my men in order of battle, in the 'brush,' placing my prisoners in line, and thus displaying a force of sixty-four men.

"Our loose horses were sent to the rear, and thus disposed, we waited the attack of the enemy. They remained in line about half a mile from us, and then advanced into the 'brush' on our right, for the purpose of attacking us in the rear. Discovering this movement, I started our loose horses, mules and prisoners across Spring river towards Fort Scott, sixty miles distant, placing them in charge of a corporal and six men. With twenty-one men I now drew up, on the north bank of the river referred to, and determined to dispute its passage at all hazards, and cover, if possible, the retreat of the prisoners and stock. The enemy soon appeared in sight, approaching the ford, but one volley cooled their ardor, and they fell back halting about seven hundred yards from the river. They there remained, apparently in consultation, about two hours, and then withdrew entirely from our sight. We were not strong enough to pursue, and resuming our march, arrived safely at Fort Scott, on the evening of the twelfth of the month, without having lost a man or a horse."

Thus ended one of a series of scouting expeditions on the border, which, however it may have been at variance with the modes of regular warfare, gave aid to Union men, and in the army parlance of the South-west, "everlastingly woke up" the rebels. On the 4th of March Mr. Worthington left camp alone, under orders from Colonel Deitzler,[20] commanding the forces in Southern Kansas, to proceed to the Arkansas line, and ascertain carefully the quantity of forage and the probability of sustaining a cavalry force in the country. He was absent five days, and returned, reporting favorably. No events worthy of special notice had occurred. His mission, however, was perilous, and called for the exercise of that coolest type of courage, the daring of the scout.

Early in the month, the Fifth Kansas Cavalry and three companies of the Sixth moved southward from Fort Scott, under command of Lieutenant Colonel Clayton of the Fifth,[21] and established a post at Carthage. The three companies of the Sixth were shortly afterwards at Bower's Mill, on Spring river, fifteen miles further east, and making that point their base of operations, were actively engaged in clearing the surrounding country of guerilla bands and in giving aid to the militia then enrolling in South-west Missouri, until the 8th day of April, when they were ordered to Fort Scott, and the Fifth Kansas to Rolla. On the 2nd of the month, Mr. Worthington had been dangerously wounded in a skirmish, and when his company moved, was lying at Mount Vernon, unable to accompany it. About the 1st of June, being now able to ride on horseback, he set out with Colonel

Richardson of the 14th Cavalry, Missouri State Militia, on an expedition to Neosho. Approaching Granby, Mr. Worthington was sent forward with twenty-five men to attack the notorious marauder
Livingston, who, with his band were supposed to be hovering in its
vicinity. They were fallen in with, when a sharp running fight ensued,
and five of the gang were killed. A ball, fired by Livingston himself,
grazed Worthington's cheek, but beyond this, no injuries were
received by him or his party. They now followed the main command
which had moved on to Neosho. Here, three days later, Colonel
Richardson was attacked by Coffee and Waite, with a force of twelve
hundred men, whites and Indians. His own mustering but one hundred and seventy-five men, fit for duty, he was compelled to return,
which he did without serious loss.[22]

Mr. Worthington remained for a time in and about Mount Vernon,
scouting with the militia, and waiting for an opportunity to go to
Paoli, fifty miles north-west of Fort Scott, where his regiment was
then stationed. On the 21st of July he received authority from Colonel
M. LaRue Harrison, commanding the First Arkansas Cavalry, to raise
a company for that regiment. Knowing that there would be no difficulty in obtaining a discharge from the Sixth Kansas, if he succeeded
in this new enterprise, he immediately went to work with great vigor,
and so well did he succeed that on the 7th of August his company was
mustered into service. In the latter part of this month it was deemed
advisable to send a scouting party into Carroll county, Arkansas, and
a force of one hundred men from the First Arkansas Cavalry was
ordered out, commanded by Captain Charles Galloway, with Capt.
Worthington as second in authority.

Leaving Springfield, Missouri, they moved rapidly to Berryville, in
Carroll county, without meeting opposition, or discovering any but
straggling marauders, thence still more speedily to Carrollton, the
county seat. Here they observed a guerrilla band strongly posted on a
bluff, a short distance east of the town, and partially concealed by a
rude breastwork of logs. They had evidently intended to "stand," and
seemed to think themselves secure against cavalry. Captain Worthington
was ordered to gain their rear, if possible, by a flank movement to the
right. The nature of the ground not admitting this, he dismounted his
men, and advanced thirty-six to within two hundred yards of their
position. They still betrayed no signs of fear, and were evidently in no
hurry to get away. Unfortunately they were not prepared for the range
of the Whitney rifle,[23] with which the First Arkansas is armed, and

very soon concluded that safety lay in flight. Immediate pursuit followed, but the usual celerity of "bushwhackers" saved all but two, who were taken prisoners. Several horses and guns, and some camp equipage were captured.

Learning that a force much larger than his own was in the vicinity, Capt. Galloway deemed it prudent to retire. He then fell back to a strong position on Yokumn's Creek, and awaited their advance, expecting a night attack. They came, in fact, within two miles of him, but anticipating, apparently, an ambuscade, and believing, doubtless, that discretion was the better part of valor, fell back. Galloway now hastened to Springfield, losing neither man nor horse, having penetrated eighty miles into the enemy's country, carrying terror to the marauders with whom Carroll county was infested, and enabling a number of Union families to escape from further persecution and outrage.

In September, while the rebels were in possession of Cassville, and Capt. Gilstrap, of the First Arkansas Cavalry, was stationed with his company at Crane Creek, to watch them, Galloway and Worthington, with a detachment of one hundred men, were ordered to coöperate with him in a descent on the town. Early on the morning of the 21st the dash was made. It was a complete surprise, and resulted in some excellent "skedaddling."—[From the Greek Σχεδαζὼ—to scatter.] The notorious Hawthorne was among the first to leave. Others were not so fortunate, though they seemed to prefer flight to powder and ball. Several were killed, and more taken prisoners, who, with a number of horses, were sent to Springfield.

On the 18th of October, the second battalion, to which Captain Worthington's company belonged, were ordered to Elk Horn Tavern. While there, it was engaged in numerous scouting expeditions, but especially in one to the source of the White river, and another growing out of this. The first, consisting of a detachment from the same battalion, Major Thomas J. Hunt,[24] commanding, proceeded early in November to the head of the west fork of White river, dispersing several gathering bands of home guards, and capturing a large number of horses. While returning, five men separating from the command, failed to report on its arrival at Elk Horn. A few days afterwards, it was ascertained, as the news came in, that they had been "gobbled up" by Ingraham's men, a notorious band of bushwhackers, infesting Benton and Washington counties.[25]

On the fifteenth of the month, Capt. Worthington and his command, with twenty-five men from squadron "B," under Lieutenant

Wilhite, were dispatched to "gobble up" the "gobblers." Reaching Pearson's Bend, in White river, thirty miles south of Elk Horn Tavern, Capt. Worthington learned that Ingraham, with from thirty to forty of his followers, was concealed in a cave two miles distant. The place was inaccessible to cavalry, and it was therefore necessary that the attack should be made on foot. Darkness had now set in, and the night was cloudy. Dismounting his men, and leaving a sufficient number to guard the horses, with the remainder he moved cautiously towards the cave. Advancing a mile and a half, an armed man was descried, and without ceremony shot. They now pushed forward through the darkness more rapidly, but still cautiously, the men grasping the scabbards of their sabres to prevent betrayal from that source. The "bushwhackers" heard the firing, but as men for reconnoitering purposes were kept out in different directions, they were in doubt as to its cause. The cave was defended in front by a rock, and on either side by a rough breast-work of logs.

Dividing his men, and stealing up in order, every man armed with rifle and sabre, and many of them also with Colt's "Navy sixes," the most acceptable revolver in the South-west, at ten paces from the cave a sentinel hailed them. He was answered with the crack of a Whitney rifle. Instantly the hill was lit up with the flashes of guns, and then, for the first time, the bold besiegers became aware of the formidable character of the "bushwhackers'" position, and the difficulty of driving them from their rude fortress. But they were all marksmen, and though guided alone by the most transient of lights, pressed up dauntlessly to the breast-work and endeavored, yet unsuccessfully, to scale it. The daring of the attack, however, overawed the besieged, and they fell back to an opening leading from the cave to the river. Captain Worthington now ordered his men to fire between the logs and the crevices in the rocks, and this they did with such effect, although the darkness was intense, and it was impossible to aim with precision, that in a few minutes, the "bushwhackers" retreated precipitately. Two of them were killed, five wounded, and five horses and nine guns were taken. The only casualty upon the other side was the slight wounding of G. A. Hottenhauer, First Sergeant of squadron "B." The party now returned to Elk Horn, and for a time Ingraham ceased to be troublesome.[26] Captain Worthington continued in active service at Elk Horn, now sitting on a military commission, and now scouring the adjacent country, until the day before the advance in that direction, of the second and third divisions of the Army of the Frontier, a short time prior to the battle of Prairie Grove. He was present with his command at that engagement, but it being almost exclusively a contest with infantry and artillery, he was not ordered under fire.

He now commands the Provost Guard of the divisions mentioned, and is energetic and efficient in the discharge of his duty. Quick to discern and prompt to execute—a safe counselor and a bold leader, he is admirably fitted for the service of the South-west; and if life and health are spared, will yet make the foes of the government feel the force of his avenging arm.[27]

CAMP AT PRAIRIE GROVE, ARK.,
December, 1862.

THIRTY DAYS AT ELK HORN TAVERN.

ON THE 10TH of November, 1862, the writer was ordered from Springfield, Missouri, to Elk Horn Tavern to take command of the first and second battalions of the First Arkansas Cavalry Volunteers, then holding the post. At that time, the second and third divisions of the Army of the Frontier had fallen back into Missouri, and the first, Gen. Blunt commanding, was in camp on Lindsey's prairie, near the line between north-western Arkansas and the Cherokee Nation. Elk Horn Tavern, situated on Pea Ridge, Arkansas, and itself the centre of the fiercest fighting of the three days' conflict of March last, is a rude old fashioned structure, on the Virginian model of a hundred years gone. Its overhanging roof and capacious chimneys, built up sturdily from the outside, as though scorning modern improvements, give it an air of comfort, and in the days of the overland mail, its good cheer was most ample.

At the time we mention, it was an outpost for the main body of the Army of the Frontier, then lying from forty to fifty miles east of it. Gen. Blunt was forty miles nearly due-west, but relied on this post to facilitate his dispatches to Gen. Curtis, commanding the Department of the Missouri.

The military telegraph had lately been continued to Elk Horn, and it was therefore of great importance to hold the post.

There was no intermediate office between Elk Horn and Springfield —strange, too, that there was none at Cassville—and had the post been abandoned, two days' hard riding by messengers, with all the delays and dangers incident thereto, would have been added to the vexations—always numerous enough—of keeping up a long line of communication. Moreover, the place was threatened by guerrillas, an insignificant enemy when the movements of a grand army are considered, but by no means to be sneered at in defending outposts, generally weak in numbers, and always hazardous in position.

Such was Elk Horn Tavern—*a town of one house*—on the 14th day of November, 1862. Scarcely had the writer arrived, when information came in that the wires had been cut. Keitsville, as pestiferous a place as can be found above ground, lay ten miles north-easterly, and a detachment was at once sent up the road to trace the depredators and repair damages. The evidences of the mischief were discovered near the town referred to, but the wily rascals who caused it, had taken to the "brush." Administering some wholesome advice to the inhabitants of the neighborhood, that closed with the significant intimation that if the offence was repeated, not a house would be left standing for miles along the highway, the officer in command returned with his party to Elk Horn. The threat had its effect, and for weeks the line was undisturbed.

On the morning of the 15th, a scouting party was sent out under the command of Captain Worthington of company H, to scour the country adjacent to White river, to rescue five men who had recently been captured by Ingraham's band, and if possible, "take in" Ingraham himself. While out, there occurred the fight in the dark, to which illusion has already been made. Ingraham, however, was not captured, and is still at large, robbing and retreating. The same day were furnished twenty-five men to escort the daughters of Isaac Murphy to their home in Huntsville, forty miles distant. On the morrow, arriving within a mile and a half of the place, it was deemed prudent to allow the young ladies to go on alone. There were no appearances of danger, no rumors afloat, and the men were permitted to dismount. They had stopped at the base of a small hill, near an intersection of roads, and the surrounding country was favorable for a surprise. Suddenly between sixty find seventy horsemen dashed in upon them. A few sprang into the saddle. Others were unable to, and took to the woods, and still others were captured. A feeble resistance was made, and those who escaped were very much inclined to say, each to the other, *put not your trust in appearances.*[1]

The detachment, save the prisoners, seven in number, came finally into camp, and all reports concurred in the fact, that the attack was made by regulars aided by a number of home guards. The information was important enough to warrant reconnoitering, and accordingly on the 17th inst., Major Johnson, commanding the First battalion was sent out with a detachment of two hundred men, with orders to penetrate as far as Huntsville if he should consider it prudent to do so, at all events to ascertain whether any considerable force had actually moved up from below. Such a demonstration was not improbable, for many of the Missourians in the Trans-Mississippi army were known to be disaffected, and claiming for an advance in the direction of their homes. Starting in a severe rain storm that continued for thirty-six hours without cessation, Major Johnson forded White river with difficulty, and then pushed on rapidly towards Huntsville. When within ten miles of the town, he was met by loyal citizens, known to be such, who confirmed the surmises then current at Elk Horn, even among citizens of Huntsville, that there was at that place at least a brigade of rebel soldiery.

Major Johnson now threw out his scouts, placing a trusty officer in charge, who reported a confirmation of the previous statements, and added to their definiteness by rehearsing the story of certain persons, who declared solemnly that they had themselves seen cannon in the streets of Huntsville, pointed in the direction in which the Federals were expected to approach. The White river was now rising rapidly, and the danger of being cut off serious, in case a retreat should become necessary. Those who ought to know had informed Major Johnson of the condition of affairs at Huntsville, and having been ordered out to reconnoitre simply, he wisely concluded to return before the White river should effectually bar him. His command were compelled to swim the stream, as it was, and two horses were drowned.[2]

But the sequel showed how a party of reconnaissance can be deceived. There had only been at Hunstville those who attacked the escort, mostly Jackman's men,[3] and these secretly made their way into Missouri, directly after the skirmish. Madame Rumor, and citizens whose selfish fear of a foraging party was more powerful than their patriotism, ruled the hour, and dispatches were forwarded to headquarters that would have answered very well as addenda to "The Arabian Nights" or "Sinbad the Sailor."

There were at this time in confinement at Elk Horn, certain citizens of Arkansas, against whom charges had been preferred for offences known to military law.

Among them was one John Bell,[4] a tenant of David Walker, of convention memory. On the morning of the 16th his wife drove within the pickets, accompanied by a lady, well dressed and intelligent. Her conduct exciting the suspicion of John Camp, of Fayetteville, then a refugee at Elk Horn, she was arrested. Of course she must know why, and expressed very great surprise that she should be so severely dealt with. She declared positively that she came simply as a companion for Mrs. Bell, and to aid in effecting the release of her husband. Moreover, that she had left her "little one" at Fayetteville, and was very anxious to return to him. Upon further inquiry the "little one" proved to be a boy *thirteen years of age,* and her general conduct continuing to be suspicious, it was concluded that she would "do to hold."

The tavern was occupied in part by the wife and family of its owner, then in the rebel army, and with them Mrs. Vestal was domiciled.[5] She was frequently observed looking searchingly down the Fayetteville road, and often enquired for the newspapers, always wishing the latest. Like a true student of the times, she invariably scanned the telegraphic columns first, and seemed to be deeply interested in the war budget. She was a puzzle to us all, and on the 17th, Capt. Martin D. Hart, of Texas, then at Elk Horn with a number of Texans who were making their way homeward with the view of raising a regiment, was granted the privilege of taking such a course as he might choose to adopt, for the purpose of ascertaining her real character. By arrangement, it was represented to Mrs. Vestal that an imprisoned Texan captain wished, if agreeable, to have an interview with her. It had been previously ascertained that she had traveled in Texas, and the request was eagerly acceded to. Arrayed in "butternut" of the most approved color, Capt. Hart was marched to her apartment under guard, the sentry remaining at the door. He introduced himself as a Captain Watrous, of Hunt county, a veritable officer in the rebel army, and soon acquired her confidence. She now informed him that she had left Van Buren on the Tuesday previous; that between twenty thousand and thirty thousand men were assembled there and in the vicinity; that the cavalry advance was at Cane Hill, and that thirty days' rations were being prepared for a forward movement.

She further exhorted him to be of good cheer; told him that he need not be uneasy about his situation, and that if he should reach the Confederate army before she did, he must not fail to inform a certain Missouri regiment of her arrest and detention.

"But, Captain," at length shrewdly suggested his fair confidant, "I did not see you in the guard-house this morning when I visited it with Mrs. Bell."

"Oh! I am an officer," was the ready reply, "and they allow me the liberty of the camps." But the position was becoming critical, and the prisoner Hart, *alias* Watrous, thought it about time to beat a retreat. He therefore excused himself, not wishing to intrude himself too much upon the lady's time, and signifying to the guard his readiness to be taken away, bowed himself out and was formally marched off. The following morning this Vestal, in name at least, was taken to Cassville, thence to be forwarded to the Provost Marshal General at

Springfield. Mrs. Bell remained at Elk Horn long enough to find out that her husband could not return with her, when she departed for home, a sadder but a wiser woman. While Mrs. Vestal's case was under consideration, and a military commission was sitting, events were thickening below.

On the 15th, General Blunt had telegraphed that Marmaduke with five thousand cavalry and four pieces of artillery was at Rhea's Mill on the 14th, and that Hindman with a large infantry force was coming up from Mulberry creek to join him. He, nevertheless, expressed the determination to fight them, but desired active scouting in the direction of Elm springs, Fayetteville and the White river. The enemy, however, fell back across the Boston mountains, and for a time it was thought by those who wear the stars, that he would retreat, not only to Van Buren, but thence to Little Rock. These conjectures proved to be incorrect. Marmaduke again advanced, and General Blunt, to cripple the enemy before they should be able to concentrate, made a forced march of thirly-five miles, and attacked the rebel cavalry at Cane Hill, driving them back in disorder to the Boston Mountains.[6] He now took a position and waited developments. It soon became apparent that Hindman was intending a general advance, and dispatches for headquarters came "thick and fast" to Elk Horn.

Though General Blunt is the personification of bravery, and when the danger was imminent of being attacked by far superior numbers, could characteristically predict "one of the d——dest fights or foot races ever heard of," he was not unmindful of the necessity for reinforcements. More than once he telegraphed to bring forward the second and third divisions, but their advance was tardy, and when General Herron arrived at Elk Horn at noon, on the 5th of December, Blunt's pickets were engaging the rebel vanguard. While these events were passing, the cavalry at Elk Horn were not idle.

Orders were received to scout thoroughly to Yellville, seventy-five miles in one direction; to Huntsville, forty-five miles in another; and indefinitely towards Fayetteville and beyond. Aside from these orders received by telegraph, came a formal letter of instructions from the Commander of the Army of the Frontier. It ran in part as follows:

"That no misapprehension may exist, this is to inform you that your forces are expected to continually scout and scour all the country within your reach. One-half of the command may be on distant scouts all the time; the other portion should be constantly employed in your immediate neighborhood. No part of your forces should be idle at any time. You are expected to rid all the country within your reach of all small bands, guerrillas, provost guards, &c., &c. Your forces should continually harass the enemy by driving in pickets and skirmishing with advanced guards and detached parties, *capturing forage trains and commissary wagons.* No limit is placed upon the country through which you may act, but you are expected to go wherever you can, without unnecessarily jeopardizing your command. You are to relieve the Union people and punish the treasonable. Unfailing activity and the utmost vigilance are demanded at your hands. One large party, consisting of about one-half of your command, should be pushed near the enemy's lines and kept out all the time, capturing pickets, &c., and you may even go in rear of the enemy's forces, and do them all the damage you possibly can. Feel the enemy often, and communicate all information you may obtain. This force should be relieved by the other half after a scout of five or six days."[7]

All this was expected from two battalions of cavalry, who had never been *one hour* in a camp of instruction; and though now in the service from eight to nine months, under the most distressing circumstances, and called out by special order from the War Department, had, up to this time, been only partially clothed—there was not an overcoat in the line—and has never been paid. Added to this, they were not attached to any division in the Army of the Frontier. Campaigning by itself, the regiment was ordered first by one general and then another— the innocent shuttlecock between distant battledoors.

But the men knew the country where they were operating. They were on their native hills again, and were active and zealous in their efforts to support that Government, loyalty to which had caused them so much suffering. Scouting was maintained with vigor. Frequent inroads were made into the enemy's country—a party striking here to-day and there to-morrow—now moving around Fayetteville, and driving in Marmaduke's pickets at Cane Hill, and again dashing into Huntsville, or fighting the "bushwhackers" of Carroll county after their own method. At the same time men were needed to keep open telegraphic communication with the East, and occasionally to forward messages of the first importance to General Blunt.

Within the lines of the post, matters were more quiet. The "tavern" soon became a central point for the neighborhood, many of the citizens being attracted to it by their own necessities, and some, no doubt, from motives that would not bear the test of scrutiny. Women on horseback, with boys *en croupe,* and sacks in their hands, clamored for salt. Twenty-five cents a quart, payable in eggs, butter, chickens, money, the genuine ringing silver, *anything* for the saline treasure. Had Lot's wife been crystallized at Elk Horn, the monument of her disobedience would have been hailed *as manna from above.*

We had taken with us, for individual use, a bushel of 'fine table' and it so happened that just at that time, no one else had any to spare. The persistent women soon found this out, and we were compelled to go to bartering for our mess. It availed nothing to insist that we had already traded for fifteen chickens, had ten quail, and more butter and eggs than we knew what to do with.

"No, you must give me at least a quart. You have sold Mrs. Jones and Mrs. Smith some, and I need it as much as they do. Now you hav'nt got any pies, and I've some of the nicest you ever saw. I dried the peaches *myself.*" We took the pies and when that bushel of salt disappeared, made light drafts on the commissary.

Prisoners were frequently brought in, poor, ignorant deluded men, the rough work of the rebellion. Examinations were protracted or otherwise, according to circumstances, and, aside from their revelation of the dark phases of this revolt, the terrible effect of secession upon the poor and confiding, their occasional ludicrousness is deserving possibly of a passing notice.

"What is your name?" said the provost marshal, to one of them.

"Which?"

"What is your name, I say?" repeated the officer.

"Still."

"I know, but what is your first name?"

"J."

"No, it is'nt," chimed in his wife, pettishly. "Lilburn J. Can't you understand the provo?"

"Well," continued the marshal, "what does the J. stand for?"

"I don't know, I'm no scholar," replied the imperturbable Still.

"That all may be," said the marshal, now a little vexed, "but you *certainly* must know what that J. means."

"I don't sir, I did'nt put it there. You'll have to ask pap I reckon."

The provost marshal, now concluding that some other person would certainly have to be interrogated before the point could be cleared up, proceeded with the other features of the case.

One day in December, the pickets brought in a seedy, sallow vagabond looking individual, wearing an old straw hat, and clothed otherwise in the ubiquitous "butternut." He represented himself as from Lawrence county, Missouri, whither he was traveling with a sick wife. Further inquiry drew from him the assertion that he had been conscripted into the rebel service, and belonged to Bryant's battalion. He seemed familiar also with the topography of Benton county, and spoke freely of prominent rebels living there.

When brought to head quarters, it so happened that Lieutenant Thompson,[8] of company "F," itself from Benton county, was in the room. While questioning the man pretty sharply, Capt. Wimpy,[9] likewise from Benton, came to the door.

Hearing his own name mentioned, and seeing at once what was going on, a sly wink from the Lieutenant turned the case over to him.

"Where did you say you have been?"

"In the southern army; I was conscripted."

"Where do you live?"

"In Lawrence county, Missouri, when I am to home."

"They don't conscript up there," continued the captain.

"Well, I run down har to git out of the way of the army, and they picked me up," replied the prisoner not at all disturbed.

"You are acqainted in Benton county, I understand?"

"I am that," with emphasis.

"You mentioned Wimpy's name a little while ago, Wimpy, Wimpy!" said the captain, thoughtfully, "what Wimpy was that?"

"Dick Wimpy. He's a 'Fed' captain."

"You know him, of course, when you see him," continued the captain enquiringly, and looking him steadily in the face.

"I reckon I do," replied the prisoner, with a confident air. "I was at his house oncst; but I know his wife a heap better than I do him. He was away most of the time."

This was consoling, but the captain seeing that he was not recognized, began again.

"Were the 'rebs' after Wimpy?"

Prisoner, knowingly, "You bet. They watched his house."

"Who watched it?"

"Wilson Woodward was one."

"Anybody else?"

"I can't remember now."

Captain (still a little curious to see if the fellow did really know anything about him, for he told the truth when he mentioned Wilson Woodward) "What sort of a fellow is this Wimpy?"

"Well, he's a brave chap. I'd bet on him *quicker 'an I would on five aces.*"

The captain's modesty now overcame him, and he beat a retreat, not, however, until he had informed the forward individual that he was the veritable Wimpy in question.

Five minutes afterward a blank countenance went to the guard house.

While incidents of this character were arising at Elk Horn, army movements on the frontier were approaching a crisis. On the 3d of December dispatches were received, ordering all our available force, leaving barely sufficient to guard the post, to Fayetteville, from which place a strong reconnoitering party was to be sent out on the Cane Hill road. That night Colonel Harrison arrived with a part of the third battalion, and a supply of quartermaster stores. As soon as these could be issued he pressed on, leaving only a portion of two squadrons to guard the post. This was on the morning of the 5th. At noon of that day the advance of the third division, under Colonel Wickersham,[10] of the Tenth Illinois Cavalry Volunteers, galloped up. It did not come too soon. The perilous position of General Blunt had been known for several days, and telegraphed to head-quarters; and we, at Elk Horn, wondered why the army at Camp Curtis did not move. But, we were either civilians or subordinates, and in military strictness we suppose this was none of our business. The arrival of the advance was hailed, nevertheless, with delight, and when later in the day, the entire division passed by, followed hard on the morrow by the second, Colonel Huston,[11] Seventh Cavalry Missouri Volunteers, commanding, we breathed more freely.

Two days before, it was known that General Blunt confidently expected an attack within forty-eight hours, and the news had just come in of the engagement of his pickets. General Herron could not, therefore, move too rapidly. His march to Elk Horn had been quickly, very quickly made; but Blunt was in imminent peril and Herron felt the necessity of losing no time in going to his assistance. Still, his men were exhausted, and bivouacked for the night near Sugar Creek. He remained himself at the tavern, and on the following morning was off with his staff at day light.

And now we anxiously awaited the march of events as well as men. Our little post seemed like a deserted village, and was almost ready to be *driven into the ground.* The jay-hawking propensities of some of the soldiery had stripped us of our forage, burned up the fence rails which hitherto we had claimed the exclusive privilege of "guarding," killed all our "turkeys" of the porcine species, and— which last offense we charge to General Herron's *aids in black*—made off with our camp stool, broom, candlestick and two chickens that our salt had bought.

We had our humble apprehensions for the fate of the army. Blunt had been ordered to fall back two days march on Herron, but had not done so. He still stood his ground with dogged resolution that death only could overcome. Evidently it was Hindman's intention to attack and rout him before reinforcements could arrive, and had he done so, one more general would probably have been "retired," if not given the unenviable distinction of a disastrous court martial. But success is the favorite test of merit, and General Blunt's disobedience of orders, will not impair his reputation.[12]

From Sugar Creek the army under Herron marched with great rapidity, halting at Fayetteville no longer than was absolutely necessary to refresh tired men and horses. Early in the morning of the 7th he pushed on toward Prairie Grove, ten miles distant. The battle fought that day, though a decided success for the government, was a chapter of accidents. Blunt had expected to attack in a certain direction at day-light, and had sent out the night before a strong patrol to watch the road, up which the rebels were expected to come; but from some cause or other they failed to accomplish the object of their mission,[13] and before morning the enemy passed towards Prairie Grove, and attacked a portion of the Seventh Cavalry, Missouri Volunteers, who, falling back on the First Arkansas Cavalry, then by order moving with its train to General Blunt, threw it likewise into confusion, and all together retreated across Illinois Creek, skirting the northern side of Crawford's Prairie, the scene of the battle.[14] Herron, with his infantry and artillery, now came up, (the cavalry had been hurried forward to Blunt) and the rebel pursuers fell back across the creek.

It is not our purpose to enter into the details of this action. It is well known that Herron alone fought far superior numbers until late in the afternoon, when Blunt, having found *where the rebels were,* commenced a tremendous cannonading on their left, accompanied with a heavy fire of musketry.

It is said of Hindman, by those who were near his person, and endeavoring to obey his orders, that he gave them confusedly and in a high state of excitement, disheartening to his own aids, and when Blunt opened on him so terribly and the failing fortunes of the day began ominously to loom up, the pressure was too great and his self-possession seemed entirely to forsake him. For hours he had held a large force in reserve, infantry, cavalry and artillery, to attack Blunt in another quarter, and now they were too far away to successfully oppose him.[15] Herron, meantime, was hotly pressed. The daring valor of his infantry was beyond all praise, but superior numbers were telling fearfully on their ranks, and the rebels had every advantage of position.

Gen. Herron was a beaten commander, though he may not have known it, when Blunt thundered away on his right. On the other hand, had not Herron moved up so gallantly and attacked the rebels with such remarkable vigor, when we think of the wearisome march of his army—one hundred and ten miles in seventy-two hours—Blunt's position would have been extremely critical. Hindman crossed the Boston Mountains with twelve thousand five hundred effective men—no more, no less—for the express purpose of attacking Blunt, and nothing but the ken of prophecy could have foretold his fate, had the rebel general moved on the train at Rhea's mill, as he could have done, had not Herron opportunely appeared at Crawford's prairie. The relief was mutual. *Herron saved Blunt and Blunt saved Herron.*

All day long the cannonading had been terrific, and when night set in, the caissons in Herron's batteries were nearly empty. It was not known but that Hindman would attack in the morning, and had he done so, the splendidly served artillery of the seventh must shortly have been limbered to the rear for want of ammunition. Herron saw the exigency, and forthwith dispatched a trusty messenger to hasten with all speed up the Fayetteville road, and hurry forward the ammunition train. The messenger was told that he ought certain to meet it five miles beyond Fayetteville, and that it could not possibly be further away than Cross Hollows. He was directed however to ride on until he met it, and urge it, *urge it forward.*

About nine o'clock in the evening of the 8th, as we were sitting where Gen. Price was standing on the morning of the third day of the battle of Pea Ridge, when, with his batteries, Sigel opened on him so spitefully, and he thought it about time to "get out of that hotel," a weary and be-draggled man burst in and eagerly enquired for the ammunition train.

"Don't know anything about it, sir. Hav'nt been advised that one's coming."

"But there is," said the messenger, excitedly, "and Herron told me I would certainly meet it before getting to Cross Hollows. *The army is out of ammunition.*"

This startled us into a perpendicular at once, for we had heard from Prairie Grove, when it was thought the battle would be renewed in the morning. A detail was immediately sent galloping up the road to Keitsville to hurry forward the train as rapidly as mules could move it. Ten miles away they found it parked. With great haste, the teams were geared up, and the train set in motion. Shortly after daylight, it lumbered into Elk Horn *without a guard.*

Here was carelessness that might have been terrible in its consequences, and from our stand-point there was no reason to suppose the contrary. The ordnance officer in charge had been told at Springfield that a guard would speedily overtake him. In that hope he had pushed on without hesitation, though he knew it to be perilous to do so. Arriving at Cassville he was still without a guard, and none was to be had there. He moved on, nevertheless, for he knew he should be nearer the rear of the army than he then was. Ingraham's marauders were still troublesome in the neighborhood of Mudtown (euphonious name!) and Cross Hollows, and on the morning of the arrival of this train, news had been received that the day before some convalescent soldiers on their way to Fayetteville had been fired upon from the bushes, and three wounded.

A guard was now imperative, but the difficulty lay in getting it. Two detachments from our feeble post were then away on unavoidable duty, and we could only muster forty effective men for the defence of our position. We were not expected to furnish guards for passing trains, and of course were unprepared for this emergency. But the guard must be had at all hazards. Captain Galloway was ordered out with thirty-five men, Lieutenant Frank Strong, the post adjutant, accompanying, to turn the few stragglers who had come in to good account. On moved the train, and that night our defensive force was five men—the telegraphic repairer, George S. Albright, the operator, Lieut. C. C. Wells,[16] the post quartermaster, and ourselves.

Fortunately the battle was not renewed on the eighth. Of the two, the rebels were in the worse predicament as to ammunition. During the engagement a section of Murphy's battery,[17] commanded by Lieutenant Marr, had, by exceedingly well-timed shelling, killed or disabled all the horses attached to two caissons observed moving through the woods. The caissons themselves were afterwards taken and found to be well filled with grape, canister and spherical case, of the most approved *English* manufacture. This was no trifling loss for Hindman, and weakened in other respects, he retreated.

On the 10th the ammunition train reached Prairie Grove—early enough for a victory, altogether too late for a defeat. The circumstance is unimportant now, but had our arms met with a reverse, the quick decision of a court-martial would have disgraced—somebody. On the 14th of December we were ordered to Prairie Grove.

FAYETTEVILLE, ARK.
February, 1863.

CHARLES GALLOWAY.

THERE ARE SOME men to whom the busy life of a populous community is forever irksome. Aside from the demands of increasing families, a restless love of adventure urges a change of habitation, and as society becomes stable and habits of life fixed, they turn towards a wilderness. Of this class was Jesse Galloway, the father of the subject of this sketch. Residing for a time in Knox county, Tennessee, in which his son was born, October 15th, 1825, he removed thence to Morgan county in the same State, where he resided until the year 1828, when he settled in Morgan county, Indiana. A farmer by occupation, he applied himself vigorously to the needs of a large and increasing family, still his success was not equal to his wishes. Like many others, he thought he could do better, and hearing of the mild climate, the richness of soil, and the abundant natural productions of Southwestern Missouri, he determined to seek again a home.

Leaving Indiana in 1834, he settled upon Flat Creek, in what was then Barry county. The country was wild in the extreme. Deer were abundant on the hills and in the valleys; game of all kinds abounded; the forests were rich in the dainty sweets of bee-trees; grapes hung purpling in the woods ungathered and unsought; the air was vocal with the melody of a thousand songsters, and the climate itself knew neither rigor nor disease. Here Charles Galloway received the impressions that moulded his character. The boy of a frontiersman, he soon became bold, daring, venturesome. The ever faithful rifle was his constant companion, and the lonely rambles of early manhood became a fitting pupilage for the stirring scenes of his latter life.

The Mexican war breaking out, he enlisted as a private in Company "G," Third Regiment of Missouri Mounted Volunteers, Colonel Rawles commanding. This company, raised in the vicinity of Springfield, Missouri, was commanded by Samuel A. Boake, then a well known citizen of the Southwest.[1] Rendezvousing for the purpose of organization at Independence, on the Missouri river, the regiment was ordered thence to Fort Leavenworth. There its commissary stores were supplied, and other preparations made for war with the Indians. At this time the Apaches, Navajoes, and other tribes were especially troublesome, and while heavier military operations were going on below, it was necessary that the remote frontier should be carefully guarded. To that end the regiment to which young Galloway belonged was ordered first to Santa Fe. There a post was established and Colonel Rawles placed in command. From this point a portion of the regiment moved northward, Captain Boake's company included, established a post seventy-five miles higher up the Rio Grande river, and from that time until the close of the war, was actively employed in operations against the Indians. Young Galloway was frequently detailed for this service, and distinguished himself by his intrepidity. In an engagement with the Apaches he was painfully wounded in the foot, an injury from which he has never fully recovered.

Alternating thus between extreme peril and the leisure that a soldier often enjoys, when not in action or preparing for it; at one time boldly following the wily sons of the forest, reckless of ambush or assistance, and at another down at Santa Fe living in an Adobe house, and dancing with Mexican women; he returned at length with the regiment to Independence, and was there mustered out. Starting immediately for Springfield, he arrived on election day, and voted for Cass and Butler.[2] His democracy, sealed as it had been, with his blood, and thus speedily finding its true expression in the ballot-box, became a fixed principle of conduct, and nerved and sustained him in the trials that twelve years later were forced upon him. In February, 1849, he married, bought the old homestead and went to farming. Until the autumn of 1860 he remained quietly at home, pursuing his avocation and dealing in stock, when the approaching cloud in the political sky admonished him of the necessity for action, prompt and concerted.

The Flat Creek country, commonly so called, was then within the boundaries of Stone county, and had been settled by a class of men who mainly performed their own labor. They were hardy, industrious and honest—neither filling the community with backwoods gamblers nor lawless desperadoes—and in politics were almost, without exception, followers of Stephen A. Douglas. In the general election of that year, the county showed itself to be strongly Union—Flat Creek precinct, in which the subject of this sketch resided, polling a unanimous vote for Douglas and Johnson.

Charles Bird, then living on Crane Creek, and who had held the position of county judge of Stone county for a number of years, was elected to the lower branch of the State Legislature as a Douglas Democrat. Arriving at Jefferson City, the taint of secession infected him, and he wrote to his constituents that "secession was the popular side," advising some of them, also, of a corresponding change in his own views of national affairs. His conduct exasperated his former friends, and they manifested their disapprobation of it by returning to the State Convention, called for the purpose of deliberating upon the question of secession, a Union delegate, Judge Hendricks, of Green county. After the Convention adjourned, Judge Bird, up to this time remaining at Jefferson City, returned home a ruined politician and a disappointed man, and undertook the raising of a jayhawking and marauding company, yet under the guise of protection against jay-hawkers, bushwhackers, and other men of the like ilk.

There was associated with him one Isaac Bledsoe. By choice a minister and a Methodist, he sustained a character prior to the break-ing out of the "great rebellion," in harmony to some extent with his profession. An earnest adherent of the "Methodist Church South," he shared in the prejudices of his section, and when Missouri began to consider the question of secession, politics and the pulpit very soon became with him synonymous terms. Itinerating through Stone county, he "took his text from the Bible and preached from the news-papers," until he exhausted his piety and his purse—the latter never long—and took to bushwhacking. While raising men, however, he would be occasionally smitten with the hortative fury of his earlier days, and then disseminate treason under the cloak of sanctity and the Sabbath.

At such times he spurned all secular methods, and *the rebel in him* rising with his fervor, his defection burst every restraint, and no doubt his sympathizing hearers reflected the sentiment—

> "Heroes shall fall, who strode unharmed away,
> Through the red heaps of many a doubtful day—
> Hacked in his sermons, riddled in his prayers,
> The 'butternut' slashing what the 'shot-gun' spares."

The band known at first as Bird's, was afterwards more generally mentioned as Bledsoe's, and during the autumn and winter of 1861, ceaselessly depredated upon the property of the Union men of Stone, Christian, Barry, and other counties in south-western Missouri. So notorious, in fact, did it become, that Bledsoe's men were regarded as the central light in bushwhacking; the fruitful source of rapine and murder; the terror of Union men. In August, 1861, they murdered, in cold blood, Jesse Galloway, Charles' cousin, and then captain of a home-guard company in Christian county. Other citizens were also wantonly killed, and countless depredations committed by this band. Always dressed in citizen's clothes, the characteristic "butternut" prevailing, they moved about in the true spirit of guerrilla warfare, meeting by agreement in some secluded spot when a deed of darkness was to be committed, and separating each to his home or hiding place when danger appeared imminent. Cowardly as they were malicious, when found alone or a few together, they would insist on being orderly citizens, and unarmed, were generally "going for the doctor," or armed, were out "turkey shooting." During the summer of 1862 a military commission sat continuously at Springfield, Missouri, and no marauder's name appears upon its minutes so often as Isaac Bledsoe's.

With these men to contend against [im]mediately, and an approaching Southern horde farther off, Charles Galloway went earnestly to work. Without waiting for authority, he raised a company from Stone county, and tendered their services to Gen. Lyon, then commanding at Springfield. The company was ordered to the duty of home protection, and from that time until the battle of Wilson's Creek, remained in and near Stone county, a portion of the time held together, and again separating into small detachments for the better protection of families threatened by Bledsoe and his men. Captain Galloway, now bold and defiant, had become especially obnoxious to the rebels, and a party of sixty-three were sent by Col. Mackintosh,[3] commanding a Texan regiment in the vicinity, to entrap him.

"Joe Peevie" was employed as commander and guide. For a number of years sheriff of Barry county, he was somewhat noted in his locality, and though of low instincts and disposition, had managed to maintain a *quasi* respectability. He consorted with horse-thieves and cut-throats, and was a rabid secessionist. Possessing some influence, his tirades against negro equality won converts, and he readily raised a jay-hawking company. This was in the summer of 1861. Ennis Dixon, another notorious character, had likewise organized a bushwhacking band, and the two seemed now striving to out-maraud Bledsoe. The parson's *sanctity*, however, gave him the inside of the track, and he kept it.

Captain Galloway, having been advised of the meditated attack, called to his aid a few home guards, and thus feebly reinforced took position in the vicinity of Clark's Mills, on Flat Creek. About this time he had been personally threatened by William McKenney, a notorious rebel, living on Rock House Creek, nine miles northeast of Cassville, and knew that a determined effort would be made to take him. The imminence of his danger had only permitted him to gather forty-five men, and with these he prepared for a fight in the most approved bushwhacking method. Peevie, accompanied by "Wild Bill Price," well known in the Southwest, was cautious, yet he attacked with spirit, and Captain Galloway's reinforcement fled. His men reduced now to thirty, but animated by their intrepid leader, fought bravely. For half an hour the woods resounded with musketry, Galloway's men taking every advantage of trees, logs and thickets, and only firing when they could "draw a bead." The deadliness of their aim soon had its effect; "Wild Bill Price" vindicated his soubriquet, and the redoubtable Peevie turned his back on Clark's Mills, reflecting possibly upon the vanity of human hope. A horse had been shot under him, fifteen of his men killed, and a number wounded. Captain Galloway's loss was but one killed and three slightly wounded. Not knowing but that this attack came from the advance of the rebel army, ascertained to be near by, he fell back and moved hastily to Springfield.

Reporting in person to General Lyon, he was at once employed as a scout, and directed to find out accurately the position of General Price and his forces, then supposed to he marching towards Wilson's Creek. Starting southward, in company with Dr. Philip M. Slaughter, of Stone county, and avoiding the highway, they discovered near the house of John I. Smith, off the Cassville road, thirty-five miles below Springfield, the rebel advance under General Rains. Hastily dispatching Dr. Slaughter to General Lyon, Galloway struck again into the woods in the direction of Flat Creek. Stealthily moving about here and there, now on the flank of the enemy, and now in their rear, he soon acquired very valuable information as to their disposition and numbers, and made all haste to General Lyon. He met him two miles west of Springfield advancing upon the enemy. During the eventful 10th of August he was eight miles south of Wilson's Creek, having been sent in that direction after the Dug Spring skirmish, and was making his way back to General Lyon when the battle began. As soon as he learned the day was irretrievably lost, and the death of General Lyon, from whom the Southwest expected so much, certain, he sorrowfully turned his steps towards Stone county. There again he gathered a company, and when Frémont came to Springfield, tendered its services to him, and was frequently employed on scouting expeditions under the superintendence of Colonel John M. Richardson, now of the Fourteenth Cavalry, Missouri State Militia, then chief of scouts.

As we have elsewhere had occasion to state, the removal of Frémont, and the retirement of the grand army first assembled under him, left Southwestern Missouri in a most pitiable condition. The policy of the government was only manifest in the failing fortune of its cause, and the numerous arrests of loyal citizens, or their hurried departure from home. The men who had repeatedly rallied under Galloway became disheartened, and some of them, no doubt, compromised their patriotism for the sake of domestic security. The company disbanded, and Captain Galloway was shortly arrested by a party of one hundred and fifty men, sent into Stone county to "break him up." With twenty others he was taken to Keitsville, placed in a corn-crib, held there two days and a night, allowed one meal for every twenty-four hours, and was then taken before Judge Bird, heretofore mentioned, for examination. When asked if he was willing to join the Southern army, and replying that he was not, he was rudely told to stand aside—a direction which he construed to mean hanging. Some of his old friends, however, men who were under obligations to him for favors shown before the war, interceded in his behalf, and he was permitted to go home.

He remained there until fourteen days before the battle of Pea Ridge, when he was again employed is a scout, and a few days later was mainly instrumental in saving a large train, then in great danger of being cut off before it could reach the army. After the battle of Pea Ridge, he returned home, and there remained, endeavoring to restore his shattered possessions, until the summer of 1862, when he was tendered a captaincy in the First Arkansas Cavalry. Accepting the proffered appointment, he speedily raised a full company, and on the 7th of August was mustered into service. In the latter part of the month he signalized himself by a daring foray, with one hundred men, into Carroll county, Arkansas, dealing a severe blow to rebel influence in that section, and relieving many Union families.

Not long afterwards the notorious Coffee[4] appeared near the Arkansas line, moving northward. His destination, or the number of his men, no one seemed to know. Strange stories were told of his movements, and wild conjectures indulged in. At Springfield even, we were directed to be in readiness for an attack at a moment's warning, and shortly came the news that Cassville had been evacuated by order of the General commanding the district. Coffee, however, kept on until his discomfiture at Lone Jack compelled a precipitate retreat.[5]

The abandonment of Cassville was a serious blow to the buoyancy of Arkansas men, nearly a thousand of whom were now at

Springfield. Cassville was fifty miles nearer their homes, and they regarded that post as an indispensable link in the chain of communication that would ultimately re-unite their native hills and valleys to fatherland. A mad Convention had usurped the prerogative of the people, and the bitter fruit of secession was being tasted by the innocent and the unoffending. Making no concealment of their loyalty, they had been compelled to flee from their homes, and burning for the hour of return, the retreat from Cassville struck them like a cold chill. Whether politic or not, we do not assume to say. Generally speaking the abandonment of an outpost is an unwise measure. The motive will always be misunderstood. Speculation will draw the most extravagant conclusions, and rumor begotten of fear will circulate a thousand falsehoods, yet you cannot forget them.

The occupation then of Cassville by the rebel forces, shortly after the Federal troops retired, was to Arkansians and the loyal Missourians of the Southwest an eye-sore of the worst description. On the other hand military circles were not long disturbed, and a force was sent to Crane Creek with directions to keep out scouts below. Their intelligence was reliable that Cassville was held by a small detachment only, and it was, therefore, determined to make a descent upon the town. Leaving Springfield on the 19th of September with one hundred men, of the First Arkansas Cavalry, and obtaining at Crane Creek a reinforcement of seventy-five, under Captain Jesse M. Gilstrap, of the same regiment, Captain Galloway passed the Federal pickets and struck over the hills for Cassville. All regularity of movement was now disregarded, and dividing his men into two parties he approached the town from opposite directions. Lying in the adjacent woods during the latter part of the night of the 20th, early on the morning of the 21st he dashed into town from a southerly direction, Captain Worthington accompanying him, and leading a portion of the men, while Captain Gilstrap simultaneously hurried forward from the North. Between one hundred and fifty and two hundred rebels, reposing in confident security, were holding the town. They were the advance of a much larger force a few miles away to the South-West, and having their pickets out on the usual approaches, were unprepared for a sudden attack. Had a meteor fallen in their midst, it could not more thoroughly have startled them. Some, hastily mounting their horses, made all speed for a safer portion of "Dixie"; others trusting to the agility of the natural man, clambered up a convenient hill-side, while still others commenced an annoying fire from houses, the only display made of even the lowest type of courage.

Meanwhile Captain Galloway was hurrying his men into town. Tactics were "thrown to the winds," and above all the noise and confusion rose his shrill and peculiar voice—

"Charge 'em, boys, G——d d——n 'em, charge 'em!"

Language, we admit, more forcible than moral; but the boys "charged," gathering some of the escaping, hurrying others up the hillside with accelerated speed, and driving the remainder from their shelter, killing fifteen and capturing twenty. Captain Gilstrap co-operated well, and the victory was complete. Fugitives had now carried the news below, and an immediate retreat was necessary. Retiring over the hills, the next day Captain Galloway arrived at Springfield. Cassville was speedily filled with rebels, but they found nothing to fight.[6]

On the 18th of October, Captain Galloway was ordered to Elk Horn Tavern. While the battalion to which he was attached remained there, he was almost constantly engaged in the perilous duty of scouting. About the 1st of December he was sent out with about one hundred men, with Lieutenant Thomas Wilhite as second in command, and who was thoroughly acquainted with the country, to endeavor to break up a notorious company of marauders, known as Enyart's band.[7] Falling in with them on the main fork of White river, fifteen miles south-east of Fayetteville, a spirited skirmish ensued, in which Stephen Enyart, the Captain of the band, and one others were killed, and a few wounded. The rest precipitately fled towards the Boston Mountains.

To repulse the marauders of the South-west they must be met in their own way, and no men were better qualified for these hazardous operations than Galloway and Wilhite. The former now remained at Elk Horn until the 14th of December, when he was ordered temporarily to Cassville. Remaining there but a few days, he moved with his company to Fayetteville. Arriving again in Arkansas, he was put at once upon active duty, and took a prominent part in the forays made during the winter to the Arkansas river. He dashed into Ozark on the morning of the 4th of January, 1863, was halted by the pickets, but gave his characteristic order to charge, and drove a detachment of rebels out of the town; captured several prisoners and horses, broke up a score of shot guns, and destroyed a quantity of commissary stores. His own force was twenty-two men.[8]

The latent loyalty of north-western Arkansas breaking out in the most cheering manner in the latter part of January, but still requiring the support of the military arm, Captain Galloway, with a sufficient force, was present at Huntsville on the 31st, for which day a public meeting had been called. He left Fayetteville also for another purpose. It had been ascertained where the notorious Peter Mankins,[9] with a band of desperadoes, were secreting themselves in the South-eastern corner of Crawford county, and it was determined upon, "to break up the nest." This was a part of Captain Galloway's duty, in the discharge of which be was to receive co-operation from Captain Robert E. Travis, of the same regiment, who had magnanimously offered to go as a spy into the dangerous cane.

Born, we believe, in or near Indianapolis, and passing his entire life in the West, Captain Travis at the breaking out of the rebellion was a dealer in stock in Northern Missouri. For a time employed as a spy for the original army of the Southwest, he afterwards enlisted as a private in company "A," of the First Arkansas Cavalry. Subsequently receiving authority to raise a company, he did so, and at the time of which we speak was commanding squadron "M." We were then on detached service at Fayetteville, and well remember the appearance of the captain in our office the afternoon of his departure. Dropping in but for a moment, he pleasantly drew our attention to his habit, now completely that of a backwoodsman. Every garment of the army blue had disappeared, and we could not help thinking of Joseph's coat of many colors. No spy was ever more appropriately clothed. Suggesting that he be very cautious, for he was about to deal with the most desperate men on the border, and wishing him a successful enterprise and a safe return, he left the room.

We now quote from the report of Captain Galloway to Colonel Harrison, commanding the post at Fayetteville.[10]

"The first night after leaving I encamped on the Huntsville road, about two miles from that place. The next day I reached Huntsville at 11 o'clock, A.M. There being no rebels in force in the vicinity of the town, I remained there until the morning of the 1st inst., at which time, in obedience to your order, received at Huntsville, I started for Williams' farm. A little while after dark, of the same day, I reached Allison Hill's farm, about eighteen miles distant from Ozark, and twenty-five miles from Williams' farm, to which I intended to go. There it was rumored that there were one hundred rebels in Ozark, and three steamers above the place. I proceeded at once to Ozark, arriving just at break of day. I there found a rebel captain, whom, with a lieutenant I had captured the day before, I paroled. I also paroled four rebel privates. I remained at Ozark until 1 o'clock, P.M., waiting for the steamers, but they did not come down, and I started for Williams' farm. When I had proceeded seven miles, my advance drove three rebel pickets, whom I supposed to be patrols. The advance soon came in contact with the main force of the enemy, who charged, and it fell back to the main column of my forces, now forming in an advantageous position. The enemy came up to within one hundred and fifty yards of my line and opened, when the contest fairly commenced. After thirty minutes' severe fighting I repulsed him with loss. At this time I would have charged had I not feared an ambuscade. The enemy retreated with great precipitancy, breaking into small squads as they retreated, which scattered to the right and left of the road. From the most reliable information, I found that the rebels numbered one hundred and eighty men, and were commanded by Colonel Dorsey.[11] I could not accurately ascertain their losses, as they carried off their dead and wounded. Ours was one slightly wounded.

"The rebels were informed of our presence in the vicinity, and of our advance, and had been waiting for us one or two hours. From here I started to Williams' farm, reaching it about dusk. At eight o'clock a spy, who had been co-operating with Captain Travis, came into camp, and at nine the captain himself arrived. They had learned that Mankins' band, numbering thirty men, was immediately beyond the Arkansas river, and his (Captain Travis's) plan was to proceed at once to the river with his whole force, leaving one-half on this side to guard the horses, and sending the other half over the river to capture the guerrillas. This plan I considered defective, since I supposed that the rebels with whom we had the fight would probably return reinforced to their encampment, two miles from us, and not more than two from the ferry where we would have to cross the river. Moreover, my men were very tired, as also the horses, having had no rest since we had left Huntsville. My design was to attack the rebel camp in the morning, if they were not too strongly posted, but finding by one o'clock at night that the rebels had not returned to their encampment, and still considering it imprudent to move part of my forces across the river, I determined to start for Fayetteville in the morning.

"Captain Travis insisted on taking the men into the cane-brake for the purpose of capturing five or six of the enemy, who, he said, were to meet there to organize a band. He wanted no more than ten. I considered his proposed expedition nothing more than a small scout, and believing that there was no rebel force in the vicinity, granted his request. He was to rejoin me five or six miles from Williams' farm, and about the same distance from where he was going. He insisted, on starting out, that if he did not meet me there, I should go on, and he would overtake me. A little before daybreak I started for Fayetteville, and having marched about twenty miles, halted and fed. Some of the party now came up and gave information that Captain Travis and four of his men were killed or mortally wounded.

"The facts, as I gathered them from the men who escaped, were these: Captain Travis, leaving us in camp, proceeded at once to the cane-brake, two and a half miles distant. Finding some indications of an enemy in the vicinity, he marched until break of day, when he dismounted his men, hitched his horses, and began to search for them. He came to their camp, which was about one hundred rods from where he alighted, and found thirty horses tied to the bushes. Leaving one man to guard them, he proceeded with seven others to attack the rebels in their fortifications, whom he knew from their horses to number about thirty. When a hundred yards from the fort, a sentinel descried them and gave the alarm. The rebels sprang to their rifles and commenced firing on our men, who, opening fire in return, continued to advance until within thirty yards of the fort. At this time, when three or four of our men had fallen, the captain ordered a retreat, and while himself in the act of turning, received a mortal wound. His remaining men moved him about one hundred rods distant, where, after staying with him ten or fifteen minutes, they left him apparently dying. They overtook me at noon the next day. When informed of this disaster, I would have returned at once and recovered the wounded, if still living, and interred the dead, but owing to the fatigued state of my men and horses, I deemed it best to move on to Fayetteville. Entrusting the disposal of the dead and wounded to a citizen, and pledging him to attend to them, I moved on."

Poor Travis! he fell a victim to his own rash bravery, yet all honor to the man who could divest himself of his command, and so cheerfully volunteer to ferret out and rid that section of country of its most dangerous enemies. If he could not succeed, he could fight, and he paid the penalty of his daring with his life. A few days later an avenging expedition softened the remembrance of this disaster, by converting the block house in the canebrake into a mass of ruins, and driving its hated defenders ignominiously across the Arkansas river.[12]

We now leave Captain Galloway at Fayetteville, ready to render any service that may be required of him. We do not claim in his behalf the precision or the punctilio of the martinet, which very often, to secure the shadow, sacrifices the substance, but in those sterling qualities that adapt a man to the irregular warfare of the Border, enabling him to snatch victory, when the mere disciplinarian would suffer defeat, he has few equals and no superiors.[13]

FAYETTEVILLE, ARK.,
February, 1863

THOMAS WILHITE.

THE SOUTH WEST has given birth to no more daring spirit than the subject of this sketch. Born in Washington county, Arkansas, on the 23d of September, 1836, and reared upon the Border, early manhood found him a true representative of frontier life. Hiram Wilhite, his father, was one of the earliest settlers in Washington county, emigrating from Tennessee first to Frog Bayou, in its southeastern corner, and thence, eighteen years since, to Fall Creek, twenty-one miles south of Fayetteville. There the impressions that make the "child the father of the man" were imprinted on the character of young Wilhite, and he grew up as robust and vigorous as the forest trees that surrounded the paternal dwelling. A farmer's child, his boyhood was quite like that of most other boys, and had not the dogs of war been let loose some years later, at his own door, he might still be following the plough, or roaming over the Boston Mountains, a keen huntsman and a dead shot.

In politics, his father was a democrat of the Jeffersonian school, and young Wilhite early imbibed kindred views of public affairs. In the campaign of 1860, both father and son were warmly interested as Union men, nor were they at all timorous in the avowal of their sentiments. The all-absorbing topic of the time was the question of negro slavery in some form or other, and the utterance of views antagonistic to its extension, or even in opposition to the secession of the slave-holding States, was met first by contumely, then with hate and persecution. As between immediate and unconditional secession, and co-operation with the Border States, a phase which the troubles of the time assumed, the Wilhites favored the latter. They were, notwithstanding, unconditional Union men, and when in February, 1861, the people were called upon to send delegates to a State Convention to consider the grave question of separation, they worked zealously for Union nominees.

One of the candidates was Thomas M. Gunter,[1] a lawyer of position, residing in Fayetteville. Opposed to him was Wilburn D. Reagan,[2] another Fayetteville attorney, and a bitter, uncompromising secessionist. At a public meeting held at the place just mentioned, during the canvass, and conducted on the Southern plan, Gunter was called out, after a rabid speech by Reagan, made beneath a secession banner. He responded to the call, but declined speaking under the "damnable rag," pointing to it, and an adjournment took place to the Court House. In the crowd that followed him were Wilhite and a score of well-armed men, who were determined that he should speak without molestation, as now some symptoms of trouble were breaking out. Gunter began. To repeat the humble saying of the time, he told the boys to "stick up" for him and he would for the Union, and that he would suffer his right arm to he taken from his body sooner than cast a secession vote. This "Gunter's scale," however, proved to be of the sliding order. He sat in the Convention, cast his vote for the fatal measure that went like a knell to the prosperity of the State, and returning home, had the ignoble privilege of meeting those whom he had betrayed. The delegates from Washington county to this Convention seemed, before their election, happily to unite in denunciation of the suicidal doctrine of secession. The pure air of the White river hills apparently stimulated the noble spirit of self-sacrifice, and the determination to suffer their bodies to be maimed, at least on the part of David Walker and Thos. M. Gunter, rather than aid in taking the State out of the Union, was especially commendable. But the cotton lands of the valley of the Arkansas neutralized White river; Little Rock overawed Fayetteville, and the outstretched arms that had so patriotically been offered as a holocaust upon the altar of the Union, still obey original will, bodies and members committing treason together. After the secession of the State, Gunter returned to Fayetteville and accepted a captaincy in the Third Regiment of Arkansas State Troops. His defection was now complete, and whatever claims he may once have had to the suffrages of Washington county, his treason had obliterated every sense of obligation, and he stood condemned by his friends of a lifetime.

Whether on duty or otherwise, it so happened that he was in Fayetteville, when in July, 1862, Major Hubbard, of the First Missouri Cavalry, and Major Miller, of the Second Wisconsin, dashed into the town, with a very considerable scouting party, creating some consternation and more "skedaddling."[3] Though the occurrence took place early in the morning, Gunter was on the street, and discovering the approaching cavalry, hastily made a dissolving view of himself. When danger is imminent and one is flying from it, speed is everything, and the ex-delegate was very soon snugly stowed away in the attic of the house of a rebel friend, one Isaac Taylor. Why he did not seek his own home history does not inform us; quite possibly it was inconvenient for him to do so. Then again he might be caught *in transitu*, and hurried off to Springfield under circumstances that would compel him to leave his command behind, a conjectural condition of things more probable than pleasant. All day long the obscure but friendly attic concealed its strange inhabitant. The lower story was frequently searched for the occupant of the house, but the persistent Federals at length became satisfied that he was not at home. They little thought of the specimen of half suspended animation so short a distance above them, and for whom they had elsewhere looked in vain. Towards night "an intelligent contraband" disclosed his whereabouts, and he was dragged to the light, though he "loved darkness rather." Taken to Springfield he was there exchanged, and is now a colonel in the rebel army.

Such was one of the prominent leaders of the Union party in Northwestern Arkansas, but thanks to the sturdy common sense of the masses, his defection did not carry with it the majority of those who had determined, through weal or woe, to stand by the old flag. They have, however, cause enough to curse the day they voted for Thomas M. Gunter. The ruined farms and the desolate households of a once prosperous and happy community, will, for long years, couple his name with those of David Walker and John Parks,[4] a triumvirate of treachery. But we are digressing. Gunter was permitted to continue his speech, and the meeting adjourning, the people separated to their homes congratulating themselves upon the *firmness* and *devotion* of one of their principal leaders.

Shortly after this occurrence and before the secession of the State, Wilhite attached himself to a company of minute men, who were to be ready at a moment's warning to respond to the call of public danger. The most of the company were at heart Union men, and they secretly resolved to make their organization subservient to their own wishes. While matters were in this situation, one James M. Scott raised a secession flag in Cove Creek Township, and called on the minute men to rally beneath it. The *minutes* just then became hours, and Wilhite and his companions made haste to rally *very slowly*. In fact they flatly refused to do so, and Mr. Scott's banner hung lazily from the staff, looking for all the world as though it had been brought out to droop and die. Wilhite had now thoroughly committed himself to the Union cause, and it behooved him to look well to his personal safety. The rebel element predominated in his neighborhood, and the "strikers" and "tools" of the secession leaders, were implacable in their resentments. Not considering, however, that his immediate personal peril was so great as to warrant an abrupt departure from the State, and yet feeling that he must never go about unarmed, Wilhite remained at home and prepared to "make a crop." When following the plow a trusty rifle was invariably slung from his back, and a brace of revolvers were belted about him. At night the rifle stood at the head of the bed, and he often slept with his revolvers on. Several times when in the field he descried men coming to take him prisoner. He would then leave the plow in the furrow, slip into the woods and remain there until his enemies went away. There was no danger of their interfering with the horses or the plow. They knew too well the deadliness of his aim, and the disagreeable doubt as to who would be his victim, kept them all away from the peril.

One day in June six rebels, whom for the satisfaction of their friends, we will name, Gilhamton Walker, Calvin Walker, George Bell, Alfred Strickler, John King and William Sharp,[5] knowing that he was at home rode hastily up to take him, but he was too quick for them, and dodging around a corner of the house, with his rifle and revolvers, held his advantage while a parley took place. *They* informed *him* that they had come to arrest him because he was a Union man. *He* informed *them* that they would have to reinforce and come again, that six men were not enough for the business, and that if any of them "dropped a gun," one man would fall *sure,* and they would not know beforehand who it was to be. Like their predecessors who scouted the corn-field, they returned as wise as they came, even requesting that they might ride away unharmed.

Not long afterwards another squad rode up to the house for a similar purpose. Fortunately Wilhite was absent, but to his mother was *considerately* shown the rope with which they intended to hang him. Going during the same summer to Kidd's mill, near Cane Hill, for flour for the family, a knot of men gathered around and "allowed" to take him prisoner. On the other hand, he "allowed" that if they made any such attempt, he should defend himself to the last; that he had thirteen shots, and should try his best to make some of them "tell," and that they could not take him alive. His determination subdued the crowd somewhat, and T. K. Kidd, a merchant of the place, interceding in his behalf, on the ground that he might yet make a *good southern soldier,* he was permitted to transact his business at the mill and return home.[6]

There was living at this time not far away from Wilhite, a Baptist minister, known by many as "Old Tommy Dodson, the preacher," otherwise rejoicing in the christened name of Thomas. He was a violent secessionist, and preached whenever audiences could be assembled, whether on the Sabbath or during the week; nor did he confine himself to Biblical teaching. The sword of the spirit was not, in his judgment, the only weapon to be wielded for the Confederacy. His tirades were frequent and unsparing against Union men and Black Republicans, who, if they did not recant, were to be driven off or shot. On one occasion Wilhite attended his services, held at the house of Benjamin Strickler, on Fall Creek. The congregation was quite large for the locality, and in it were several soldiers belonging to the regular rebel army. The preacher's harangue savored, as usual, of public affairs. The secession of the State was justified; the public functionaries at Richmond lauded; a highly wrought prophecy of the grandeur of the New Republic was pronounced, and then fell the ministerial denunciation on all those who still clung to the old government. Warming with his subject, and evidently growing indignant, he exclaimed—

"If there is a Union man within the sound of my voice, I want him to leave the house, and leave it now—a."

Thinking it about time to depart, and having no reluctance to define his position, Wilhite started for the door.

"Then, go—a," resumed the excited and now somewhat exhausted preacher, moving towards the retreating Federal, "and darken not again the house of God. And do you, my brave boys," pointing to the rebel soldiers, "fight on for the glo-o-o-rious Southern Confederacy. The Lord is on our side. The Lord will help us to gain the independence of the South." By this time Wilhite was in the yard, and the Rev. Thomas Dodson began slowly to return to his normal condition. Eighteen months later, the same clerical gentleman was an inmate of the guard-house at Fayetteville, under charges for trial before a military commission, to sit at Springfield, and Wilhite was officer of the guard.

Alas! the mutations of sublunary affairs.

The summer and autumn passed without any special peril to Wilhite, other than what we have referred to, except that the necessity for vigilance was greater, so much, in fact, that in November he was compelled to "lay out." Anticipating a winter of trouble, unless he were to take unusual precautions against it, he had, by night, hauled one hundred bushels of corn and some other forage to a secluded spot

on the Boston Mountains, intending to pass the winter in a cave and
subsist a few horses. In this manner he lived, occasionally going home
clandestinely, until the month of May, 1862, when he secretly made
his way to Springfield, Missouri, with William Zinnamon,[7] who, for
a time had been his companion in the cave.

Colonel M. La Rue Harrison was then organizing the Arkansian
refugees into what subsequently became the First Regiment of
Arkansas Cavalry Volunteers, and Wilhite at once identified himself
with the project. Being empowered not long afterwards as a recruiting officer for the regiment, he left Springfield on the 5th of July, with
Dr. Wm. Hunter, of Washington county, and Thomas J. Gilstrap, of
Crawford county, afterwards respectively assistant surgeon and a lieutenant in the same regiment. Falling in with the expedition commanded by Major Miller, they proceeded with it to Fayetteville,
whence they moved on to the head of White river.

Recruiting in Arkansas for the Union Army was at that time it
perilous undertaking. Loyal men avowed their principles at the hazard of life, and the greatest difficulty to be overcome was in getting
recruits to the rendezvous of the regiment for which enlistments were
being made. The Provost Marshal's department of Arkansas, as
organized by Major General Hindman, then commanding the trans-
Mississippi district, was in active operation. Numerous companies of
provost guards had been formed, and, under color of orders, were
robbing Union men and committing all manner of outrages. They
were especially zealous in their efforts to check the growing tendency
to enlist in the "Abolition Army," as they termed it, and hunted with
the eagerness of a bloodhound those Union men who, first cautious,
and then expeditious, abandoned their homes for the woods, and the
woods for the Federal pickets. The general order that thus gave
license to rapine, and stimulated the blind zeal of a prejudiced people,
ran as follows, not omitting the italicized phrases as they appeared in
the original publication:

"GENERAL ORDERS NO. 17.

"HEAD QUARTERS, TRANS-MISSISSIPPI DISTRICT,
"*Little Rock, Ark., June 17, 1862.*

"I. For the more effectual annoyance of the enemy upon our
rivers and in our mountains and woods, all citizens of this district,
who are not subject to conscription, are called upon to organize themselves into independent companies of mounted men or infantry, as

they prefer, arming and equipping themselves, and to serve in that part of the district to which they belong.

"II. When as many as ten men come together for this purpose, they may organize by electing a captain, one sergeant and one corporal, *and will at once commence operations against the enemy,* without waiting for special instructions. Their duty will be to cut off Federal pickets, scouts, foraging parties, and trains, and to kill pilots and others on gun-boats and transports, attacking them day and night, and using the greatest vigor in their movements. As soon as the company attains the strength required by law, it will proceed to elect the other officers to which it is entitled. All such organizations will be reported to these head-quarters as soon as practicable. They will receive pay and allowances for subsistence and forage, for the time actually in the field, as established by the affidavits of their captains.

"III. These companies will be governed in all respects by the same regulations as other troops.

"Captains will be held responsible for the good conduct and efficiency of their men, and will report to these head-quarters from time to time.

"By command of Major-General Hindman:

"R. C. Newton, *A. A. Gen'l.*"[8]

By arrangement, Wilhite and Gilstrap, having for recruiting purposes gone into different neighborhoods, were to meet at the house of one Spencer Bullard, on Fall Creek, in Washington county, and there concert measures for the removal, or getting northward rather, of their recruits. For some reason or other, Gilstrap had departed on Wilhite's arrival, and the latter having with him twenty-eight men, determined to retire into the White River Hills and the Boston Mountains, and collecting from the adjoining settlements still other men who were anxious to get away, bide his time for departure. At first he went to Winn's Creek, at the head of the west fork of White river. His re-appearance in a country where he was so well known, and his object thoroughly understood, caused great watchfulness on the part of the secession element. One Doctor H. Spencer in particular, now a citizen prisoner, at Springfield, Missouri, under the general charge of robbing Union men, was very active in his endeavors to find out how many recruits Wilhite had. An old, vindictive man, with a countenance that would have betrayed him in a church, we well remember his appearance when brought before us for examination.

He had hunted Wilhite and others as the woodman seeks his game, and we made short work of preliminaries. Spencer, a home guard himself, and co-operating with the bands now organized and organizing under the general order that we have inserted, placed every impediment possible in the way of the daring recruiting officer.

There were now in Crawford and Washington counties, carrying out the spirit, if not the letter, of the order, no less than six companies led by Frank Oliver, Peter Mankins, and four other notorious marauders, all of whom were on the track of Wilhite. He still, however, succeeded in avoiding capture. His rendezvous was the wilds of the Boston Mountains; his subsistence the irregular hospitality of secretly Union men, and his comrades now together and now apart, increased their numbers and their resolution alike by daring and danger. His camp of instruction was a thicket or a hill, and his times for drill the opportune moments when provost guards came within range, and his trusty weapons made targets of traitors.

Lying in the woods one day in August, near the house of William Strickler, in Mountain Township, Washington county, with six men, a blood hound was heard baying in the distance, and apparently on his track. Like a general in the field, Wilhite immediately made his "dispositions," each man taking a tree and re-examining his weapons. Their horses were tied in a thicket a short distance off, and they now awaited the approach. Presently a number of men were observed advancing; the hound had been called in and they moved very cautiously, dismounting when they observed Wilhite, and creeping warily towards him. Discovering three men evidently endeavoring to get a safe shot at him, he anticipated their design by commencing hostilities with both barrels of his shot gun. Wounding two, the third placed a tree between himself and danger, and afterwards still further increased his chances for life by slipping away entirely.

This attack, more sudden and effective than they had anticipated, cooled the ardor of the home guards, and though a number of guns were fired, which but for the friendly protection of the forest would have been deadly in their effect, they fell back, remounted their horses and rode off. Wilhite now assumed the offensive, and approaching the highway by a devious but rapid and effective movement, came suddenly upon his foes of the hour before. Singling out Woodruff himself, (the leader of the party,) as the object of his personal aim, he missed the man, but killed his horse. Several others, however, were wounded, but succeeded in escaping. This little affair roused the leaders again, and vigilance was redoubled. Rallying under Sutton F. Cotterill,[9] of Van Buren, the provost marshal of Crawford county, two hundred camped one evening at the three forks of Lee's Creek, in the county last mentioned. From a high bluff adjacent to, and overlooking their camp, Wilhite had watched them for several hours, and when night set in, knowing that he could not attack, for he had but two men, he nevertheless determined to acquaint them with his proximity. Hallooing with all his might, he informed whom it might concern, that if they wanted him they must catch him, as it would be unpleasant just then to surrender.

How or why we are unable to say, but early on the following morning the guards decamped. Possibly they feared an attack; and then again, should they assume the offensive, the disagreeable uncertainty of the bushes was too fresh in memory to be rashly courted. Wilhite lingered long enough to see his enemies disappear, when he dashed again into the woods. A short time after this occurrence his father was arrested while moving along the highway near the west fork of White river. There was with him a small boy, who, not being interfered with, hastened as expeditiously as he dared to the hiding place, not far away, of two of Wilhite's men. They were there, fortunately, and knowing where Wilhite then was, lost no time in acquainting him with his father's arrest. Hurriedly collecting four of his men, he started down the Van Buren road, and after a sharp run of nine miles, overtook his father, then guarded by seven men. Four of the guards "broke" for the woods, and the remaining three were taken, dismounted, relieved of their arms and then set at liberty.

About this time a warrant for the arrest and execution of Wilhite was procured from the rebel military authorities by Frank Oliver,[10] a heretofore mentioned leader of home guards. It proving somewhat difficult to proceed under this warrant, according to its exigency, General Hindman offered a reward of seven thousand dollars and three honorable discharges from the Confederate service to any man who would bring in Wilhite, living or dead. Notices to this effect were numerously posted along Cove, Fall, and Lee's Creeks, and the west fork of White river. Scouting about one day in September, with a number of his men, and having occasion to cross Lee's Creek, near the base of the southern slope of the Boston Mountains, Wilhite discovered one of these notices tacked to a tree. Claiming the right to "cross-notice," he appropriated the margin to his own use, by inscribing thereon a notification to this effect: that his men and himself

claimed forty square miles of the Boston mountains, and that if
Hindman and his provost guards trespassed upon their dominions,
they would seek to drive them into the valley below, and there assume
the offensive. He now takes from his pocket the Jack of diamonds,
nails it to the tree, and writing above the head of this well-known
gentleman the significant word "Union," informed "Squire" Hindman
that if he wants him he must first catch him, and to be careful at
the same time that he does not "catch a Tartar."[11] The party now
rode off.

A few days later, when Wilhite was lying in the woods near the
summit of the Boston Mountains, word came to him that General
Hindman himself had just eaten dinner at a house not far distant, and
that he was then on the road to Fayetteville, moving in a carriage with
a body guard of but six men. Hastily gathering a few of his companions Wilhite took up the pursuit. Bearing still further from the highway than he then was, he thought to strike it again in advance of the
general, but in this he failed. In the distance, however, he descried the
coveted carriage, and hastened forward with all speed. The pursued
now took alarm and hurried away northward. The chase was becoming exciting, but unfortunately for the pursuers they were nearing the
rebel pickets at Hog Eye, twelve miles south of Fayetteville. Conscious
that they had no time to lose, Wilhite and two of his men took as
steady aim as circumstances would admit, and away whizzed a ball
after the carriage, a second and then a third. But General Hindman
was still safe, though the pursuit did not cease until the pickets, his
body guard and the carriage went pell-mell into the poetically named
village so conveniently at hand. The pursuers now wheeled about and
hied away to their fastnesses.[12]

Leading thus a life of wild adventure, Wilhite passed his time on,
and in the vicinity of the Boston Mountains, until the advance into
Arkansas of the Army of the Frontier in October, 1862. His escapes
from peril were manifold. His superior knowledge, however, of the
woods, and his consciousness of the fact that nature would permit
only a few men to operate against him at a time, gave him confidence
and strength, and though there were hundreds of rebels on all sides of
him, to the Boston Mountains he did not bid adieu, until of his own
volition he reported with a small squad of men to General Herron at
Cross Hollows, twenty-eight miles south of the Missouri line. As early
as August it had been found impracticable to take a number of

recruits northward in a body, and Wilhite had accordingly determined to remain in the mountains, annoying the enemy and taking vengeance upon those who had so cruelly robbed and maltreated Union men, until his passage could be safely and easily made.

From Cross Hollows Wilhite proceeded to Elkhorn Tavern, where he rejoined his company, and was at once appointed its first lieutenant, a position that had been left vacant for months in the hope that he would yet arrive to fill it. From that time onward Wilhite has been constantly engaged in active service, always entering with zest upon the adventures for which there is so much incentive on the Border. On one occasion while scouting below Fayetteville, and not far from his haunts of the summer previous, he drove in Marmaduke's pickets, and then suddenly wheeling, was off again to the northward. He participated in the nocturnal skirmish elsewhere mentioned, and while out made a descent into a cave, under circumstances worthy perhaps of a relation. The cave in question was located about six miles southeast of Black's Mills, in Benton county, and was one in which men were known to occasionally secrete themselves. To it, on the afternoon preceding the skirmish, the detachment was conducted. Arriving at its mouth, and observing traces of the recent entrance of some one, the men were disposed semi-circularly around it, and the unknown individual told to come out. No response. The order was repeated. Still no answer. Wilhite now volunteered to crawl in. Buckling a brace of revolvers firmly about him, and grasping a third in his right hand, he commenced operations. Advancing on all fours, and moving about seventy-five yards into the cave, situated on a hill side he discovered a man crouching in apparently great fear. Breaking the silence by ordering him out, the figure began to move and he to follow. As the unknown individual approached the light, the men brought their pieces to the shoulder and awaited his appearance. Presently emerged a head, then shoulders, arms and hands. At sight of the men and their weapons, the unknown stopped while yet midway between the upper and nether earth, rested himself firmly on his hands, and looking queerly up and around him, exclaimed, "Well! this beats me!" He was beaten surely enough, but found his captors inclined to treat him kindly. Taken to Elkhorn he was afterwards released, but cautioned to refrain in the future from running when he saw Federals. We know the man, and thus far the advice has been heeded.

We now leave the subject of this sketch. Rebels call him a desperado, but he has fought only, and is now fighting, for "The Union, the Constitution, and the Laws."[13]

FAYETTEVILLE, ARK.,
February, 1863.

A PROVOST MARSHALSHIP.

ON THE EIGHTH day of January, of the present year, an order of the
Provost Marshal General of the Army of the Frontier made us Provost
Marshal of the post of Fayetteville, Arkansas. The position, under no
circumstances a sinecure, was now doubly onerous. The returning
loyalty of North-western Arkansas was eager to express itself, yet a
vein of interest withal ran through the crowd, who daily thronged our
"sanctum." Claims also of every description were presented, some
serious, some farcical, and it was not always easy to adjust them. The
summariness of martial law, however, enabled us to come to quick
conclusions, and men very soon found out whether they "could or
they could'nt."

The duties of the office illustrated the multiform phases of public
affairs. Exercising the functions of judge, jury and sheriff; empowered
to arrest deserters, whether regulars, volunteers or militia, and all disloyal persons; to enquire into and report upon treasonable practices;
to seize stolen or embezzled property belonging to the Government;
to detect spies of the enemy, and put a stop to miscellaneous pillaging
by lawless soldiery, a provost marshal in the enemy's country has
enough to employ and quite sufficient to harass him. Added to these
labors, bonds are to be taken and safeguards given; a general pass system devised and occasionally re-constructed; oaths of allegiance
administered and paroles subscribed; proofs of loyalty made and
endorsed on vouchers, and vouchers themselves procured—in short,
there is imposed upon him the general administration of law during a
suspension of civil process.[1]

Every section has its peculiarities, and war makes them more
prominent. In the South-west the men and women of the rural districts go to their centres of trade almost universally on horseback, and
Saturday, when peace reigneth, is the merchant's harvest time.

> "Day of all the week most profitable,
> Ever longed for, but hebdomadal."

Then, too, in time of war, a provost marshal's office is most crowded.
As many birds as possible must be killed by the same stone, and while

the good wife is making the most of her opportunities to gather the news of the town—often rumor of the most extravagant kind—her liege lord presents himself to the "*provose,*"and wants to prove his "*loy-al-i-ty.*"

"Well! have you been in the rebel army?"

"No."

"Have you any sons?"

"I have two."

"Where are they?"

"I suppose they are in the Southern army, but they were conscripted."

"When did they enlist?"

"Last July, I reckon."

"But the conscript act wasn't then in force."

"Oh! well," said the old fellow, not at all discomfited, "they enlisted rather than be compelled to."

Such was the character of countless conversations, accumulating at last to such an extent, that we offered a pecuniary reward to the orderly who would bring before us a father willing to acknowledge that his son had *volunteered* in the rebel army. We nevertheless strove, of course, to do justice in these cases, not considering it necessary to visit the iniquities of the children upon the fathers, unless it was clearly proper that they should atone for filial misconduct.

The Government of the United States is not vindictive. It is sincerely desirous that those who have been led astray should return to their allegiance, and that a large proportion of the masses in the Southern States have been, there can be no reasonable doubt. Convince them that we are fighting for the "Old Constitution" *as we are,* and they will turn from the miserable will-o'-the-wisp that they have been following, and like the prodigal son, gladly return to their father's house. The *Richmond Dispatch* does not speak *ex cathedra* in the following editorial:

"We warn the democrats and conservatives of the North, to dismiss from their minds at once, the miserable delusion that the South can ever consent to enter again, upon any terms, the old Union. If the North will allow us to write the Constitution ourselves, and give us every guarantee we would ask, we would sooner be under the government of England or France."

Very probably the leaders of this rebellion, the "*fire-eating,*" slavery-perpetuating politicians of the South would. *Their* treason is too high-handed to overlook, and there is nothing strange or unnatural in their evident unwillingness to place their rebellious necks beneath the axe of offended law. The common people think differently, where they are permitted to think at all. Nothing but the grossest misrepresentation keeps them in the ranks. Strike off the fetters that have converted public opinion into the will of the aristocratic few, let facts go before the people of the Southern States, and their army will melt away as General Hindman's dissolved after the battle of Prairie Grove—we had *almost* called it the sixteenth decisive battle of the world.[2]

We repeat the idea, therefore, that the Federal Government does not cherish unreasonable animosities; and that commander of an army or a post makes a great mistake who puts forth no effort to conciliate the inhabitants of a seceded State. It will not answer, on the other hand, to indiscriminately receive back into the fold those who have rebelled. The truly repentant must be distinguished from fawning hypocrites, and if, in the former case, a safeguard is given, a commensurate obligation, enforceable against property, should be received. Here again the provost marshal is resorted to, and has often to draw the bond not only, but sign and witness it, as Mr. A. writes a *"slow"* hand, or Mrs. B. has the palsy. While this operation is going on, perhaps a dozen or more crowd around him, clamoring for "protection papers,"or something else, and getting a little excited, he breaks out—

"Now, see here men, stand back. One at a time if you want to do business."

"Are you the *"provose?"* interposes a rough looking specimen, just from the Cherokee line.

"Yes. What do you want?" relenting a little.

"Them ar Pin[*] Ingins are pesterin me a heap, and I want a safe ge-ard."[3]

"Have you proven your loyalty?"

"I can, I reckon."

"Well, go into the back room and try,"and off he went.

"Look he-ah, Mister, 'tend to me now," said a stout farmer, watching his opportunity.

Not fancying his style of approach, we told him *we would if we agreed to.*

---

*The Pin Indians are Cherokees, so called from wearing pins on their hunting shirts, to distinguish them from the rebel members of their tribe. They belong to the John Ross party, and are staunch adherents of the Government

"Is this where you get passes?" cried an elderly woman, holding her riding dress in one hand, and a bag, supposed to contain salt, in the other.

"Orderly! show the lady into the other room."

"Now sir," to the farmer, "I'll attend to you."

"I wan ter know," said he, with great deliberation, and settling himself slowly into a chair, "I wan ter know whether this 'ere oath will prevent my givin a meal of vittals to my son, and keepin' him over night, should he come home from the Southern army? Now I want to do what is right."

We told him it would not; that such conduct would be humanely construed, but that he must endeavor to keep his son from going back, and induce him to deliver himself up.

"Now, another thing," said the farmer, with equal if not greater deliberation: "I've lost a horse."

We suspected as much, for these conversations were generally kept up by the spur of pecuniary interest. We resumed however.

"Have you any idea what became of it?"

"Not certain, but some of them soldiers have got it, I reckon they're right smart stealers."

Advising him to hunt for his horse before we gave the matter any further attention, we told him to call again.

"But—" beginning anew, and showing no inclination to rise.

"No matter about your 'buts,' we can do nothing for you now."

At this he partially raised himself by the elbows of the chair, his countenance falling as his body rose.

"It was my last filly."

"Can't help it, sir. It will be your *first* when you get it."

He now departed, and as he left the room a stalwart "Pin," belonging to Col. Phillips' Indian brigade,[4] stalked in. Evidently wandering about to see what he could discover, as our eyes met, he came to a halt.

"What can we do for you?" we said, with as much of the *suaviter in modo* as we could command.

"Ugh!" responded the savage, blowing off an apparent surplus of breath.

The ejaculation we knew to be undoubted Indian, but could not see its application as a response to our question. We therefore determined to try again, and as our knowledge of Cherokee was very limited, fell back on the Anglo Saxon.

"What do you want?

"Me Ingin," striking his breast. "BIG INGIN! Me much jay-hawk—steal horses!"

We thought as much, but in the absence of complaint had the aboriginal jay-hawker escorted to the street.

Such is a faint reflex of the scenes enacted under our eye. They were not, perhaps, unusual, for the peculiar characteristics of the business of provost marshalships are co-extensive with their existence. With all that is humorous or indecisive, justice is summarily administered, and the Gordian knot often cut, when in time of peace it were vain to attempt to untie it. Law, in fact, loses none of its majesty in the despatch of its operations, and the quick settlement of a difficulty the earlier buries it in oblivion.

FAYETTEVILLE, ARK.,
February, 1863.

DE WITT C. HOPKINS.

"Wild oats," to use a familiar phrase, are not always sown by the time an impulsive young man has attained his majority. A rash and boyish adventure occasionally begets a liking for peril, and from that time the staid and sober joys of home are apt to lose their charm, and the inclination of the hour becomes the impulse of a lifetime. In early boyhood the subject of this sketch launched his bark upon the world's turbulent sea, and it has been tossing about ever since. De Witt C. Hopkins was born at Franklin Mills, Portage county, Ohio, on the 8th of November, 1840. His father, Benjamin F. Hopkins, a successful merchant, had him taught the rudiments of a good education, but from extreme youth he was rash and impulsive, and though quick of apprehension, was always restless and uneasy in the school room. As generous, however, as he was headstrong, he often gave to his companions the sly assistance, that the son of a man in easy circumstances has so many opportunities of extending.

In March, 1852, he ran away. At that time "filibustering" possessed all its attractions. Dreams of adventure and conquest disturbed the thoughts of too many young Americans, and numbers enlisted under Walker and Lopez.[1] Three young men from Portage county, a few years older than himself, induced young Hopkins to accompany them to New Orleans, thence to embark for Cuba. Under these circumstances he left his father's house, taking with him seven hundred and fifty dollars in money, to pay the expenses of the party and procure an outfit in the Crescent City. Arriving there without molestation, the young men soon made the acquaintance of Lopez, and tendered to him their services. A few days later the steamship Dancing Feather cleared from New Orleans with as precious a cargo of rash humanity as ever walked the decks of a vessel. When fairly in the Gulf, Lopez addressed his men, telling them that Cuba belonged naturally to the United States, and that the present was the time to wrest her from imperious Spain. He told the men also, that the object of the expedition was more particularly to seize the Governor General of the island, which done, and he taken away, negotiations could the more advantageously be entered into, or war the better prosecuted.

Not long afterwards the steamship cast anchor in a secluded cove on the northwestern side of the island, but a day's march from Havana. The party, numbering between three and four hundred men, now landing, speedily put themselves in readiness for a forced march on the capital. It was the intention to enter the city by its main gate, and proceed at once to the house of the Governor General, situated near the Grand Plaza, seize him, and hurry out of the city with their prize before a general alarm could be given. Approaching this gate, therefore, just after dark, the sentinel gave an alarm, but was instantly shot, when Lopez hurried forward to the house of the Governor General. Arriving there a few minutes later, a quick but thorough search was made for him, yet to no purpose.

Warning had been given, and he was now arousing the soldiery and populace for the capture of the bold adventurers. In an incredibly brief period of time the Grand Plaza was thronged with maddened men, and the "fillibusters" were speedily compelled to see each to his personal safety. Leaving their guns in the house of the Governor General, and determining to keep together if they could, young Hopkins and his three friends, with pistols belted about them, stealthily moved off. Their boyish appearance saved them in a measure from suspicion, and they succeeded in reaching uninjured the suburbs of the city. Concealing themselves beneath fig trees until day-light, they then hurried to the beach, striking it near a bath house, where from a distance they had observed a boat fastened to a stake.

About this time they were discovered, when they made all haste to put to sea. As the boat was being cast off, and just as Albert Clark, one of their number, was about to enter it, he was mortally wounded. The living had now no time to attend to the dying, and barely saved their own lives by putting boldly to sea, some oars having fortunately been left in the boat. They rowed hard, exerting all their strength to keep away from the shore, preferring very decidedly the perils of the sea to those of the land. On the evening of the next day, and when nearly exhausted, they were picked up by the steamship Mexico and taken to New Orleans.[2]

For a boy twelve years of age, as young Hopkins was, this was an adventure quite unusual, to say the least, and seemed to have had a salutary effect upon him. He telegraphed promptly to his father that he was in New Orleans, and a few weeks later was again beneath the parental roof. He now remained at home, going most of the time to school, until the month of April, 1854, when the family started southward, journeying for pleasure and the health of his mother.

Sojourning some weeks at Havana, Hopkins became acquainted with a dashing young Spaniard, for whom, not long afterwards, he acted as a second in a duel fought with another Spaniard. Making their preparations according to the "code," the parties repaired to a secluded spot in the rear of Moro Castle, and with short swords commenced paying tribute to honor. After cutting and guarding, thrusting and parrying in true Castilian style, for several minutes, a fortunate lunge for young Hopkins' principal ended the affair. One carriage drove to a grave-yard, the other to a restaurant. A few weeks later Mr. Hopkins sailed with his family for Indianola, in Matagorda Bay, and from there went up the bay to Port la Vaca. After bathing one day a difficulty sprung up between young Hopkins and a son of Dr. Johnson, residing in the place. Hopkins challenged the other boy; the challenge was accepted; pistols and knives were chosen; the beach was selected as the place for operations, and the duel was to be fought at once. At a given signal each party was to fire three shots, and if ineffective the duel was to be terminated with knives at close quarters, the left hands of the combatants being tied behind their backs. The firing took place without result, and just as the maddened boys were about to "close it," some men appeared upon the scene of action, took forcible possession of the young duellists, and without hesitation threw them both into the bay. The men did not interfere, however, with their struggles after *terra firma,* and for the time being the effect of this involuntary baptism was salutary.

Later in the day the boys came together again, and undertook anew the vindication of their injured honor. At the second fire Hopkins wounded his antagonist in the left arm, when the whole party suddenly decamped. This rash affair came near seriously troubling his father, but was finally adjusted to the satisfaction of all concerned. From Port La Vaca, the family went to a plantation near Victoria, when young Hopkins, becoming involved in a difficulty with its proprietor, suddenly started for the City of Mexico. Temporarily away from the plantation, on returning, Mr. Hopkins, senior, learned from his younger son the course De Witt had pursued, and having previously intended to visit the Aztec Metropolis, followed, in a few days, his wayward boy. He arrived at the city two weeks after De Witt, who by this time had become quite familiar with the amusements of that "free and easy" capital. Of cock fights and bull fights he could talk like a connoisseur, and behaved very much as do other ardent young men amid the surroundings of a seductive city.

The sojourn of the family in Mexico was brief, and embarking at Corpus Christi, they shortly afterwards reached New Orleans. From thence they traveled at their leisure up the Red River to Shreveport, Louisiana; thence again to the Hot Springs, in Arkansas, and from there to Louisville, Kentucky, where it had become necessary for the father to transact some business. This disposed of, the family turned their faces anew to the South, and passed the approaching winter at Holly Springs, Mississippi. In the spring they returned home, where young Hopkins remained until the year 1858, when, his mother's health continuing poor, his father, with a view to a change of residence that should bring relief, purchased a section of land in McDonald county, the extreme southwestern portion of Missouri, and during the year settled upon it.

Mr. Hopkins had chosen a very eligible location upon Buffalo Creek, a small stream emptying into the Cowskin or Elk river, was himself extremely well pleased with the country, especially in its climate and soil, and hoped to have no occasion for the old cause to recommence a traveling experience. His farm was situated three miles from the Cherokee line, and two and a half from the Council House of the Seneca Nation. To young Hopkins this proximity of the Indian tribes soon became attractive, and his adventurous inclinations were often gratified by lengthened excursions into the interior of their country. To pleasure, however, he added profit, moving about as a trader from place to place, bartering especially among the Creeks, Cherokees and Osages, and thus acquiring a familiar knowledge of their languages and habits, that in his subsequent adventures proved to be of great value.

In the spring of 1861 he made arrangements to participate with a band of Osages in a grand buffalo hunt to the Rocky Mountains, but the war breaking out the project was abandoned. From council fires he returned home, and though rebel influence was powerful in McDonald country, he took no part in the earliest events of rebellion in the Southwest. In June, 1861, he was living quietly at home determined, nevertheless, to avail himself of the first opportunity to render his country a substantial service. During this month the armies of Price and McCullough concentrated on Cowskin Prairie, a few miles from Mr. Hopkins' farm, and for two weeks the family mansion was appropriated as General Price's Head-quarters. While the house was thus occupied, young Hopkins had frequent opportunities of learning rebel intentions, and ascertaining one day, that a junction was to be immediately effected with troops under Governor Jackson and General Rains, then moving southward from the Missouri river, he determined to apprise a Union force at Neosho, twenty miles north-easterly, of the fact, and also of their own imminent danger. He had, moreover, observed during the day, strong patrols going up the Neosho road, and conjectured that a movement was on foot.

Waiting, therefore, until nearly midnight, he mounted a horse, and spurring over the hills, arrived at Neosho before day-break. A Teutonic captain was in command, holding the town with a force of one hundred and fifty men only. Hopkins warned him of his danger; told him that the rebels were advancing in overwhelming numbers, and that he ought, by all means, to at least send out mounted patrols. But the wrong-headed German would take no advice, and Hopkins galloped on to overtake Colonel Sigel, then marching on Carthage to intercept Jackson and Rains. Coming up with him on the morning of the fifth of July, and while actually engaged in battle, he informed him of the movements of Price and McCullough. A messenger was imme-diately dispatched to Neosho, but to no purpose. He was captured before arriving there, and when the town itself had been several hours in possession of the rebels. The valiant captain and his entire com-mand were now prisoners of war, and under guard at Neosho, were having ample time to reflect upon the unpleasantness of a situation as disgraceful as it was unnecessary.[3]

From Carthage, Col. Sigel fell back to Mount Vernon, young Hopkins acting as a guide. The latter now determined to revisit his home, and if possible put himself in such an attitude that he could remain there until other opportunities should be presented to give information to the Federal army. To this end he arrayed himself in the home-spun of the country—a process, however, that required but slight modifications of his former garb—and started out alone and on a circuitous route, first for lower Kansas and the Indian Nation. Arriving at Humboldt he struck thence for the Neosho river, down that to Grand River, and from the latter stream wended his way to the Grand Saline, (salt works,) in the Cherokee Nation. He now pur-chased a pair of Indian ponies, with the view ostensibly of selling them to the Confederate army, when he should have reached it from below. From the Grand Saline he went to Telequah, and from thence to Maysville, Benton county, Arkansas.

Learning now that the rebels were concentrating again and re-organizing their forces on Cowskin Prairie, he entered the camp from the South-West, leading one pony and riding the other. Meeting a number of old acquaintances, he regretted *very much* his inability to be at the Carthage fight, and rejoiced with them over the easy surrender of the redoubtable Teuton, who commanded at Neosho. His character as a sympathizing Indian trader giving him ready currency, he sold one of his animals, and retaining the other, passed on homeward, but soon found that he could not remain there in safety. His sudden disappearance at a critical juncture had been observed, and he saw that he was an object of suspicion. A very few days, in fact, sufficed to warn him of his danger, and he was compelled to abandon his father's roof for the woods hard by.

On one occasion he was near the house, when a party of men rode suddenly up and demanded his forthcoming. Listening to their conversation with his father, he gathered enough of it to induce him to show himself, to prevent the burning of the house, but in such a way that his presence should be *felt* as well as seen. He was well mounted, an intrepid rider, and flashing past them, discharged both barrels of a shot gun, and spurred into a thicket. Attention was now directed from the house, the party riding after him, save two crippled rebels, who were the unfortunate recipients of this unexpected salutation. Escape, nevertheless, was easy, and as soon as his pursuers were baffled, young Hopkins cautiously approached the house of Small Cloud Spicer, acting Chief of the Seneca Nation.[4] A minor, Curly Eye Butterfly, was the heir apparent, but to Small Cloud was entrusted the management of the affairs of the tribe, and Hopkins, previously acquainted with him believed his protection to be worth the seeking. It was cheerfully but cautiously accorded, and to avoid suspicion, a hiding place a short distance off, near the Cowskin river, was pointed out. There Hopkins secreted himself for several days, his food being brought to him by an Indian maiden, daughter of Small Cloud, when learning that his enemies had left the vicinity, he ventured to return home.

Shortly after this occurrence, a dancing party assembled at the house of a Captain Parks, in the Cherokee nation. Ascertaining in advance that a number of rebel officers were expected to grace the occasion with their presence, Hopkins determined to attend, for the double purpose of enjoying himself and gathering information of army movements. Inviting an Indian girl, he led her in due time to the floor, but had scarcely done so when a stalwart Cherokee brushed past him in a manner that, by the customs of the tribe, could only be construed into a deliberate affront. It was so intended, in fact, for the same dusky damsel had declined him as an escort to the dance, our friend having pre-occupied the ground. The insult was promptly resented, and the ball came suddenly and tragically to a close. While the company had been assembling, young Hopkins learned that a movement was in contemplation against General Lyon, but not possessed of sufficient information to warrant the hazards of a trip to Union headquarters, returning home he tendered his services to General Rains. They were accepted, and he was established at headquarters, a voluntary *aid-de-camp* without rank or braid.

On the 9th of August the rebels were so to move, as to attack Springfield at daylight on the 10th, and Hopkins becoming satisfied that such was the intention, essayed to reach the Federal lines. He was arrested, however, just outside of the rebel lines, by a patrol of Louisiana troops, and it required all his coolness and address to sustain even partially, the character of forager for the General's mess. Considered a suspicious personage he was taken to camp, and placed under guard, his case to be disposed of after the expected battle then absorbing attention. For various reasons sufficiently well known, the contemplated advance on the night of the 9th was not made, and on the following morning the battle was fought at Wilson's Creek, ten miles southwesterly from Springfield. During the engagement Hopkins was kept with Woodruff's battery,[5] but in the evening the guards left him, wild, like their comrades, over the unexpected success of the rebel arms. Springing now on to a horse he rode rapidly homeward. Alternating between the house and the woods, he remained in the vicinity until General Frémont's arrival at Springfield, an event that hastened his departure, successfully now, to the Federal lines. Arriving at Flat Creek he reported to Sigel, commanding the advance, and was placed at once in the corps of secret service men. In January following he was sent southward by General Curtis, then commanding the army of the Southwest, to proceed to the Arkansas river.

The rebels then held Arkansas and South-western Missouri; were making extensive preparations for the battle fought afterwards at Pea Ridge, and to enter their lines, much more to pass through them to the river in question, was an undertaking as difficult as hazardous. Providing himself with a suit of the most approved Confederate gray; dyeing his hair and whiskers; adjusting a pair of goggles; mounting a "C. S." horse, and assuming the character of a Missouri officer, returning from a recruiting expedition, he struck into the Indian

Nation, and then boldly southward. It required now all his address to avoid suspicion, but his confidence increased with his peril.

Courage on the battle-field, questionable oft times, as advancing columns approach each other, is thoroughly roused by a few volleys, but the cool, deliberate daring of the spy—the resolution that braves reproach, ignominy and death, belongs to men of other stamp. The services of this class are as old as war, and though the spy may occasionally fail of his object, and impart information to be received with allowances, he is indispensable, and so far as money can reward, Government looks well to his interests.

At the time of which we write, Fort Smith, situated at the junction of the Arkansas and Poteau rivers, and directly on the line between the State of Arkansas and the Choctaw nation, was a central point in rebel scheming in the Southwest; where troops were gathered; from which news of importance to the army was set in motion, and where, within the fortress of the same name, magnates of the new Confederacy met to eat, drink and plot treason. Here, in February, 1862, Ben McCullough sneered at Northern prowess, and here, in March, was buried, falling at Pea Ridge before the aim of Peter Pellican, a private of Company "B," of the 36th Illinois Infantry Volunteers. The officers' mess at the fort was kept by a Mrs. Preston, and it was customary to lay the table for supper immediately after dark. Formality in coming and going was dispensed with; the place in this particular assuming more the character of a restaurant than officers' quarters. Of these peculiarities Hopkins was cognizant, and moving rapidly through the Cherokee Nation, arrived on the evening of the fourth day out at a friendly house on the northern bank of the Arkansas, a mile from the Fort. During the night and the next day, he remained in the neighboring cane, and as darkness set in moved for the river. His garb securing ferriage across without difficulty, he rode boldly up to the main entrance, saluted the sentinel on duty as he passed, and with the air of an *habituè*, dismounted in front of the officers' quarters tied his horse, and walked with the utmost *nonchalance* into the supper room.

It so happened that the bell had just been rung, and entering with others, he quietly took a seat at the foot of the table. There were seated about it, General McIntosh (killed at Pea Ridge), Major Montgomery of the Quartermaster's Department,[6] and other prominent officers. The conversation turned upon the all absorbing events of the time; the probable advance of General Curtis, and their own state of preparation, and was in no wise restrained by the presence of the pseudo recruiting officer. The vivands disposed of, the position was becoming embarrassing, and Hopkins wished for nothing so much, as that his *brother officers* should rise and precede him from the room, but they pertinaciously clung to their seats. At length, conscious that he could remain no longer without exciting suspicion, he rose and moved unconcernedly toward the door. Now, for the first time, he arrested attention. As he passed General McIntosh, that officer turned sharply around—

"Who do you belong to?" he enquired with more emphasis than politeness.

"Quartermaster's Department, Little Rock!" was the ready response.

"What's that you say?" said Major Montgomery, starting up from the other side of the table.

Seeing, on the instant, that his affairs were likely to take a disastrous turn, and without venturing a reply, he rushed quickly out, cut the strap with which his horse was tied, and dashed for the fortress gate leading into Garrison avenue—the avenue to the river. For a few moments the officers at the fort were so startled by the strange occurrence that they lost their self-possession. Recovering it they gave the alarm; shouted to the sentinel on duty at the gate to "halt the daredevil," and harmlessly discharged one or two pistols. By this time Hopkins had passed the guard, though shot at and slightly wounded as he darted by, and was galloping at a furious rate down the avenue. Arriving at the river he spurred his horse boldly in, and sliding off in a manner not unfamiliar to those whose army experiences have compelled them to swim streams too deep to be forded, grasped the animal by the caudal extremity, and making a rudder of himself, landed finally on the opposite bank. Remaining unobserved that night and the next day in the friendly cane, while an active search was being made for him, apparently in almost every direction, he then struck northward, moving up by Frog Bayou through Crawford, Washington and Benton counties, Arkansas, and after the lapse of several days reported to Gen. Sigel.

While McCullough's army was lying at Cross Hollows in the February following, Hopkins appeared within the lines with two artillery horses for sale. Readily bargaining them away for Confederate notes, he delivered one, and at his own request was permitted to retain the other until the following morning. Meantime he quietly prepared to run the pickets, and about 9 o'clock in the evening approached those stationed on the telegraph road leading to Elk Horn Tavern.

"Who comes there?" shouted a voice from the road side.

"Friend with the countersign," was the quick reply.

"Advance, friend, and give it."

Hopkins now rode rapidly forward, answered the demand with the quick discharge or both barrels of a shot gun at the astonished soldiers, and spurring onward through the darkness, was soon out of harm's way. A month later he participated in the battle on Pea Ridge, and after that engagement, was for some time employed as a general scout for the post at Cassville. Thus engaged when Col. Harrison began recruiting for the First Arkansas Cavalry, he ardently seconded his efforts, and received power to recruit for the proposed regiment.

On the 5th of April, 1862, he left Cassville, and shortly after midnight of the same day arrived at the Widow Christie's, on Pool's Prairie, Newton county, Missouri. Tired, hungry, and drenched with rain, he roused the occupants, and was admitted to the house. His horse, upon the advice of the widow, was secreted in the neighboring bushes, as Livingston's men, notorious bushwhackers, were constantly prowling about the locality. He had scarcely disposed himself by the fire, when the house-dog raised a warning bark, that was answered by the clearly distinguishable clattering of hoofs close to the house. Verily the Philistines were now upon him, though not probably aware of his presence. His feminine friend, alarmed, nevertheless, for his safety, threw up the quilts and mattress of a bed in an adjoining room, and told him to jump underneath them. In he went with boots, spurs, hat, and a fair representation of south-western mud. The clothes were covered over him, and save a moderate increase of altitude, the bed was in *statu quo*. The approaching party were indeed Livingston's men, and a few minutes later they entered the house. The widow accounted for the light at so unusual an hour by saying that she was unwell, and had risen to prepare a warm cup of tea.

The excuse was satisfactory, and after a brief halt the marauders departed. Hopkins now emerged from his place of concealment, and shortly afterwards was galloping away to the westward. Recruiting as he passed along, he had collected between twenty and thirty men, when his services as a scout were desired by Major Hubbard, of the First Missouri Cavalry, then scouring south-western Missouri. They were promptly given, and to his intrepid guidance is due much of the praise properly accorded to our forces for their operations against Waitie, Coffee and the rebel Indians, in the spring of 1862.

After the affair at Neosho, in which Major Hubbard obtained a signal success over the enemy, Hopkins, worn down with incessant riding, left the command, and repaired to a private house for rest. A portion of the 37th Illinois Infantry Volunteers had encamped near by, and it was Hopkins' intention to move on with them in the morning to Cassville. When morning came, however, the troops had departed, and he found himself alone in the enemy's country. Nothing was left, of course, but to follow on, which he did, gaily and unconcernedly—for the rebels had been most thoroughly whipped—when suddenly there sprang from the road-side, as he was passing a secluded spot, half a dozen armed men, who checked him with the well understood "Halt!" There was no alternative, and he surrendered. This occurrence took place on the 27th of April. On the 1st of May he was sent under charges as a spy, by Colonel Waitie, to General Cooper's headquarters, on Buck Creek, in the Choctaw nation, and from there to Fort McCullough, where General Pike, as commander of the district of Indian Territory, was then stationed. Here he was detained two weeks, but uniformly treated with great kindness by General Pike. Returned then to Cooper's command, he was forwarded from it to Norfolk, on the north fork of the Canadian river, and from there to Colonel Waitie's camp, then pitched on Cowskin Prairie, in south-western Missouri.

His trial was now entered upon, but while pending, an adjournment took place, and he was sent to Fort Smith, where the remainder of the evidence against him was to be taken. At that place the trial was concluded, the prisoner convicted and sentenced to be hung, and the record sent up to General Pike, for the usual supervision of a commanding officer. With Albert Pike the discharge of such a duty was no mere formality, and the result of his reviewing was a reversal of the decision of the court below, on the ground, as we understand the point involved, that the offence committed, if committed at all, took place within the territorial limits of the State of Missouri, which, so far as the Government of the Confederate States was concerned, was conquered territory in the possession of the Federal forces; and that therefore Hopkins could not, by the laws of war, be regarded as a spy, but was entitled to the treatment and disposition given to other prisoners of war. He was held, nevertheless, but his confinement was made less rigorous, the freedom of a dungeon being substituted for the close quarters of a ball and chain, with a staple in the floor to give them locality.

About this time Majors Hubbard and Miller made their dashing entrance into Fayetteville, and the report came to Fort Smith that

Judge David Walker, whom we elsewhere mention, had been killed. The rebels at the Fort were quite naturally enraged at such a proceeding, and "blood for blood" was demanded for the supposed outrage. Hopkins was their selection, and his execution was ordered to take place one afternoon at four o'clock. Fortunately, on the morning of the dreaded day, news was received that Judge Walker was still alive and unharmed, and the execution was *indefinitely postponed.* Hopkins now received the treatment to which he was entitled, and on the 2d of August, 1862, left Fort Smith for exchange at Cassville. Reporting to Colonel Harrison at Springfield, he was promoted to the captaincy of company "I" of the regiment in which he had enlisted some months previously, and since re-entering the service has been constantly on duty, proving himself under all circumstances to be a very bold, daring, and efficient officer. He has been engaged in skirmishes without number, and as the commander of a reconnoitering party, we do not know his equal.[7]

FAYETTEVILLE, ARK.,
February, 1863

JOHN W. MORRIS.

THE EXPERIENCE OF John W. Morris constitutes a marked instance of rebel intimidation and tyranny. An order-loving, law-abiding citizen, quietly pursuing his calling, he has been made to feel the iron hand of persecution, and knows from sad reality how tender are the mercies of Southern domination. Born in Giles county, Tennessee, August 1, 1834, he emigrated, when a boy, to Searcy county Arkansas, and with the exception of two years passed in the adjoining county of Pope, has always resided there. In August, 1857, he married, and when the rebellion broke out was farming in Calf Creek Township.

In politics his relatives were nearly equally divided, and at a time when party rancor culminated in party hate, the embarrassment of such a position can only be appreciated by those who have been similarly situated. His father-in-law, John Campbell,[1] of Searcy county, was a delegate to the State Convention, of which mention has already been made, elected as a Union man, but like all his compeers, Isaac Murphy alone excepted, he "fell from grace" on the memorable 6th of May, 1861, not having the moral courage to say *no*, when the bitterness of popular excitement bade him say *aye*.[2]

At this time the "Peace Organization Society" was in operation in Searcy and the adjoining counties, and Mr. Morris connected himself with it.[3] This circumstance was not known at the time, but his conduct had nevertheless made him an object of suspicion with the rebel authorities. He was narrowly watched for some months, and on the 28th of October, 1861, was arrested at Burroughville, the county seat of Searcy. He had heard of the arrest there, without cause, of Union men, but doubting the accuracy of the rumor in its full extent, determined to ascertain for himself the true situation of affairs. Accompanied by a brother-in-law, he had scarcely entered the place, when two double-barreled shot guns were thrust in their faces, and they were insolently told that they were prisoners. John Smith and Mark Hogan, two notorious rebels of that locality, effected their arrest, and took the prisoners at once before a Colonel Alexander Ham, then organizing the militia of the county.[4] By him Mr. Morris was briefly questioned, and then taken to the Court House, where, with others, he was imprisoned for two weeks. A trial was promised but none had, and after being imprisoned as stated, he, with seventy-six other State prisoners, was marched to Little Rock, a distance of one hundred and twenty-five miles.

They were all American citizens, had injured no man, and were arrested simply for refusing to disregard the Constitution which they had sworn to support. They were *traitors to treason*, "only this and nothing more." Rebels call them Southern tories, but God never made a tory of a man who had sworn to support, protect and defend the American Constitution, and kept his oath. Let the curse of an ignominious epithet rather, rest upon the high born men of the South, who, rendered imperious by their education, and tyrannical by their insolence, have followed the *ignis fatuus* of a Trans-Atlantic aristocracy, and made the name of rebel even, a weak indication of turpitude.

Error has ever begotten outrage, and in this instance it was doubly refined. The seventy-seven were chained together two and two, with an ordinary log chain fastened about the neck of each, and for twenty-four hours prior to their departure from Burroughville were thus guarded, in two ranks, as it were, with a long chain running down the centre of the column. But rebel cruelty in this instance was foiled by its own invention, for before the party started on its toilsome march, the brutal guard discovered that this disposition of their prisoners was not at all favorable to pedestrianism. Inclination gave way to humanity, and the prisoners were fastened together by twos only, the odd man bringing up the rear with a chain encircling his neck and thrown over a shoulder, that his walking might not be impeded. Six days were spent in the march to Little Rock, and a guard of one hundred men detailed. Arriving there fatigued, worn out and still in chains, they were marched into the hall of the House of Representatives, and addressed by Governor Rector. He offered them their choice, either to volunteer in the rebel service or go to jail, and await trial for treason, giving them the *flattering* assurance that if they accepted the latter alternative, four or six months might elapse before trials could be had, and that should they insist upon them then, he was very confident that they would be hung.

Such was the conduct of the Executive of the State towards citizens whom he was bound to protect. It was coercion in its worst form; the blind zeal of infuriate fanaticism. The prisoners were helpless, and with the exception of two, who were not permitted the alternative, volunteered. These men were thrown into prison, remained

there a few months, and were then unexpectedly released. After the
prisoners had determined their choice, their chains were stricken off,
and before leaving the hall, they were organized into a company, and
a Captain and three Lieutenants appointed over them. Four days later
they left Little Rock for Memphis. Remaining there two weeks, they
were ordered thence to Bell's Station, in Kentucky, twenty-five miles
north of Bowling Green. They had previously been assigned to a
regiment commanded by Colonel, now General Marmaduke, and
insufficiently fed and poorly clothed, but well armed, they were
thenceforth placed in active service.[5]

While at this station Morris attempted an escape. Marmaduke,
learning that a detachment of Union soldiers had crossed Green river,
marched one night in January, 1862, with a detachment of six hundred men to surprise them. Our friend was one of the party, and
marched on apparently with as much zest as any of his fellows. He
shortly, however, found a pretext for "falling out," and making the
most of his opportunity, took a direct course for the Federal lines. For
several hours be hurried on undisturbed, but suddenly falling in with,
and being arrested by rebel pickets near Cave City, where he least
expected to find them, all his wits were needed to account for his
moving about alone at so late an hour of the night. He was at once
suspected and taken before the Captain of the guard, who charged
him with attempting to escape. This he stoutly denied, insisting that
he could not avoid "falling out"; that doing so he had taken the
wrong road, and when arrested was in search of his command.

The end justified the means in this extremity, but it did not protect him from ill-treatment. The Lieutenant of the guard taunted him
with being one of those "d——d Arkansas jayhawkers, sent out by
Hindman"; communicating also the *comforting* intelligence, that none
of Dawson's company should return to that State, and authoritatively
enquiring of the guard why they had not shot him.

At this juncture the Captain interfered in his behalf, and the next
day he was returned to his company. The regiment falling back to
Murfreesboro, Tennessee, he was there taken sick and sent to a hospital. Recovering, he rejoined his regiment at Corinth, Mississippi,
and was with it at the battle of Pittsburgh Landing. At that time, the
band of seventy-seven men, marched into Little Rock as related, had
been reduced by sickness, desertion and death to ten. It had been
more than decimated. Hard marching while barefooted and sore;
clothing that the Lazaroni of Naples would have spurned;[6] food that

sickened but could not satisfy, and above all a lack of confidence on
the part of officers, that converted discipline into cruelty, had made
the lives of these men miserable mockeries of existence, and the company wasted away as though swept by a sirocco.

The first day of the engagement the remaining ten men were
placed in the front rank in line of battle, officers plainly avowing that
they had no confidence in them, but that they would probably be of
some service in warding off Federal bullets from loyal Southern men.
With such encouragement they went under fire, and a few hours later
eight of the ten were either killed or wounded. Morris was wounded
severely in the foot and borne from the field. He was taken to an
apology for a hospital near by, and there permitted to remain, his
wound receiving no attention whatever until the next day. By that
time—to employ a collocation of terms somewhat common of late—
"secesh" having "skedaddled," he was hurried with their other wounded
soldiers into a cart and driven to, or rather towards Corinth; for the
rains descending and the mules miring, in a manner that the experiences of the present rebellion have rendered historical, his arrival as
hoped for was prevented. But, even misery has its mirth, and his sufferings not being absolutely intolerable, he found diversion in the
floundering of the mules; the wrathful expletives of the driver, and the
peculiar inducements to alternately go ahead and halt, that nothing
but a mule can understand. The mud, however, would not share in
the defeat of the party, and the wounded men, mutually supporting
each other, were compelled to trust to their own crippled limbs for
locomotion to Corinth. There a furlough was given to Morris, and he
went home, experiencing on the way many privations and hardships.
His wound healing, the old determination to abandon a service that
he loathed, broke out afresh. He had been forced into the rebel army,
and neither reason nor justice, demanded that he should again imperil
his life for men who had no regard for his own. Becoming once more
an object of suspicion, he soon discovered that his life was in danger,
if he remained longer at home. Determining to escape northward, and
leaving his family in as comfortable a condition as he could, he "took
to the woods," and arrived at Springfield, Missouri, on the sixth day
of July, 1862.

The First Regiment of Arkansas Cavalry Volunteers was then
forming there, and receiving authority to recruit, he aided materially
in raising Company "H" of this regiment, and was afterwards commissioned its first lieutenant—a position that he now holds.

As an officer he has shown himself prompt and faithful in the discharge of duty, but higher than this, a man whose patriotism has stood the test of adversity and persecution, and who will yet, if the opportunity be given to him, strike for his family and fireside with vigor that will be its own defender.[7]

CAMP AT PRAIRIE GROVE, ARK.,
December, 1862.

PARIS G. STRICKLAND.

LIKE THE SUBJECT of the last sketch, Paris G. Strickland, may be considered a representative of rebel oppression in Searcy county. Born in Alabama, December 6, 1831, emigrating to Arkansas when a child, and living ever on Southern soil as a Southern man, he has given his enemies no cause for distrust by reason of birth or associations. A substantial citizen and identified for years with the best interests of his section, he promptly expressed himself in favor of the Union, when secession thrust forth its hideous head. He is, in fact, one of those comparatively few men whose convictions, under similar circumstances, have not been effected by timidity or fear, and who, regardless of personal consequences, have been frank and outspoken in the demonstration of loyalty.

Of the "Peace Organization Society" he was a member, and labored industriously to disseminate its views, dominant among which was the assertion of the right of communities to combine together for the mutual protection of life and property. The society had its ramifications especially in Conway, Marion, Pope, Searcy and Van Buren counties, and members knew each other in the customary manner of secret associations. Although seeking tranquility amidst disturbances of the most alarming character, the order, if it may so be termed, was thoroughly loyal, and in a State and at a time, where and when armed opposition to the rebel powers would have been fruitless of good result, was quietly moulding a public sentiment that in time would have been able to counteract the rebellious proclivities of the locality, had it not early been betrayed.

One John Holmes, of Van Buren county, and a Mr. Garrison,[1] whose christened name and precise residence we have not learned, worthless characters both, are entitled to this miserable distinction, and should they now be living can lay claim to an amount of misery and destitution altogether beyond their feeble power of atonement. Through their instrumentality the names of a large number of men belonging to the order were reported to the State Militia, and the order itself was effectually broken up. Seventy-six loyal citizens of Arkansas, whose only offense was devotion to the flag of their fathers, were cruelly incarcerated at Burroughville, the county seat of Searcy county, and afterward, as we have elsewhere stated, marched to Little Rock. There must be, nevertheless, some excuse for such conduct, other than the fact that the arrested men were averse to bearing arms for the Southern Confederacy. The sweeping accusation of jay-hawking and robbing was preferred, and the society charged with entering into a conspiracy to plunder and murder citizens of the secession party. As cause of complaint, these aspersions were wholly groundless, yet they served admirably to stimulate the blind zeal of the ignorant instruments of the rebel authorities. Concert of action was thus, in a great measure, disturbed, yet Union men occasionally met each other, and though unable to ameliorate their condition, strengthened their loyalty by the secret but effective interchange of mutual beliefs, hopes and fears.

There has been presented to us the original draft of a series of resolutions read and approved at the house of David C. Ruff, in Calf Creek Township, Searcy county, on the 25th day of November, 1861, at an interview attended by between thirty find forty citizens of the county, Mr. Strickland among the number, and as they breathe the inspiration of a genuine loyalty—loyalty that was nourished at the hazard of home, fortune, life itself—it may not be amiss to insert them:

"WHEREAS, It is reported that many of our peaceable, orderly and law-abiding citizens have been accused of entering into a conspiracy against the secession party, for the purpose of murdering, robbing and plundering the citizens of that party; and, *whereas,* many of our citizens have already been arrested and are held in custody, or imprisoned, and denied the right of trial, or to be heard in their own defense, and that all men who are desirous of remaining peaceably at home are considered enemies of the country and guilty of treason—

"*Resolved,* First: That the charge of conspiracy for the above or any other purpose, is a gross and palpable falsehood, and that we are ready at any time to take up arms against any body of robbers, North or South, and to maintain the peace of our country and the liberties of our citizens.

"*Resolved,* Secondly: That we are willing to have a full investigation made of the object and purpose of the society to which we belonged, as we intended only to benefit ourselves, when all other resources failed us, without interfering with any seceder or his property, and claiming for ourselves the right to think and act as independent American citizens.

"*Resolved,* Thirdly: That we will not submit to be taken up and tried for crimes of which we are not guilty; and rather than submit to the high-handed oppression now going on, we will defend ourselves by force of arms, and die, if necessary, in the assertion of our liberties."

Practically, however, those who assented to these resolutions were unable to accomplish anything for the betterment of their condition. They were too weak in numbers and resources, and could only live and hope. Mr. Strickland, seeing that he had become obnoxious to the rebel element in his neighborhood, and that his life would be endangered if he remained longer at home, secretly departed, in company with L. D. Jameson,[2] Harmon Hodges, and John H. Jenkins, men who, like himself, were no longer safe where rebellion held sway.

Arriving at Salem, Dent county, Missouri, they were placed under arrest as suspicious personages, and were sent by the Commander of the Post to Rolla. There, through the intervention of one Captain Ware, who had been a member of the same organization with themselves, they were released, and shortly afterward Mr. Strickland joined the army of the Southwest at Lebanon. Attached to it for a time as teamster, and then its bearer of dispatches, in March, 1862, he was taken sick, but recovering soon after, undertook to go home, striking across the country from Keitsville.

On the 2d of April he arrived there, and was told by citizens that he was in at least no immediate danger. For a short time he was unmolested. The Sunday following his return, however, Churchill's Brigade of Texas Cavalry, arrived at Burroughville, and that night a detachment of nine of them, guided by James Shaw, Miles Thornton and Wade Griflin,[3] went to the house of Strickland's step-father, twelve miles from Burroughville, with whom he was then residing, for the purpose of effecting his arrest. Other arrests were made *en route,* and it was 9 o'clock ere the party arrived at the house, where it was intended to seize Strickland. He had not yet retired, and seeing small squads of men approaching the house from different directions, hastily passed from one room to another through an open porch, after his rifle and revolver, and when returning was hailed with the polite salutation—

"G——d d——m you, strike a light or we'll fire!"

The ruffians, immediately, pressed up to the house, and a moment later shot John Workman, the step-father of Mr. Strickland, just as the latter was handing him a gun. The women of the household now caught hold of Mr. Strickland to prevent his shooting, as men were breaking into the house from opposite doors. This demonstration saved his life, as the Texans hesitated to shoot when they saw the clinging women. He was now seized; "punched" several times with the muzzle of a gun, and at length dragged from the house and taken to Burroughville. The next day he was notified that he would have to "stand a trial," and very shortly afterward was ushered into the court room under guard, and called upon to respond to the charge of treason, before an extemporized tribunal, consisting of the most bitter rebels of the town. They sat around promiscuously, and like the minions of a barbarous despot, aggravated the injustice of their decision by the irregularity of their proceedings. It was a sort of "*free fight*" on the part of the court, every member considering himself privileged to ask all manner of bellicose questions, and that he possessed the right of unlimited abuse of the poor victim of oppression, who, without counsel or preparation, was thus called to answer a most serious charge.

The names of some of these men we insert: M. P. Hogan, *officious;* Alexander Hill, Clerk of the Circuit Court and ex-officio County Clerk of Searcy county; James D. Shaw, Gibson Parks, Terrill Young, Justice of the Peace, *very officious;* Martin Blair, John J. Dawson, John L. Russell, and William H. Jones.[4] The long scroll of infamy that the rebellion is now preparing, likewise includes them, and as the subordinate but hated instruments of a tyranny as malignant as it is hopeless, they will never be forgotten in the county of their residence. Under the general charge of treason against the Southern Confederacy, the first specification was, that the accused belonged to the Peace Organization Society; the second, that he had been to the Northern army; and the third that he was a spy. No witnesses were examined, and he was called upon substantially to convict himself. He admitted that he belonged to the Peace Organization Society; in reply to an impertinent question denied all knowledge of or complicity with jayhawkers; answered that he left his home because he became satisfied that he could not remain there, and boldly averred that he went to the Northern army for protection. In response to the interrogatory, why he did not join the Southern army, he answered that he did not like the soldier's fare, and alluded to the seventy-seven citizens who, the autumn before, had been marched like a chain-gang from Burroughville to Little Rock, and there, in the Hall of the House of Representatives, been forced to enlist or be tried for treason—a ceremonial at which Governor Rector was the high priest.

This extraordinary court now placed their heads in wise juxtaposition; asked each other if they had any more questions to put, and were about to direct the removal of the accused, when he requested the privilege of addressing them. It was hesitatingly accorded; but he had scarcely begun, when he was stopped and taken from the room under guard. Marched to Cooper's Tavern, he was allowed to remain undisturbed until 9 o'clock at night, when, with others, who had undergone a similar trial (?), he was told to get his blanket to go to jail. The prisoners' hands were now tied behind their backs, and ropes placed about their necks. They were then separated, one John W. McDaniel[5] (still living) being first taken away. Strickland was led in a direction opposite to that in which the jail was located, into a secluded hollow nearly a mile from town. The rope previously placed about his neck was thrown over the limb of a tree, and he was tauntingly asked which he preferred, to he hung or shot. Upon his replying that if nothing but his death would serve their purpose, he preferred to be shot if he could see them do it, one Captain Black, upon whom is chargeable the death of John Workman, shot as already mentioned, and who was acting a conspicuous part in the proceedings of the hour, replied that he would shoot him, but in the back.

"Down on your knees," says the brutal Captain. Strickland refused to bend, whereupon the rope being released from the limb, Black catches hold of it near his neck, and after one or two ineffectual efforts jerked him down. He jumps now upon his stomach, and then catching him by the hair of the head, draws a knife and passes it across his neck, slightly cutting the skin. Meanwhile his curses were incessant, and at length he rose and ordered Strickland to do likewise. But the latter was nearly exhausted, and replied that he could not. Black then places his foot under Strickland's neck, and by the joint action of it and a command, succeeds in getting him up. He jerks him again so that he staggers but does not fall. Ordering another man to hold the rope, he takes up his gun and fires it above Strickland's head. He now draws a pistol, remarking that "he had killed one d——d old jayhawker with it, and was going to try another"; presented it to Strickland's forehead, and snapped it several times, doubtless to annoy, however, rather than kill.

When the ropes were being adjusted at the jail, Black told Strickland that he had been condemned to be hung, and now informs him that he should proceed with the operation. Throwing the rope over the limb again, he jerked Strickland violently against the tree, and then, as if relenting, said that he hated to hang or shoot a man unless he had an equal showing with him. Apparently relenting still further, he asks him if he would go home and remain there if released. Strickland remarked that under the circumstances he would. Cautioning him against revealing the occurrences of the night, Black now sets him at liberty, together with John W. McDaniels, previously mentioned, and Martin Gillam, another citizen. Returning home that night Strickland remains five or six weeks in the vicinity, lying in the woods by day, and venturing forth even at night with great caution. He then secretly departed for White county, where he was arrested by soldiers belonging to the army of the Southwest. On hearing his story General Curtis promptly released him, when he went to Helena, thence to St. Louis, and from there to Springfield. He was lately at Elk Horn Tavern, waiting with an anxiety, that none but a refugee can feel, for the occupation of Arkansas by the Federal forces.

CAMP AT PRAIRIE GROVE, ARK.
December, 1862.

NORTH-WESTERN ARKANSAS.

WHEN GENERAL MCCULLOUGH passed through Fayetteville, on his way to discomfiture and death at Pea Ridge, he expressed the wish, that North-western Arkansas was in a place, which we shall simply designate as more hot than holy. If character and calamity on the one hand, and the Bible on the other, can determine the *post mortem* condition of a human being, "Ben McCullough," whilom somewhat famous as a Texan Ranger, is sealed with a fate that polemics cannot modify, and God will never change. Rabid secessionists have always disliked North-western Arkansas. Though bordering on the Cherokee line, it has been for years the intellectual centre of the State, with Fayetteville as the point from which its intelligence radiated. Settled principally by Kentuckians and Tennesseans, whose early teachings, under Henry Clay and Andrew Jackson, gave to their politics life, and to their loyalty vigor, attachment to the Federal Union has, from its settlement, been the prevailing sentiment of this section; a result attributable, in no small degree, to the educational institutions of Fayetteville and vicinity.

In the summer of 1839 the first school was established in Fayetteville. Its proprietress, Miss Sophia Sawyer, was well known and very favorably remembered by the early residents of Washington county.[1] A lady of indomitable energy, her experiment soon expanded into the Fayetteville Female Seminary, at the head of which she continued for a number of years, and until declining health compelled the abandonment of her enterprise to the care of others. In 1842, Robert W. Mecklin, who had been for years a prominent State surveyor, opened a grammar school three miles west of Fayetteville.[2] Shortly afterward it became the Ozark Institute, incorporated as a college in 1845. Some years later there arising a difference in views, that grew out of an act of discipline, the faculty were divided, and Robert Graham, a professor in the college, and a gentleman of culture and experience, severing his connection with it, went to Fayetteville and shortly succeeded in founding the Arkansas College, an institution that, until the rebellion broke out, thrived far beyond expectation.[3] Though on the frontier, it was not at all inferior in its course of study and thoroughness of instruction to the time-honored seats of learning that have made New Haven, Cambridge and Princeton, classic ground.

Another female institute sprang up at Fayetteville in 1858,[4] and some years earlier a seminary at Elm Spring, ten miles northwesterly, under the auspices of William Barrington, a merchant of intelligence and energy, who, looking beyond the necessities of trade, could appreciate the educational wants of a new community. The climate, moreover, of North-western Arkansas is favorable to the growth of intellect, and the surface of the country, high, bold and beautiful with here and there valleys of the richest soil, through which meander the Main, Middle and West forks of the White river, and other lesser streams, while inviting the meditation of the student secures the hygienic approval of the parent. Agriculturally, also, this section of the State possesses a variety of adaptation rarely found elsewhere. In the bottom lands, south of the Boston Mountains, cotton is raised abundantly, and north of them, in the valleys, all the cereals, and on the hillsides fruit, superior to any that either New Jersey, or Western New York can produce. Grapes likewise grow wild in great abundance, and if given any attention are very superior in flavor. The vine-grower could there find his paradise.[5]

Such briefly is the natural aptitude of the section, and when the rebellion broke out, nature and intelligence seemed to be vying with each other in making the people contented and their homes happy. Arkansas College and the female seminaries at Fayetteville were busy with the hum of earnest voices, participating in which was the well-pronounced English of native Creeks, Cherokees and Choctaws, young ladies, many of them who, but for faint traces of their origin, would have passed, in parlor or hall, as high born dames of Anglo-Saxon blood.

In February, 1862, and before its re-organization near the base of the Boston Mountains, a short time prior to the battle of Pea Ridge, the rebel army retreated through Fayetteville. Going northward, before that event, McCullough had stated, that if he should be compelled to return, he would burn as he went, and he kept faith with his threat. The Arkansas College, the Fayetteville Female Seminary, a large steam flouring mill, and four ware-houses, became heaps of ruins, to say nothing of the numerous private dwellings that were sacrificed upon the altar of his spleen. North-western Arkansas will long remember the irascible Texan, but for the brilliancy of his fires not his genius.[6] In politics, also, the section has been equally prominent. A strong Union feeling has ever been its dominant characteristic, and notwithstanding the defection of leaders, when firmness was most needed, the masses are loyal still, and while we write are coming up nobly to the support of the Union of their fathers. When South Carolina seceded in December, 1860, the rash act was nowhere more severely reprobated than in North-western Arkansas, and when a few weeks later, the Legislature of the State passed an act calling a convention, the object of which was to take into consideration the secession of the State, the Union element was eager for the polls. The election of delegates was to take place on the 18th of February. Public excitement was running high, and "straight out" secessionists were straining every nerve to elect unqualified disunionists. The most extravagant statements were made. Every supporter of the Administration was termed a Black Republican. The idea of negro equality, which, by the way, has always thrived far more in the apprehensive minds of Southern men than anywhere else, was expanded into a system of adverse laws and ordinances, and Union men derided as spiritless and unequal to the emergency of the time. But the inoculating material was vicious, and the impulses of the people shrank from the noxious touch. The Union delegates received large majorities, and with the Hon. David Walker, of Washington county, at their head, walked into the Convention, proud recipients of the confidence of a patriotic constituency.

The Convention met on the 4th of March, 1861, and during its brief, but stormy session, the Union men stood firmly by their colors. Every conceivable pressure was brought to bear upon them, culminating at length in a proposed ordinance of secession, and threats to take the State out of the Union by force, if all other methods should fail. The public mind on the other hand, was strongly inclined to co-operation, and the Union delegates sought to defer the action of Arkansas, until the result of a Convention of the Border slave-holding States, to be held at Frankfort, Kentucky, on the 27th of May, should become known. On the 20th of March, therefore, the day before the adjournment of the Convention, the following ordinance was passed:

"An ordinance to provide for holding an election in the State of Arkansas, for the purpose of taking the sense of the people of the State on the question of co-operation or secession.

"SECTION 1. *Be it ordained by the people of the State of Arkansas in Convention assembled:* That an election shall be held in all the counties in this State on Monday, the third day of

August, 1861, at which the question of "co-operation" or
"secession" shall be submitted to the people of this State; which
election shall be held and conducted, in all respects, in accordance with the laws of the State now in force prescribing the manner of holding elections; *Provided,* that the sheriffs of the several
counties shall be required to give at least thirty days' notice of
the time and places of holding said election, by advertisement
thereof, as required by law for ordering elections.

"SEC. II. *Be it further ordained,* That the ballots or tickets to
be used in said election, shall be endorsed 'for co-operation,' or
'for secession,' from which ballots count shall be made by the
Judges, and they shall ascertain how many votes are cast for 'co-
operation,' and how many are cast for 'secession' at their respective precincts, and shall duly certify the result of said counts, and
make returns thereof to the clerks of their respective counties,
who shall open and compare said returns, as they are now
required by law to open and compare the returns of other elections; and each clerk shall make an abstract of the vote of his
county upon the question of 'secession' or 'co-operation,' and file
the same in his office; and shall also at the same time make out
under his seal and deliver to the delegate or delegates from his
county to this Convention, a copy of said abstract, to be
returned by them to the office of Secretary of State, as hereinafter
provided.

"SEC. III. *Be it further ordained,* That the delegates to this
Convention, shall be made special returning officers, to bring up
the certified vote of their respective counties, on the question of
'co-operation' or 'secession,' to the office of the Secretary of
State; which vote from all the counties shall be opened and
counted by the Secretary of State, in presence of the Governor,
Auditor, and Treasurer, or any two of them, on Monday, the
19th day of August, 1861; and said officers, or any three of
them, shall certify to the President of this Convention, when the
same shall be again convened, as hereinafter provided, the whole
number of votes cast in the State 'for co-operation,' and the
whole number of votes cast 'for secession,' and if from any cause
any delegate shall be unable to bring on the vote of his county,
as herein provided, he shall have power and it shall be his duty,
to appoint a special messenger to be the bearer of the same in his
stead; and if from any cause, there should be no delegate from
any county, then the clerk of said county shall appoint a messenger to bring up the vote thereof.

"SEC. IV. *Be it further ordained,* That the delegates, or other
messengers, who shall bring up the vote of the different counties,

shall receive the same mileage as is provided to be paid to returning officers by the act of the General Assembly calling this
Convention.

"SEC. V. *Be it further ordained,* That if it shall appear, when
the result of said election shall be made known to this Convention, that a majority of all the legal votes cast in the State,
shall be for 'secession,' then, in that event, such vote shall be
taken to be an instruction to this Convention to pass an act of
immediate secession, and the Convention shall at once pass an
ordinance dissolving the connection existing between the State of
Arkansas and the Federal Government, known as 'The United
States of America'; but if a majority of all the legal votes shall
have been cast for 'co-operation,' then this Convention shall
immediately take such steps as may be deemed proper, to further
co-operation with the Border or unseceded slave States, in the
effort to secure a permanent and satisfactory adjustment of the
sectional controversies disturbing the country.

"SEC. VI. *Be it further ordained,* That the President of this
Convention be, and he is hereby instructed to issue his proclamation, within ten days after the adoption of this ordinance, to
the sheriffs of the several counties in the State, requiring them to
hold an election in their respective counties, in conformity to the
provisions of this ordinance.

"SEC. VII. *Be it further ordained,* That when this Convention
shall adjourn, it shall adjourn to meet on the 19th day of
August, 1861."

By section six of this ordinance, the President of the Convention
was instructed to issue his proclamation for holding an election,
whereupon the following was generally circulated:

*"Proclamation of the President of the Convention of the people
of the State of Arkansas, to the sheriffs of the several counties, greeting:*

"WHEREAS, The Convention of the people of the State of
Arkansas did, on the 20th day of March, A.D., 1861, pass and
ordain an ordinance, entitled 'An ordinance to provide for holding an election in the State of Arkansas, for the purpose of taking the sense of the people of the State on the question of
"co-operation" or "secession"'; and, *whereas,* the provisions of said
ordinance require an election to be held in said State, upon said
question, on the first Monday in August, A.D., 1861. Therefore,
I, David Walker, President of the Convention, under the authority and in accordance with the provisions of said ordinance, do

hereby declare and make known that such election will be held in the State of Arkansas, on the third day of August, A.D., 1861, upon the said question of 'co-operation' or 'secession'; and the sheriffs of the respective counties in the State, are hereby required and commanded to cause said election to be held according to the said provisions of said ordinance published herewith. [The two were published together.]

"In testimony whereof, I have hereunto set my hand as such President of the Convention, at Little Rock, Arkansas, this 22d day of March, A.D., 1861.

"DAVID WALKER.

"By E. C. BOUDINOT,[7]
"Secretary of the Convention."

The Convention having now adjourned, both parties went busily to work to fashion public sentiment. The Union men remained firm, and great hopes were centered in the coming Convention at Frankfort. On the other hand, the rebel element in the State strained every nerve to precipitate secession. All the appliances that art could devise or ingenuity invent, were brought to bear upon the people. The thorough canvassing of the State was projected, and prominent politicians rode hither and yon, assuming to rouse the people from a lethargy *that they had never felt.*

Meanwhile there appeared a pamphlet, entitled "State or Province, Bond or Free," written by Albert Pike, of Little Rock.[8] It was a very specious argument for secession, but a re-production of the political heresies, that thirty years ago called down on John C. Calhoun, the anathema maranatha of Andrew Jackson. It was passing strange too that Albert Pike, of all men, should thus have written. The treason of the great South Carolinian, gigantic in conception if not in execution, had hardly passed into history, when there appeared from Pike's pen the following stanzas, entitled—

DISUNION.

"Ay, shout! 'Tis the day of your pride,
　　Ye despots and tyrants of earth;
Tell your serfs the American name to deride,
　　And to rattle their fetters in mirth.
Ay, shout! for the league of the free
　　Is about to be shivered to dust,

And the rent limbs to fall from the vigorous tree,
    Wherein liberty puts her firm trust.
Shout! shout ! for more firmly established, will be
Your thrones and dominions beyond the blue sea.

    "Laugh on! for such folly supreme,
        The world has yet never beheld;
    And ages to come will the history deem,
        A tale by antiquity swelled;
    For nothing that time has upbuilt
        And set in the annals of crime,
    So stupid and senseless, so wretched in guilt,
        Darkens sober tradition or rhyme.
It will be like the fable of Eblis' fall.[9]
A by-word of mocking and horror to all.

    "Ye mad, who would raze out your name,
        From the league of proud and the free,
    And a pitful, separate sovereignty claim,
        Like a lone wave flung off from the sea.
    Oh! pause, ere you plunge in the chasm,
        That yawns in your traitorous way!
    Ere Freedom, convulsed with one terrible spasm,
        Desert you forever and aye!
Pause! think! ere the earthquake astonish your soul,
And the thunders of war through your green valleys roll.

    "Good God! what a title, what name
        Will history give to your crime!
In the deepest abyss of dishonor and shame,
        Ye will writhe till the last hour of time,
    As braggarts who forged their own chains,
        Pulled down what their brave fathers built,
    And tainted the blood in their children's young veins,
        With the poison of slavery and guilt;
And Freedom's bright heart be hereafter, ten fold
For your folly and fall, more discouraged and cold.

    "What flag shall float over the fires
        And the smoke of your patricide war,
Instead of the stars and broad stripes of your sires?
        A lone, pale, dim, flickering star,

With a thunder cloud veiling its glow,
   As it faints away into the sea;
Will the eagle's wing shelter and shield you? Ah, no!
   His wing shelters only the free.
Miscall it, disguise it, boast, rant as you will,
You are traitors misled by your mad leaders still.

"Turn, turn then! cast down in your might
   The pilots that sit at the helm,
Steer, steer your proud ship from the gulf which dark night
   And treason and fear overwhelm!
Turn back from your mountains and glens,
   From your swamps, from the rivers and sea,
From forest and precipice, cavern and den,
   Where your brave fathers bled to be free.
From the graves where those glorious patriots lie,
Re-echoes the warning, 'Turn back or you die!'"

Though still a young man, we doubt whether a more vivid picture of the arch traitors of the present time, or of Albert Pike's own utter defection, could be drawn in verse. The chasm that yawned in the traitorous way of Calhoun and his confreres, has opened beneath his own feet, and the "folly supreme" of the poet, is now the *supreme folly* of the man. Many of Mr. Pike's warmest friends regret exceedingly that he should pursue the course he has, since the rebellion began. He is a genius of the first order, and wherever he is known, this is admitted. His "Hymns to the Gods," published in Blackwood in 1839, gave him an enviable Trans-Atlantic reputation, and a volume of poems entitled "Nugae,"and printed in 1854 for private distribution only, breathes the inspiration of a master spirit. The muses, however, were but the companions of his leisure. A lawyer by profession, he located long years ago at Little Rock, and speedily built up a reputation co-extensive with the south-west. Nor was his practice confined to Arkansas. To New Orleans he was often called professionally, and now and then could be seen in a quiet and secluded room in the Capitol at Washington, urging the cause of a client, before the most majestic tribunal in the world. *He is the first lawyer of the south-west.*

Socially it is hardly possible, we are informed, to meet a better companion. Generous to a fault, prodigal of money, of a buoyant disposition and warm in his attachments, he made friends wherever he met men. In 1859 the newspapers killed him off, but he still persisted in treading the firm earth. Wandering on the hither side of Styx, he appeared unto John F. Coyle, of the *National Intelligencer,* who, according to the Philadelphia *Press,* "in pity to one whom he had loved while in the flesh, and mourned when numbered among the dead, resolved to *wake* him." The peculiar privilege of the children of the Emerald Isle, was now trenched upon, and a "wake" that would have aroused St. Patrick himself was *solemnized* not a thousand miles from the capital. There was indeed a spirit moved, but that of "St. Peray,"[10] and the bibulous fullness of the wit, eloquence and genius gathered about the table of "Johnny Coyle," breaking forth at length in song, Pike's own lines were sung to the air of "Benny Havens O!" We will be pardoned, we trust, for inserting some or them, with the comments made by the chronicler of the occasion:

"A gentleman from Arkansas, not long ago, 'tis said,
Waked up one pleasant morning, and discovered he was dead.
He was on his way to Washington, not seeking for the spoils,
But rejoicing in the promise of a spree at Johnny Coyles.
    One spree at Johnny Coyles, one spree at Johnny Coyles,
    And who would not be glad to join a spree at Johnny Coyles."

"He awakes on board the ferry boat which crosses the Styx; is informed by Charon that he is dead; laments that if so, this little accident may make him miss the frolic at Coyles; resists all entreaty from Horace and Anacreon to remain with them, crosses

"'The adamantine halls, and reached the ebon throne,
Where gloomy Pluto frowned, and where his Queen's soft beauty shone.
'What want you here?' the monarch, 'Your Majesty,' said he,
'Permission at one frolic more at Johnny Coyles to be.'"

"He promises to return, as Orpheus did, if allowed to revisit Coyle, and adds:

"'Tis not for power, or wealth or fame, I hanker to return,
Nor that love's kisses once again upon my lips may burn.
Let me but once more meet the friends that long have been so dear,
And who, if I'm not there, will say, 'would God that he were here.'"

"He complains that if dead, be has not been '*waked* and buried dacently'; declines nectar and ambrosia, preferring the canvas-backs, terrapins and St. Peray of his friend Coyle, and swears that better company than Pluto can boast, he can find at Coyles."

The personal descriptions that follow, we omit, remarking, however, that Philip Barton Key is styled the "Roman Tully's peer,"[11] and
Robert Johnson, United States Senator from Arkansas, *the bravest
of the brave, the truest of the true(?)."*

"The list of prime fellows rehearsed, Pluto affrighted, announces
his intention of taking them by installments, and of not letting Pike
return to upper air. But fair Proserpine coaxes her swarthy and regal
husband, and prevails on him to allow Pike to be present at his own
wake.

> "'How can you say me nay?"
> I'm sure you do not love me; if you did you'd not refuse,
> When I want to get the fashions, and you want to hear the news.
> And so at last the Queen prevailed, as women always do,
> And thus it comes that once again, this gentleman's with you.
> He's under promise to return, but that he means to break,
> And many another spree to have, besides this present wake.'"

Well had it been for Albert Pike, had Pluto adhered to his original
intention. The mythical Proserpine as the Goddess of secession, may
be said to have detained him in the upper air, long enough to enable
him to out-live his better self. "State or Province" is sharing the fate
of Calhoun's heavy volumes, and its author is now supposed to be at
Little Rock, fulminating his wrath against Generals Holmes and
Hindman, an indication of the severity of which, and of Pike's treatment in his operations among the Indians, can be gathered from the
following communication, the interest of which to us is our excuse for
its insertion.

We copy from the *Arkansas Patriot*, of February 19th, 1863,—a
southern sheet published at Little Rock:

"ALBERT PIKE'S LETTER ADDRESSED TO MAJ. GEN. HOLMES.
          "LITTLE ROCK, ARK., *December 30th,* 1862.

"When Mr. C. B. Johnson agreed in September to loan your quartermaster at Little Rock three hundred and fifty thousand dollars of
the money he was conveying to Major Quesenbury,[12] the quartermaster of the department of Indian Territory, *you promised* him that
it should be repaid to Major Quesenbury as soon as you should
receive funds, and before he would have disposed of the remaining
million.

"*You got the money by means of that promise; and you did not
keep the promise.* On the contrary, by an order that reached Fort

Smith, three hours before Mr. Johnson did, that compelled Major Quesenbury, the moment he received the money, to turn every dollar of it over to a commissary at Fort Smith, *and it was used to supply the needs of General Hindman's troops;* when the Seminoles, fourteen months in the service, have never been paid a dollar, and the Chickasaw and Choctaw Battalions, and Chilly McIntosh's Creeks, each corps a year and more in the service, have received only forty-five thousand dollars each and no clothing.

"Was this violation of your promise the act of the Government? To replace the clothing I had procured for the Indians in December 1861, and which, with near one thousand tents, fell into the hands of the troops of Generals Price and Van Dorn, I sent an agent in June to Richmond, who went thence to Georgia, and there procured some six thousand five hundred suits, with about three thousand shirts, and three thousand pair of drawers, and some two or three hundred tents. These supplies were in Monroe early in September, and the Indians were informed that they and the moneys had been procured and were on the way. The good news went all over their country, as if on the wings of the wind, and universal content and rejoicing were the consequences.

"The clothing reached Fort Smith, and its issue to General Hindman's people commenced immediately. I sent a quartermaster for it, and he was retained there. If *any* of it has ever reached the Indians, it has been only recently, and but a small portion of it. You pretended to believe that the Indians were in a 'ferment' and discontented, and you took this very opportune occasion to stop all the moneys due their troops and for debts in their country, and to take and appropriate to the uses of other troops, the clothing promised to and procured for *them.* The clothing and the money were *theirs;* and you were in possession of an order from the War Department forbidding you to divert any supplies from their legitimate destination,—an order which was issued, *as you knew,* in consequence of *my* complaint, and to prevent moneys and supplies for the Indians, being stopped;—*and you stopped all.*

"You borrow part of the money, and then seize the rest, like a genteel highwayman, who first borrows all he can of a traveler, on promise of a punctual re-payment, and then claps a pistol to his head, and orders him to 'stand and deliver' the rest. And you did even more than this. For you promised the Acting Commissioner of Indian Affairs, when he was at Little Rock, about the 1st of October, on his way to the Indian country, to give the Indians assurances of the good faith of the Government—*you promised him, I say, that the clothing in question should go to the Indians.* He told the Chickasaws and Seminoles at least of this promise. You broke it. You did *not* send them the clothing. You placed the Commissioner and the Government in an admirable attitude before the Indians; and the consequence has been, I understand, the disbanding of the Chickasaws, and the failure of the Seminole troops to re-organize. The consequences will be far more serious yet. Indians cannot be deceived, and promises made them shamelessly broken with impunity. While *you* were thus stopping their clothing, and robbing the half-naked Indians to clothe other troops, the Federals were sending home the Choctaws, whom they had taken prisoners, after clothing them comfortably and putting money in their pockets.

"No one need be astonished when all the Indians shall have turned their arms against us. Why did you and General Hindman not procure by your own exertions what you need for your troops? He reached Little Rock on the 31st of May. You came here in August. I sent my agents to Richmond for money and clothing in June and July. I never asked either of *you* for *anything.* I could procure for *my* command all I wanted. You and he were Major Generals; I only a Brigadier, and Brigadiers are as plenty as blackberries in their season. It is to be supposed that if I could procure money, clothing and supplies for Indians, you and he could do so for white troops. Both of you come blundering out to Arkansas with nothing, and supply yourselves with what I procure. Some officers would be ashamed *so* to supply deficiencies caused by their own want of foresight, energy or sense. *You* do not even know you need an engineer until one of mine comes by with twenty thousand dollars in his hands, for engineer service in the Indian Territory, some of which belongs to *me* for advances made, and with stationery and instruments procured by *me* for *my* department, in Richmond, a year ago; and *then* you find out that there are such things as engineers, and that you need one; and you seize on engineer, money and stationery.

"You even take, notwithstanding paragraph VI, of General Orders, No. 50, the stationery procured by me for the Adjutant General's Office of my Department, by purchase in Richmond in December, 1861; for the want of which I had been compelled to permit my own private stock to be used for months. I no longer wonder that you do these things. When you told me that you could not judge me fairly, because I told the Indians that others had done them injustice, you confessed much more than you intended. It was a pregnant sentence you uttered. By it you judged and convicted yourself, and you pronounced *your own sentence,* when you uttered it. The Federal authorities were proposing to the Indians, *at the very time when you stopped their clothing* and money, that if they would return to the old Union, they should not be asked to take up arms; their annuities should be paid them in money; the negroes taken from them restored; all losses and damages sustained by them be paid for, and they be allowed to retain as so much clear profit, what had been paid them by the Confederate States. It was a liberal offer and a great temptation to come at the moment when you and Hindman were felicitously completing your operations, and when there were no breadstuffs in their country, and they and their women and children were starving and half naked. You chose an admirable opportunity to rob, to disappoint, to outrage and exasperate them, and make your own Government fraudulent and contemptible in their eyes. If any human action *can* deserve it, the hounds of hell ought to hunt your soul and Hindman's for it, through all eternity.

"Instead of co-operating with the Federal authorities, and doing all that he and you *could* to induce the Indians to listen to and accept their propositions, *he* had better have expelled the enemy from Arkansas, or 'perished in the attempt,' and you had better have marched on Helena, before its fortifications were finished, and purged the eastern part of the State of the enemy's presence. If you had succeeded as admirably in that as you have in losing the Indian country, you would have merited the eternal gratitude of Arkansas, instead of its execrations, and the laurel instead of a halter. I said that you and your Lieutenant had left *nothing* undone. I repeat it. Take another *small* example: Until I left the command at the end of July, the Indian troops had regularly had their half ration of coffee. As soon as I was got rid of, an order from General Hindman took all the remaining coffee, some three thousand pounds, to Fort Smith. Even in this small matter he could not forego an opportunity of injuring and disappointing them. You asked me in August, what was the need of any white troops at all, in the Indian country, and you said that the few mounted troops I had, if kept in the northern part of the Cherokee country, would have been enough to repel any Federal force that ever would have entered it. As you and Hindman never allowed any ammunition procured by me to reach the Indian country, if you could prevent it, whether I obtained it in Richmond, or Corinth or Texas, and as you approve of his course, in taking out of that country all that was to be found in it, I am entitled to suppose, that you regarded ammunition for the Indians as little necessary as troops to protect them in conformity to the pledge of honor of the Government. One thing, however, is to be said of your next in command. When he has ordered anything to be seized he has never denied having done so, or tried to cast the responsibility on an inferior.

"After you had written to me, that you had ordered Col. Darnell to seize at Dallas, in Texas, ammunition furnished by me, you denied to him, I understand, that you had given the order. Is it so? and *did* he refuse to trust the order in your hands, or even to let you see it, but would show it to General McCullough? Probably you know by this time, if you are capable of learning *anything,* whether any white troops are needed in the Indian country. The brilliant result of General Hindman's profound calculations and masterly strategy, and of his long contemplated invasion of Missouri, is before the country, and the disgraceful route at Fort Wayne, with the maneuvers and results on the Arkansas, are pregnant commentaries on the abuse lavished on me for not taking the line of the Arkansas, or making headquarters on Spring river, with a force too small to effect anything, anywhere.

"I have not spoken of your martial law and provost marshals in the Indian country, and your seizures of salt-works there, or in detail, of your seizure of ammunition procured by me in Texas, and on its way to the Indian troops, or of the withdrawal of all white troops and artillery from their country; of the retention for other troops of the mountain howitzers procured by me for Colonel Waitie, and the ammunition sent me for them, and for small arms from Richmond. This letter is but part of the indictment I will prefer, by and by, when the laws are no longer silent, and the Constitution, and even public opinion no longer be paralyzed under the brutal heel of military power, and when the results of your *im*policy and *mis*management shall have been fully developed. But I have a word or two to say as to myself. From the time when I entered the Indian country in May, 1861, to make treaties, until the beginning of June, 1862, when General Hindman, in the plenitude of his self-conceit and folly, assumed absolute control of the military and other affairs of the Department of Indian Territory, and commenced plundering it of troops, artillery and ammunition, dictating military operations, and making the Indian country an appanage of North-western Arkansas, there was profound peace throughout its whole extent. Even with the wild Camanches and Kiowas I had secured friendly relations. An unarmed man could travel in safety and alone, from Kansas to the Red river, and from the Arkansas line to the Wichita Mountains. The Texan frontier had not been as perfectly undisturbed for years. We had fifty-five hundred Indians in service, under arms, and they were as loyal as our own people, little as had been done by any one, save myself, to keep them so, and much as had been done by others to alienate them. They referred all their difficulties to me for decision, and looked to me alone to see justice done them, and the faith of treaties preserved.

"Most of the time without moneys, (those sent out for that Department generally failing to reach it,) I had managed to keep the white and Indian troops better fed than any other portion of the troops of the Confederacy anywhere. I had twenty six pieces of artillery,—two of the batteries as perfectly equipped and well manned as any, anywhere. I had on hand and on the way an ample supply of ammunition, after being once plundered. While in command, *I had actually procured, first and last,* thirty-six thousand pounds of rifle and cannon powder. If you would like to know, sir, how I effected this, in the face of all manner of discouragements and difficulties, it is no secret. My disbursing officers call tell you who supplied them with funds for many weeks, and whose means purchased horses for their artillery. Ask the Chickasaws and Seminoles *who* purchased the only shoes they have ever received, four hundred pairs at five dollars each, procured and paid for *by me* in Bonham, and which I sent up to them after I was taken 'in personal custody' in November.

"*You* dare to pretend, sir, that I might be disloyal, or even in thought, couple the word treason with *my* name! What *peculiar* merit is it in *you* to serve on, once in this war? You were bred a soldier and your only chance for distinction lay in obtaining promotion, in the army, and in the army of the Confederacy. You *were* a Major or something of the sort, in the old army, and you *are* a Lieutenant-General. Your reward, I think for what you have done or have not done is sufficient.

"I was a private citizen over fifty years of age, and neither needing nor desiring military rank or civil honors. I accepted the office of Commissioner at the President's *solicitation*. I took that of Brigadier General with all the odium that I knew would follow it, and fall on me as the leader of a force of Indians, knowing there would be little glory to be reaped, and wanting no promotion, simply and solely to see *my* pledges to the Indians carried out; to keep them loyal to us; to save their country to the Confederacy, and to preserve the western frontier of Arkansas and the northern frontier of Texas, from devastation and desolation.

"What has been my reward? All my efforts have been rendered nugatory, and my attempts even to collect and form an army frustrated by the continual plundering of my supplies and means by other Generals, as your and their deliberate efforts to disgust and alienate the Indians. Once before this, an armed force was sent to arrest me. You all disobey the President's orders, and treat me as a criminal for endeavoring to have them carried out. The whole country swarms with slanders against me, and at last because I felt constrained reluctantly to re-assume command, after learning that the President would not accept my resignation, I am taken from Tishomingo to Washington, a prisoner, under an armed guard, it having been deemed necessary for the sake of effect, to send two hundred and fifty men into the Indian country to arrest me. *The Senatorial election was at hand.* I had, unaided and alone, *secured* to the Confederacy a magnificent country, equal in extent, fertility, beauty, and resources, to any one of our States—nay superior to any. I had secured the means, in men and arms, of keeping it. I knew how only it could be defended. I asked no aid of any of you. I only asked to be let alone. Verily I have my reward also, as Hastings had his, for winning India for the British Empire.[13] It is *your* day *now.* You sit above the laws, and domineer over the Constitution. 'Order reigns in Warsaw.' But by and by there will be a just jury empanneled, who will hear *all* the testimony and decide impartially—no less a jury than the people of the Confederate States, and for their verdict as to myself, I and my children will be content to wait; as, also, for the sure and stern sentence and universal malediction, that will fall like a great wave of God's just anger on you and the murderous miscreant by whose malign promptings you are making yourself accursed.

"Whether I am respectfully yours, you will be able to determine from the contents of this letter.

"ALBERT PIKE
"*Citizen of Arkansas.*

"THEOPHILUS H. HOLMES,
"Major General, &c."

The only heart burnings are not in Washington, and if the chief instruments in south-western rebelliousness will but continue to cherish their *evident friendship* for each other, the Army of the Frontier will have no occasion to march down the valley of the Arkansas.

But to return. While "State or Province, Bond or Free" was being industriously circulated, Union men were not idle. Forty delegates to the recent convention at Little Rock, united in an address to the people of Arkansas, that was extensively published in the newspapers of the day, refused, however, by the organs of secession.

"UNION ADDRESS TO THE PEOPLE OF ARKANSAS.

"The undersigned, Union members of the Convention which met on the 4th, and adjourned on the 21st of March, deem it their duty to issue an address, briefly stating the action of the Convention on the subject confided to it; and offering a few suggestions as to the course to be pursued in future, in view of the circumstances now surrounding our State.

"Upon assembling at the Capitol on the 4th of March, we found a clear majority of Union delegates had been elected, representing a majority of more than *five thousand* of the votes cast, though but little over two thirds of the votes of the State were polled. The path of duty to us was clear, and the ordinance of secession was voted down; but there being a large majority of delegates, representing a respectable minority of the votes polled, it was deemed most wise as well as just,—in view of the fact that the new Administration had but lately been installed, and its policy to a great extent undeveloped,—not to place the State in a condition that she could not act upon any new exigency that might arise, without the expense and delay of an extra session of the Legislature, and a new election for delegates to a convention; and with a view of obtaining a full and fair expression of the opinion and wishes of the people after the policy of the new Administration had become known.

"Resolutions in favor of a National Convention and declaring what, in our opinion, would be a proper basis of settlement of the differences between the slaveholding and non-slaveholding States were adopted in substance: That the Constitution should be so amended, that the President and Vice President should each be chosen alternately from a slaveholding and non-slaveholding State, and in no case both from either: Admission of the territories prohibiting slavery north of 36 deg. 30 min. north latitude, while the same remains under territorial government, and recognizing it south of that line, and providing for its protection by Congress and the territorial government, until the territory shall have sufficient population to apply for admission into the Union, and that when any territory north or south of said line shall contain the population requisite for a member of Congress, it shall be admitted a State, with or without slavery, as its constitution may prescribe: The denial to Congress of all power over slavery, except to protect the citizen to his right to property in slaves: That where the arrest of fugitive slaves is prevented by violence, or they are rescued after the arrest, the owner shall be paid the value of the slave by the United States, who may recover such value from the country where the arrest is prevented, or rescue occurs: That the Constitution shall not be so construed as to prevent any of the States from having jurisdiction concurrent with the United States, to compel the delivery of fugitives from labor: The citizens or slaveholding States shall have the right of traveling and temporarily sojourning with their slaves, in the non-slaveholding States: That the elective franchise and right to hold office, State, Federal, or Territorial, shall exist in white persons only, and negroes and mulattoes be excluded: And that these amendments and the third paragraph of the second section of the first article of the Constitution, and the third paragraph of the second section of the fourth article, are not to be amended or abolished, without the consent of all the States.

"Other resolutions were adopted, approving the call of Virginia for a convention of delegates from the Border slave-holding States, at Frankfort, Kentucky, on the 27th of May, in which Arkansas will be represented by delegates elected by the Convention; and providing for the submission to the people at the ballot-box, on the first Monday in August, of the question: 'Shall Arkansas coöperate with the border or unseceded slave States, in efforts to secure a permanent and satisfactory adjustment of the sectional controversies disturbing the country, or immediately secede?' To give effect to the wishes of the people thus expressed, the Convention will reassemble on *the third Monday* in August. Other resolutions declaring against coercion of the seceded States, and protesting against the quartering of the United States troops in places owned by the United States in the Southern States, to coerce seceding States or prevent secession were also adopted.

"Thus, it will be seen, that while Arkansas is not committed to the doctrine of secession, she condemns coercion by the Federal

Government, and recommends the removal of causes that might lead to a collision; and the adoption of constitutional means to restore peace and fraternal relations between the sections, and happiness and prosperity to our once united, but now distracted country. Four months will intervene before the election, affording ample time for reflection, and the formation of a just conclusion. None can complain that the people—the source of all power in this country—have not been consulted, or their voice stifled, and it is to be hoped that the expression thus fairly obtained will be respected, and the decision acquiesced in by all.

"Fellow citizens: Your destiny is in your own hands. The vote on the first Monday in August will seal the fate of the State, and in all probability determine whether the Union shall continue to exist and shed its blessings upon millions of people, or cease to occupy a place upon the map of nations: whether our national greatness is to be perpetual, affording a bright example and living evidence that man is capable of self-government, or be destroyed in the morning of its existence, and prove the truth of the theory of those who advocate the divine right of kings and the enemies of free government. We cannot doubt the result. Your verdict we shall await with confidence that you will not determine to destroy that government, which has bestowed upon us so many blessings, and secured to us so many rights not enjoyed by any other people, without uniting your efforts with those of the people of Virginia, Tennessee, Kentucky, Missouri and other slave-holding States still in the Union, to secure our rights and at the same time to preserve that Union. We make no appeal to your passions. To your patriotism, love of country and reverence for the memory of your fathers, who handed it down to you to be transmitted as a sacred inheritance to your children, none is needed. Everyone should know and understand the danger that surrounds us and the interests involved, and determine to act as duty dictates; know what our Government is, and its value, and what will follow its destruction. What the future will develop, once the work of disintegration passes to a point beyond control, *which it surely will,* if Arkansas secedes, is beyond the wisdom of man to determine. Secessionists cite the acts of Northern men, in and out of Congress, to excite our indignation, and convince us there is no hope. If we are to take the mad ravings of Phillips, Garrison and other disunionists at [*sic,* of] the North, as an index of the sentiment of the Northern people, we would be forced to despair of the Republic.

"But it is as unjust to judge the great mass of the Northern people by these men, as it would be to judge the people of the South by the declarations of our politicians of the ultra school. The politicians are one thing, the people another. The politicians have created the difficulty, and will never settle it. They stand between the people and the sections and stifle their voice. Until the voice of the people of the North, expressed in a constitutional way, can be heard, we should not conclude that they are blind to their own interests, or deaf to the appeals of patriotism and justice. The authors of the present difficulty, North and South, unite in opposing all propositions of compromise and settlement, for the obvious reason that if such an one as is proposed by your Convention is adopted, the slavery question, the fruitful source of contention, and favorite theme of the demagogue, call never figure as a question of national politics—their vocation will be gone and they fear, as well they may, their places will be filled by men after the order of the statesmen of the better days of the Government.

"The secessionists say the Northern people are aggressive, and we have often demanded our rights, even implored them to do us justice. True it is, that the conduct of some of the Northern States and finally, the election of a President upon a sectional platform by a sectional vote, evidence that there is danger of aggression on their part, and for our future security we demand additional guaranties, and this, when made, will be the only demand properly made. These we demand, and for the purpose of making such a demand as will be satisfactory to all, and of presenting it to the Northern people, we responded to the call of Virginia for a convention at Frankfort, and recommended that a national convention be held. That the Frankfort convention composed, as it will be, of delegates, from the slave-holding States, the most deeply interested in the subject of controversy, will mature a plan of settlement that will be satisfactory to all men in the South, who desire to see the Union preserved, we cannot doubt, notwithstanding it is alluded to as a trick, a sham, and every possible effort made to forestall its action and prevent its favorable consideration by you.

"It may be hardly respectful to you to enquire, whether the demand will be acceded to by the Northern people, for we feel assured that you will not despair until the last means provided by the Constitution are exhausted, and every reasonable expectation disappointed, following the example of the citizens of the greatest republic of the olden time, who awarded a public reception to one of their

Generals on his return from a disastrous campaign, which had resulted in the destruction of the army under his command, because he did not *despair of the republic*. But as it is urged as a reason why Arkansas should secede, that all appeals have been unheeded, all propositions rejected, we trust it is not improper to allude to the condition of things since the secession or disunion movement commenced; events that have transpired and the probable future. Previous to the presidential election, there were very few men in the South who took the ground that the election of Mr. Lincoln would justify a destruction of the Union, though his election was hardly doubted by any, for several weeks before the election. But scarcely had the result been announced, when we were startled by the cry raised in every town, village and hamlet in the entire South. In but little over one month after the election, and but one week after the assembling of Congress, South Carolina called a convention, and twenty days later adopted an ordinance of secession, and unexampled efforts and appliances were used to precipitate other States after her, and several followed in rapid succession. There was no statement of grieveances, no demand for redress by the seceding States. Of course there could be no united action. *The seceding States defeated it.* Virginia called for what is known as the Peace Conference, which unfortunately met at Washington, where, being surrounded by the same corrupt influences that had produced the lamentable state of the country, and composed, also, principally of delegates elected by legislatures, or appointed by Governors, elected the summer preceding the Presidential election, and representing their views, not the people's, forbade our expecting much from it, though we looked to it with some hope. It reported a plan for settlement, which it is not necessary to discuss here. But no matter what its merits or demerits are. The *extremists* leading the disunion movement North and South, denounced the Convention, and predicted its action would prove an abortion, in advance, and now, with marvelous consistency, complain that it did not receive the favorable consideration of Congress. There was still less reason to expect any favorable action from Congress, then in session, than to expect the Peace Conference to present a satisfactory plan of adjustment for its action, composed as it was, to a great extent, of extremists from both sections, elected in time of high party excitement, when the existing state of the country was not anticipated, working for a common purpose, making inflammatory speeches to be scattered broad-cast over the land, and keeping alive sectional excitement. Even if there had been a disposition to act, there was not sufficient time to discuss the amendments proposed to the Constitution.

"During the session of Congress, petitions, signed by thousands of Northern people, praying for a settlement were presented. There is still the deepest interest manifested by them. Many of their ablest and best men are engaged in the work. Several State legislatures have repealed or nullified their offensive legislation. Indiana, Illinois and Ohio have, by resolution, requested the calling of a national convention; the President and many of his leading political friends have expressed themselves in favor of the proposition. Nor is this all. The Federal troops have been, or very soon will be, withdrawn from Fort Sumpter, and thereby the danger of a collision avoided. Moreover, by the withdrawal of Southern Senators and Representatives from Congress, the Republicans had a decided majority in both houses, and the power to pass any law they chose, notwithstanding they refused to put into the hands of the President the means of coercing the seceded States, and by a two-third vote of both houses, passed an amendment to the Constitution, declaring that no amendment shall be hereafter made to authorize or give to Congress the power to abolish or interfere within any State, with the domestic institutions thereof, including persons held to labor or service by the laws of said State. We do not infer from this that the Republican leaders have abandoned any of their dangerous dogmas, but that they have found that their own people will not sustain them in their ultraism, and are disposed, by concession, to accommodate and settle the difficulties between them and us.

"The question is now plainly presented for your action. Be not deceived by the delusion that it is necessary for Arkansas to secede, in order to secure the united action of the South. Once out of the Union, the designs of the disunion leaders are accomplished. By a vote upon resolutions declaring it to be the sense of the people of this State, that the Union ought to be preserved if possible, on terms consistent with the rights of all sections, and that it is more in harmony with the spirit of our Government to amend the Constitution in such respect, as it may by experience prove deficient, than to overturn and destroy it, the secession members are fully committed against the Union. *Twenty-five* voted *against* these resolutions, *one* voted *for* them, and *eight* were absent or did not vote.

"By these resolutions disunion was unmasked, and the true object and character of the movement disclosed and shown to be a total overthrow and entire dismemberment of the Constitution and Union. It is hard to credit that any desire such an end, and we feel confident that there is not one in a hundred of the people of the South who does not desire the prosperity of the Government and the Union, if the rights and interests of all can be preserved. We believe it can be done, and appeal to you to make the effort. If successful, your interests are secured and your honor is imperishable, for we shall not only see the people of the South still adhering to the Union, once more united, prosperous and happy; but our brethren, the people of the seceded States, will arise in their majesty and decree that they shall resume their places in the sisterhood of States, and under one glorious national flag we will resume our march to national greatness; the star of our destiny will re-appear, and its splendor, temporarily obscured, illuminate the path and cheer the hearts of all people thirsting after liberty.

"DAVID WALKER, of Washington.

"J. H. STIRMAN,   "

"J. A. P. PARKS,   "

"T. M. GUNTER,   "

"J. H. PATTERSON, of Van Buren.

"J. N. CYPERT, of White.

"W. H. SPIVEY, of Yell.

"JOHN CAMPBELL, of Searcy.

"E. Z. WALKER, of Scott.

"W. M. FISHBACK, of Sebastian.

"S. L. GRIFFITH,   "

"WM. C. STOUT, of Pope.

"S. KELLY, of Pike.

"J. DODSON, of Newton.

"A. W. HOBSON, of Ouachita.

"I. MURPHY, of Madison.

"H. H. BOLINGER, "

"J. F. AUSTIN, of Marion.

"M. D. BAKER, of Lawrence.

"ALEX. ADAMS, of Izard.

"F. W. DESHA, of Independence.

"U. E. FORT,   "

"M. S. KENNARD,   "

"JOSEPH JESTER, of Hot Springs.

"A. H. CARRIGAN, of Hempstead.

"R. H. GARLAND,   "

"J. W. BUSH, of Greene.
"W. W. MANSFIELD, of Franklin.
"JESSE TURNER, of Crawford.
"HUGH F. THOMASON,"
"J. H. BRADLEY, of Crittenden.
"J. A. STALLINGS, of Conway.
"W. W. WATKINS, of Carroll.
"B. H. HOBBS,   "
"A. W. DINSMORE, of Benton.
"H. JACKSON,   "
"H. W. WILLIAMS, of Poinsett.
"JABEZ M. SMITH of Saline.
"A. H. GARLAND, of Pulaski.
"J. STILLWELL,   "

Not long after the appearance of this address, many Southern men took umbrage at the non-evacuation of Fort Sumter, and the evident disposition on the part of the authorities of the United States to hold it. Great indignation was excited also at the President's call for seventy-five thousand men, to retake the forts and arsenals in the seceded States and enforce the laws.

But there certainly was nothing coercive in this. The forts and arsenals were national property, and he who, as the executive head of the government, proposed to retake them, had been constitutionally placed in the presidential chair. Moreover, to enforce the laws was simply his duty, and he would have been an unprofitable servant had he made no attempt to do so. Men seemed to have been blind to the condition of the seceded States at this crisis. They certainly were at war with chronology, and in their excessive eagerness to crown their thoughts with acts, drew the sword before a *casus belli* could be defined, with either historical accuracy or clearness of comprehension. Let the address, which we have inserted, speak again upon this point: "In but little over one month after the election, [that of President Lincoln,] and but one week after the assembling of Congress, South Carolina called a convention, and twenty days later adopted an ordinance of secession, and unexampled efforts and appliances were used to precipitate other States after her, and several followed in rapid succession. *There was no statement of grievances, no demand for redress by the seceding States.*" Why not? Because the leaders of this rebellion had determined upon a separate sovereignty, come weal or come woe.

Their pride was humiliated by the growing strength of the Free States. They saw that by the inevitable law of emigration, they were sinking into a hopeless minority, but they flattered, and still flatter themselves, that they call build up on the soil, dedicated nearly a hundred years ago to freedom of speech, thought and action, a government that shall effectually crush out all three. For, whatever may be the present *status* of the American slave, a government whose cardinal idea is his *perpetual* bondage, will meet with a fate that shall be

"Like the fable of Eblis' Fall,
A by-word of mocking and horror to all."

On the other hand, there are but few men who are inclined to disregard the rights of slaveholders, as they exist under the Constitution, and still fewer who deny that the provision therein for the rendition of fugitives from labor, applies to negro slaves. The great mistake we humbly submit was this; that the seceding States gave President Lincoln no opportitnity to announce the policy of his administration. He was their firm friend but they cast him off. He would have exceeded any of his predecessors in the honest effort to secure every privilege and every right, but the demon possessed them, and they made no effort to exorcize him. With them rests the responsibility of this causeless, *wicked,* TERRIBLE war, and into which they have precipitated thousands of Southern men, with whom they are no more in sympathy than the Pope with reformers. The copperas-clothed can fill the ranks, brave the dangers and endure the hardships of war, but command, power and place are the peculiar privilege of the pampered few, who define labor with a sneer, and industry with an oath. Nor can the latter say that the encroachments of Federal power have placed them in their present position. Nevertheless this is the plea, and in north-western Arkansas some of the very men, who in April, 1861, signed the Union address to the people of that State, in May of the same year were loud in their denunciation of assumed coercion by the North, and among others the Hon. David Walker President of the Convention to which reference has been made.

It will be remembered, that by section three, of the ordinance providing for holding an election in Arkansas, for the purpose of taking the sense of the people of the State, on the question of "coöperation" or "secession," the delegates to this Convention were made special returning officers, to bring up the certified vote of their respective counties, the election at which the said vote was to be taken, to occur on the first Monday in August. If the power to call the Convention for a time prior to that mentioned in the ordinance, to wit: the nineteenth of August, 1861, resided any where, it was doubtless in its President. It was a power, however, to be exercised with extreme care, and only in extreme peril. David Walker was the first to sign the Union address, and is believed to be one of its principal authors. The coercion of which he afterwards complained, was the attempt of the Federal Government to restore what South Carolina and the other seceded States were attempting to destroy, and because they failed to make that "statement of grievances," or "demand for redress," of which he and thirty-nine others, delegates to the convention, and prominent citizens of Arkansas so ably complained. But the call for the seventy-five thousand was the justification of his course. He forgot the attitude of South Carolina and her sisters in error, and in the latter part of April, called the Convention for the sixth of May. There was no adequate time to instruct the delegates before the Convention would assemble, yet David Walker, a few days prior to his departure for Little Rock, issued the following address:

"TO THE PEOPLE OF WASHINGTON COUNTY.

"Under existing circumstances, I feel it to be my duty to take your advice upon some important questions which will, in all probability, arise for the consideration and action of the Convention, now shortly to be convened. Your delegates were elected under a pledge to coöperate with the Border Slave States, in an effort to settle our difficulties with the Northern States upon honorable and just terms, and under no circumstances to vote for an ordinance of secession, unless the same was referred back to you for your rejection or approval. The majority received by myself and colleague was very large, so great as to leave no doubt but that you heartily approved our position. You will see by reference to the journals of the Convention, that our grievances were defined, our rights asserted by way of instructions to commissioners to be elected to coöperate with the Border Slave States in an adjustment of the questions at issue between the North and South. Commissioners were elected to meet at Frankfort, Kentucky, on the 27th of May, and after full consideration it was left to a majority of the voters of the State to say whether they would coöperate with the Border States in such settlement, or would secede.

"Thus matters stood, and the friends of Union and coöperation, and of secession, had taken the field upon this issue, when the news reached us that the United States troops had not been withdrawn from Fort Sumter, and that in anticipation that supplies, if not also reinforcements, were to be sent, a fight ensued, which resulted in the destruction and evacuation of the fort, since which time has followed a proclamation of the President, calling for troops to retake the forts in the seceded States, and enforce the laws. Amongst other States, Arkansas was called upon to furnish a regiment for that purpose. The reports as to the grounds upon which the fight was commenced are contradictory, as well as to the extent of the preparations for a general war, between the Slave and Free States, but enough is known to leave but little doubt that there is imminent danger of a protracted and deadly civil war. Against the coercive policy of the Government, this, as well as the other Border Slave States, protested, and by a resolution of our Convention, we declared that we would resist coercion if attempted. In view of these facts, and after seeking information as well from the Border States as to their action, as from citizens of this State, I felt it to be my duty, in obedience to an ordinance for that purpose, to call the Convention together, to meet on the 6th of May. The question presented for your consideration is, under existing circumstances, what will you have your delegates do? Shall they still adhere to the position taken by them before the election, and which you so unanimously endorsed, or will you expect of them to vote for an unconditional ordinance of secession, which is not to be referred back to you for approval? Do you wish to remain in connection with a government, that if not already at war with a large portion of the Slave States, is threatening and preparing to engage in such war? Or would you prefer to cut loose from the old confederacy, and free yourself from all further allegiance to it? The effect of this act would be, on the one hand, to release you from all obligations to the old Government, and on the other, to deprive you of its protection and aid; such as its military defense on our borders, its Federal courts, land office, mail service, &c. Of this you will consider.

"But again, will you secede and maintain an independent position, and await some general settlement and coöperation of all the slave States, or will you secede and unite at once with the Confederate States? Should you prefer the former, that is, to maintain an independent position until a government may be formed by the Border States in common with the seceded States, and act in concert with them, you will necessarily incur the expense of supporting your own government and of defending it; but should you, on the other hand, prefer to unite with the Confederate States, and make common cause with them, you will necessarily assume the responsibility of furnishing men and money to aid them in the support and defense of their government.

"I am induced to call your attention particularly to this matter, because I find a strong, if not a prevailing opinion here, that in no event should troops be drawn from this portion of the State; that our exposed condition in the event of secession, will demand that the troops in this part of the State should be kept here for our own defense. None should be misled or deceived in this matter. If the State unites with the Southern Confederacy, she must necessarily come under obligations to furnish troops to fight at any and all points, at home and abroad, wherever required. And the fact is not to be disguised, that as the northern and western counties have the largest white population, a heavy demand must be made on them. There is but little hope, for a time at least, of a re-union of the States under the old Government, and as the Border Slave States contain, according to the late census, two million eighty-five thousand eight hundred and fifty-eight more inhabitants than the Confederate States, we call readily see, that should they act together in the establishment of a government, composed of the fifteen slave States, they will have it in their power, in such organization, as far as may be practicable, to protect our rights, and promote our interests in common with theirs.

"I have thus hastily and imperfectly presented for your consideration, the outlines of our present condition, and of the prominent question likely to be considered by the convention. There never was a time when we should act with more prudence than the present, and as our interests are one, we should, if possible, act as a united people. I desire to know your will, what would you have me do? I hope you will act at once, and can, in conclusion, pledge myself to obey your instructions, and reflect your will fearlessly and faithfully. I have intentionally omitted a reference to the original cause of our present difficulties, or to those upon whom rests the fearful responsibility of destroying and breaking up our once glorious and happy, but now prostrate and ruined Government. You all know my sentiments. I have endeavored to avert the calamity that is now upon us, with regard to which my mind has undergone no change. But it would be useless and improper to dwell upon the past. Our duty to ourselves and our country demands all our thoughts and all our energies. Let its look to the present and the future, and do all that we can to save our people from the calamity of civil war and utter ruin. *For weal or woe, my destiny is yours.*

"Your obedient servant,

"DAVID WALKER."

This address, it will be observed, bears no date, and we are informed, by those who know, that it was first circulated at Fayetteville, about the 26th of April, and from that place information of its purport was to be taken to the different townships of the County. On Thursday or Friday David Walker said to his constituents at Fayetteville, "I desire to know your will," and on the following Monday starts for Little Rock. The matter was of the first importance to north-western Arkansas, of which Washington county was, as it were, the life and soul. The citizens had been lulled into security by the ordinance of the 20th of March. They were anticipating a full and fair expression of their views on the first Monday in August at the polls, and this premature and fatal call of the Convention was, their interests considered, the exercise of bad judgment and the most deplorable management.

They sought, nevertheless, to meet the emergency, and immediate steps were taken to instruct David Walker in accordance with his request. Union men rode night and day about the county, urging the people to assemble with all possible despatch in their township capacities. They did so, but before their instructions, in most cases, could reach Little Rock, the Convention had assembled, and with unbecoming haste, that history will ever reprobate, carried the State out of the Union, so far as a convention by no means plenary in its powers, could accomplish so rash an act. In a few instances instructions were received, we believe, before Mr. Walker left Washington county.

On the 27th of April the voters of West Fork township in that county, assembled in mass meeting in response to his call, and passed the following resolutions:

"*Resolved,* 1ST, That we are opposed to any ordinance of secession.

"2D, That we utterly oppose any action in the State Convention that will sever the State of Arkansas from the Federal Government, without a full and fair expression of the loyal voters of the State.

"3D, That in case of an ordinance of secession, we wish to co-operate with the other Border State or States.

"4TH, That we are opposed to any act of the Convention that would unite us with the Southern Confederacy as it now exists."

Conduct so resolute and loyal deserves to be commemorated, and we take pleasure in giving the names of those who took the most active part in the meeting.

C. G. GILBREATH, *Chairman.*[14]

W. R. DYE, *Secretary.*[15]

J. C. STOCKBURGER,[16]

D. E. ROBINSON,[17]

A. W. REED,[18]   } *Committee*

JOHN A. RUTHERFORD,[19]   } *on*

THOMAS McKNIGHT,[20]   } *Resolutions*

W. D. DYE.

Resolutions from other localities, kindred or otherwise, may have been received, but one thing is certain, the people not only of Washington, but of the other counties in north-western Arkansas, were overwhelmingly opposed to secession, even after the bombardment of Fort Sumter and the President's call for seventy-five thousand men. And had David Walker from his "throne" in the convention, denounced the course of South Carolina, as in his Union address *he did* a month previously; had he advised the delegates to delay action until President Lincoln should make *a single positive encroachment* upon southern rights, instead of urging those members who had voted "no" upon the ordinance of secession to a change of opinion, that he might have the poor satisfaction of beholding a State unanimous in its defection, north-western Arkansas would not to-day rise up against him as the head and front of all its misery and all its desolation. The closing sentence of his address, "For weal or woe, my destiny is yours," dictated, it may have been, by the best of impulses, will appear in judgment against him, a lasting commentary upon his utter faithlessness. Months ago be crossed the Boston Mountains, and since his descent into the valley of the Arkansas, has raised neither arm nor voice for the restoration of law and order to that people to whom he owes his elevation, *but not his fall.*

On the eighth ultimo we went officially to his mansion on the west fork of White River, three miles from Fayetteville, to take possession of it, and what other property might be found. The house was that day to be vacated as a hospital, and we started for it early in the morning. Soon assuming control, we wandered through its generous apartments; looked from a balcony that swept a farm of a thousand acres, and then sauntering into the cabins, saw nothing there but a sad and silent negress. We thought of the Union Address, the circular to the people of Washington county, and the sixth of May, and involuntarily there flashed up the vision of "Marius sitting on the ruins of Carthage,"[21] though we took no part in causing the desolation of the place. A piano, two pier-glasses, a treatise on the laws of war, (valuable just at present), and Albert Pike's response to a petition for re-consideration in the case of "The Heirs of Mathew Cunningham, *vs.* Roswell Beebe and the Heirs of Chester Ashley," were all the effects that we could rescue, save brick walls, and half-demolished out-buildings.

> "Facilis descensus Averni:
> Noctes atque dies, patet atri janua Ditis;
> Sed revocare gradum, superasque evadere ad auras,
> Hoc opus, hic labor est."[22]

The Convention over, and the act of secession passed, the ultraist went to work more vigorously than ever. Systematic attempts were made to subdue and overawe Union men. Organizations were effected, whose object was to arouse the people and advance the Confederate cause, and no men were more active or bitter than Wilburn D. Reagan, a prominent attorney of Fayetteville, and Alfred M. Wilson,[23] United States District Attorney for the western district of Arkansas. The property of Union men was taken by a process called confiscation, but which violated all rules of law, order, and common sense. Their lives, also, were put in jeopardy, and when, yielding to the instinct of self-preservation, they sought safety in flight, armed men would follow, divest them of the means of self-defense, and not unfrequently terminate a chase with a tragedy. Thus passed a year and a half. The occasional dash of a Federal scouting party would, for a time, suspend operations, but the interruption over, they were prosecuted more vindictively than before.

Meanwhile, warlike movements, on a more honorable basis, were vigorously made, and aside from rebel activity in the army proper, citizens, whose circumstances or inclination forbade the courting of death at the cannon's mouth with that prospect of success which regular warfare holds out, organized themselves into squads as emergency men. Their deeds, we believe, are not recorded. On a flank or in the rear they were very superior. "Trees" were not the only things to be seen by them in "bushes," and quite often "Birnam wood came to Dunsinane."[24] At the Battle of Oak Hill (Wilson's Creek) they hovered near the army, and when Sigel unexpectedly commenced his cannonading, "advanced" with all haste on the Missouri line; among others Wilson and Reagan, the two Fayetteville attorneys who, as rumor hath it, did not draw the rein until they reached Dug Spring, eighteen miles distant.

"In extremis, salus corporis suprema lex."[25]

Passing south of the Arkansas river, the Union element was also observable, in spite of every exertion to suppress it. There were, and are, many loyal men in Franklin, Johnson, Scott, Sebastian and other counties, but the constant exhibition of rebel diabolism compelled them to a course that policy alone could justify. Even the love of home and kindred, however, and the desire to protect what a life-time had acquired, lost, at length, their power of attraction to the soil. The alternatives were rebellion or active loyalty, and the exodus began. Some time previously militia companies had been formed, but when the people understood their real, but not ostensible object, many abandoned them and prepared for flight. At the head of one of these organizations, in Franklin county, was William C. Parker,[26] and active in it four brothers Lee. For want of ammunition the company was disbanded, and Parker, the Lees, George A. White, Tipton White,[27] and a few others, effected the difficult task of reaching Springfield, Missouri.

On the 2d of August, 1862, there followed Samuel Lee, the father, and the two elder brothers, James H. Lee and Sir William Lee.[28] We well remember their appearance in camp. On the 15th of the month, a hot and sultry afternoon, they walked wearily in; the father, a poor decrepid old man, past three score years and ten, hobbling painfully along, but still resolute and still loyal; the sons in the prime of life, yet wan and worn with the fatigues of their sad and perilous journey. They had walked the entire distance from their home in Franklin county, two hundred miles; had crossed the Arkansas river at night, on a rude raft, constructed in darkness, of logs bound together with withes; had climbed the Boston Mountains, and then pushed anxiously on, avoiding highways, and rarely moving by day-light, until their star of hope stood still over Springfield. After their departure, the mother, an old lady of seventy, was arrested and taken to Fort Smith, and informed that she would be held until she should tell where her husband and sons had gone. A negro girl, belonging to the family, was also brutally maltreated in an attempt to accomplish the same

object, but the ruffians, active among whom in this scandalous transaction were two murderous miscreants, John Parker and William
Vaughan, were foiled. Samuel Lee and two of the sons have ceased to
be troubled. The worn out father died at Elkhorn Tavern in November,
1862, returning homeward from exile, himself a tried patriot, who, at
New Orleans, had stood behind the cotton bales when Pakenham
moved so disastrously forward. The sons died in the service; but four
brothers still remain, who, with arms in their hands, have sworn not
only to protect and defend the Constitution of the United States, but
to have satisfaction for family outrages in personal vengeance.[29]

While Union men were overcoming, as best they could, the serious obstacle of the Arkansas river, those north of the Boston
Mountains were fully alive to the peril of their position, and the
necessity of effort, at least to the extent of self preservation. In
Washington county, Thomas J. Hunt, William J. Patten and George
W. M. Reid, the first mentioned, Major of the Second Battalion, First
Arkansas Cavalry, and the latter two, Lieutenants of the line, were
especially active. They were zealous, earnest men, and when compelled to flee, their influence bore away many others. Prior to the
secession of the State, and when that calamity was imminent,
Lieutenant Patten was untiring in his efforts to arouse the people to
the extent of the impending peril.

There often accompanied him, in riding about the county to meet
appointments and extemporize public gatherings, one Stephen
Bedford of Fayetteville.[30] In turn a school teacher, a farmer, a lawyer,
a merchant, and a minister, he possessed withal an aptitude for talking, and was a very earnest Union man. In fact, there were none more
so. He favored the uniting of northwestern Arkansas to Missouri,
should the State secede, or if that act proved to be difficult of accom-
plishment, the independence of his section, rather than submission to
the will of a seceding majority. As troubles thickened, however, his
patriotism became less ardent, and when later, Rains and Coffee were
encamped in the vicinity of Fayetteville, and doubts were thrown
upon his fidelity to the South, he made a speech to the soldiery that
satisfied even the most exacting.

Whatever he *might* have been, he was now a rebel, and possibly
congratulated himself upon his idiosyncrasy that enabled him so easily to adapt himself to circumstances. His versatility was clearly his
strength, for those who know him, *know him,* and they all seem to
concur in their estimate of his character.

It so happened in February of the present year, that Mr. Bedford was inconsiderately arrested at Fayetteville. He was at once put to labor, and before his release could be effected had done good service in carrying water from a well to a hospital. Tall in stature, with a countenance that once seen can never be forgotten, a white hat that had no regard for the seasons, and a diminutive guardsman following him around with a huge musket and serious look, he was a picture to behold, if not a pattern to imitate. His arrest annulled, he walked light-heartedly homeward, and though he has since retired within himself, never visiting those places where he once was an oracle, his indecision is still his failing. But we drop the episode. "Stephen is joined to his idols, let him alone."

Lieutenant Patten, on the other hand, continued as he began, and outspoken in loyalty, never shrank from the proper avowal of his sentiments. He early saw the fallacy of secession, and born and reared in northwestern Arkansas, knew that it was in utter disconsonance with her interests. In June last, while in the employ of the Government, he was heedlessly shot in the vicinity of Cassville by a bugler named Kline, of the First Missouri cavalry. At the time, he was thought, to use the phraseology of war, to be a "secesh," and no opportunity was given for an explanation. Very remarkably the wound was not mortal. The ball had passed transversely through the head, severing the optic nerve of the left eye, and of course destroying sight. Otherwise no permanent injury seems to have been done, and the wound has healed. Lieutenant Patten is now in active service, and from his intimate knowledge of the country and people, it would be difficult to find better men to aid in bringing order out of confusion, and restore quiet and harmony in the distracted section where his regiment is at present operating.

Major Hunt, born in Washington county, and catching the inspiration of a loyal life from an earnest, intelligent and patriotic father, William Hunt of the Middle Fork of White river, known well and favorably throughout northwestern Arkansas, early gave indication of that force of character which has enabled him to brave the storm before which many of his friends and neighbors went down. When the troubles of his locality were fresh, and the militia was organizing, he raised, with others, a company of one hundred men, but in reality for the purpose of aiding the Union movement, and when expected to report to Colonel Henry Rieff,[31] rebel enrolling officer at Fayetteville, he found a more congenial place *further northward*. His influence and decision determined the course of many others, and to him is attributable in no small degree the regeneration of Washington county.

George W. M. Reid, a lineal descendant of one of those men, whose signature to the Declaration of Independence has forever made him illustrious, has likewise been active in defense of his government.[32] Born in Franklin county, Arkansas, from which his father shortly afterwards emigrated to Washington county in the same State, young Reid grew up upon the border, passing a portion of his early manhood among the Cherokees. Like many other adventurous spirits, who have strayed beyond the line that divides the States from the Territories, he has his Indian broils to remember, and though troubles of this description were, prior to the rebellion, personal simply, they were all the more violent, and on the one hand more savage. Living afterwards near the Cherokee line, the Indians became at length so annoying that young Reid settled upon a farm in Washington county, nine miles from Fayetteville. His life was barren of special interest until the rebellion broke out. Not long afterwards, however, being then Captain of a militia company, and commissioned as such by Elias N. Conway when Governor of the State, he was ordered to report with his command at what was called a battalion muster, by Col. Reiff, the enrolling officer already mentioned. Refusing to do so, and thus becoming a special object of suspicion, he nevertheless made no effort to disguise his sentiments. With John A. Rutherford and William Dye, two well known citizens of Washington county, he concerted the raising of a company of Union men, and in a brief period there arose a power whose hostility to the growing phrensy of the time was by no means insignificant. Yet Mr. Reid and many others were at length compelled to *"lay out,"* and finally to flee northward for security. While still secreting himself in the vicinity of his home, Reid one evening ventured to the house, resolved to remain until morning, unless some untoward event should drive him away. Late at night he was aroused by a loud noise at the door, and a ruffian voice demanding admission. Noiselessly slipping on his clothes, grasping a rifle and adjusting a revolver at his side, he directed his wife to open the door at which entrance was demanded, while he moved silently out at another. His departure was unobserved and fortunate. A prowling band of rebels were in search of him, but they saw in the house no traces of his recent presence. Interrogation of the wife resulted in neither clue nor disclosure, and in the morning, after compelling Mrs. Reid to procure their breakfast and forage for their horses, the men rode sullenly away. Reid observed them, and after their disappearance, ventured from his hiding place.

We cannot dwell, however, upon his adventures. Let it suffice to say that he was ultimately compelled to flee as stated. He is now an officer in the First Arkansas Cavalry, and doing good service in the vicinity of his old home. We could wish to increase the length of this sketch, and insert others of Jesse M. Gilstrap,[33] Thomas J. Gilstrap[34] and Samuel P. Lane,[35] of Crawford county, and Jacob Yows,[36] of Washington county, but we forbear. The patriotism of these men has been tried by fire, and has come forth from the furnace of persecution, outrage and disaster, doubly refined. The Gilstraps and Lane have been shamefully incarcerated for their political faith, and Yows has lived for months on the White river hills and the Boston Mountains. They all subsequently entered the service, and Thomas J. Gilstrap died with the harness on, a brave, true man.

Others still have felt as did they, the distressing pangs of separation from home and family, and the gloomy uncertainty of the future. North-western Arkansas has been full, in fact, of incident, adventure, trial and privations for the last eighteen months. Nearly every Union man is a hero, if a just cause and suffering in its defense can make one. As the old attachment to the Union began to break out, where for months it had been smothered, rebel persecution became more ingenious and vindictive. Traps were laid and subterfuges resorted to. Loyalty to the old Government was regarded as a crime, and hundreds of men were annoyed and outraged. Opportunities were sought to betray Union men into the avowal of their sentiments, and then every advantage was taken to persecute and oppress. We present a signal instance of this treatment in the experiences of James Thompson, Esq., of Fayetteville, for many years a resident of Washington county, and prior to the supercession of civil law, and the abstraction of the public records, Deputy Clerk of the Circuit Court of the county. We insert his own statement:

"About 11 o'clock at night, on the 10th of August, 1862, two men, named Lewis and Mickle, armed with guns and revolvers, entered my house in Fayetteville, Arkansas, and when I got up, one of the men represented that they were expressmen, and had a letter from Major William H. Miller, of the Second Wisconsin Cavalry, commanding at Cassville, Missouri, directed to and intended for me, and placed, or rather pushed, said letter into my hands. I replied that I had no acquaintance with Major Miller, and was surprised that he should send a letter to me. I now lit a candle, and at a glance knew the letter to be a forgery. It was dated the 10th of August, the day of this occurrence, and was in substance as follows:

"'HEAD-QUARTERS, CASSVILLE, MO., AUGUST 10, 1862.

"'*James Thompson, Esq.:*

"'I am at this place with seven hundred men, and desire to know if it would be safe to visit your section of country with this number of men. You will, therefore, give me information as regards the numbers, disposition and movements of the Confederate forces in your section.

"'Respectfully,

"'WILLIAM H. MILLER,

"'Major, 1st Battalion, 2d Wis. Cav.

"'Per Expressman.'

"The letter was enclosed in an envelope, and directed to 'James Thompson, Esq., at or near Fayetteville, Arkansas.' One of the men now began to ply me with questions, wishing to know if there were not Confederate troops about fourteen miles west of Fayetteville, at a place called Camp Rector, and also at other points in its vicinity. I replied that I had heard so, and that probably there was a right smart force there. The pretended expressman asked several other questions, showing a familiarity with the number and positions of the Confederate troops, of which I had no knowledge whatever, even from rumor. One of the men had meantime remained silent, standing a few paces distant on my right, and with a gun constantly in his hand. The spokesman approached on my left.—The latter now asked me how many troops Major Miller ought to bring with him if he came to Fayetteville. I answered that he could judge as well as myself, as he appeared to know more about the Confederate forces than I did.

"'You will reply to the letter,' said the man authoritatively.

"I answered that he had made his communication verbally, and that there was no necessity of my writing.

"'It is expected that where a letter is written and sent by an expressman to any one, that a reply will be made in writing,' was the suggestive retort.

"I then told him that he could inform Major Miller, *or those who sent him,* that no necessity existed for an answer from me.

"'But you *must* answer the letter, and in writing,' was the imperative response, the other man at the same time throwing himself, with gun in hand, into a menacing and threatening attitude. I now became alarmed, and knowing, as I said before, that the letter was forged, for I had previously on several occasions seen Major Miller's chirography, and not wishing to answer in writing, remarked that I had no pen, ink, or paper.

"'Here, this will do,' was the answer of the *obliging* expressman, handing me a pencil and a slip of paper, tearing it from the Miller letter, 'Now answer that document at once.'

"Seeing that I was in their power, I hurriedly wrote the following, designedly omitting to address it to any person:

"'FAYETTEVILLE, ARKANSAS, AUGUST 10TH, 1862.

"'I do not think it would be safe or prudent, to I visit this section with less than five or fix thousand troops. The Confederate forces are stationed fourteen miles west of this place, on or near the road leading to Cane Hill.

"To this production I declined signing my name.

"'Sign it,' said the expressman threateningly, 'You must; it is expected of you.'

"Satisfied that these men would do me violence if I did not, I now, under protest, signed my name. They immediately departed, in a state of great satisfaction, and that night reported the occurrence to Col. Armstrong.[37] Before doing so, however, they went to the house of James P. White,[38] to palm off on him the same miserable subterfuge, but the trifling occurrence of having left their pencil with me, seems to have prevented the execution of their design.

"About 11 o'clock on the following night I was arrested, by crder of Colonel Armstrong, of Texas, commanding at Camp Rector, and placed under strict guard. Ten days later, charges in writing were preferred against and given to me, and I was told to be ready for trial by Court Martial on the following morning. I remonstrated against this insufficiency of time; asked for an extension, and leave to send for witnesses. I was answered that the 'trial must take place to-morrow.'

"I was charged first, with holding correspondence with and giving information to the enemies of the Confederate States of America, concerning the numbers, movements and disposition of their forces, and secondly, with giving them aid and comfort; in this, that I fed the pretended expressman and his comrade while at my house. By permission I sent to Fayetteville for a few of its prominent citizens to testify as to my general character, and without other preparations awaited my trial, trusting that the cross-examination of the two principal witnesses against me, the men who came to my house on the evening of the 10th, would result in my favor. The trial was to take place on the confines of the camp, in the open air, and the court, respectable in numbers and appearance, having been duly sworn, the case was proceeded with. Passing over the minutiae of the examination in chief of the witnesses of the rebel government, the expressman and his comrade, I ventured personally upon their cross-examination, preferring my own inexperience to the dubious assistance of the Judge Advocate.

"*Question* (to Mickle, the expressman.) 'Did you ever know of my receiving a letter from Major Miller, of the Federal army, commanding at Cassville, Missouri, or of my having written a letter to him, giving information of the numbers, movements, or disposition of the Confederate forces?'

"*Answer.* 'Never, except the one of the 10th of August, 1862, in reply to the one I handed to you at that time.'

"*Question.* 'Do you know of your own knowledge whether I, at any time before the 10th of August, and before you put said letter into my hands, or subsequently, gave information, either directly or indirectly, verbally or in writing, to any Federal officer or soldier, of the movements, number or disposition of the Confederate troops in this section of country, or elsewhere?'

"*Answer.* 'I do not.'

"*Question.* 'Are, or were you ever an expressman for Major Miller, of the Federal army?'

"*Answer.* 'No.'

"*Question.* 'Did you ever have the pleasure or *honor* of seeing a Federal officer?'

"*Answer.* 'I never did.'

"*Question.* 'Where do you live?'

"*Answer.* 'In Crawford county.'

"*Question.* 'Do you now, and did you not on the 10th of August, 1862, belong to the Confederate service?'

"*Answer.* 'I do and did.'

"*Question.* 'Did you ever see me before the night of the 10th of August, 1862?'

"*Answer.* 'I never saw or knew you before that time.'

"*Question.* 'At what time did you receive the letter purporting to come from Major Miller?'

"*Answer.* 'About four o'clock on the morning of the 10th of August, 1862.'

"*Question.* 'Who gave you that letter?'

"*Answer.* 'Col. Armstrong, at his quarters.'

"*Question.* 'Who wrote the letter?'

"*Answer.* 'I do not know.'

"Such was the character of Mickle's testimony, and that of the man Lewis was only corroborative. The evidence adduced to support the second charge was simply ridiculous, and was so considered by the court. I was now permitted to speak in my own behalf, having first introduced the testimony of James H. Stirman,[39] Dr. T. J. Pollard[40] and W. L. Wilson,[41] prominent citizens of Fayetteville, as to my general character. I insisted briefly that the charges had not been sustained by the testimony; that a systematic attempt had been made to place me in a false position; that I was not personally acquainted with Major Miller; had never thought even of holding a correspondence with him upon army matters, and that the whole transaction was a farce. The trial here closed and I was again ordered under guard, beneath the trees. In ignorance of the decision of the court—an ignorance not yet dispelled—I was sent a few days later to Fort Smith, on the Arkansas river, and thrown into a dungeon, where remaining four or five days, I was removed to an ordinary guard-house. My health was quite poor, still I was kept in close confinement, and allowed none of the privileges accorded to other citizen prisoners.

"About the 15th of October I was sent with others to Little Rock. We were taken to the State Penitentiary and placed in different cells. I was there imprisoned for fifteen days and nights during weather unusually cold for the latitude, was allowed no blanket or other covering, and when taken out was actually frost bitten. In November I was released by order of the General commanding, and directed to go home as soon as able. While at liberty I was treated very kindly by Capt. Stephenson, the assistant provost marshal; was furnished with meals at the guard-house and allowed to move about the town without annoyance. In the latter part of December, 1862, I started for Fayetteville, where I arrived on the morning of the 27th of that month."

Such was the experience of a quiet, law-abiding citizen of the United States. Nor was his treatment as harsh by many degrees of injustice and inhumanity as that of others, who were thrown into prison or driven into the mountains. The system of persecution inaugurated nearly a year since, is now producing its legitimate results. While regular warfare has been pushed to the Arkansas river and beyond, the woods swarm with guerrillas, the sure offspring of Hindman's General Order, No. 17, elsewhere appearing. As the trees throw out their verdure and the bushes become defences, these desperadoes of the frontier, emboldened by their knowledge of the country, and smarting under occasional losses, startle the passer-by with the unexpected crack of a rifle, or at the dead hour of night awaken the household of the backwoodsman with the presaging cry of robbery and devastation.

But not alone in the fields and the woods have the Union people of Arkansas been intimidated and outraged. The General Assembly of the State has fulminated its wrath against the loyal citizens, in an act passed hardly four months ago. We give it entire, not for its present effect, for, as a law, it is scouted and defied in North-western Arkansas, but to show the exhaustive malice, the diabolical ingenuity of those men who only need the power, to disgrace and destroy their State.

"AN ACT TO PREVENT THE GIVING AID AND COMFORT TO THE ENEMY.

"Be it enacted by the General Assembly of the State of Arkansas:

"SEC. I. That any and every person in this State who shall conspire with any other person or persons, to subvert or destroy or impair the authority of the Government of the Confederate States of America, whether any act be done in pursuance of any such conspiracy or not; and any person who shall join or who may hereafter be a member of any society or association, whether open or secret, and by whatsoever name called or known, the object of which, in whole or in part, is, or may be, to subvert or destroy or impair the authority of the Confederate States of America, or to re-establish in whole or in part, or to any extent, the authority of the Government of the United States of America, or to aid and assist the said United States of America, or any officer, soldier or emissary thereof, in the prosecution of the existing war against the Confederate States of America, or to withdraw the allegiance and fidelity of any citizen or citizens of the Confederate States of America, or of the State of Arkansas, from the governments thereof respectively, or to induce the people of the State of Arkansas, or any one or more of them, to adhere to or expect protection from the Government of the United States of America; any such person or persons so offending, shall be deemed guilty of a felony.

"SEC. II. That any person within this State, not being an officer or soldier in the military service of the Confederate States of America, or the State of Arkansas, who shall counsel, persuade, advise or assist any officer or soldier in the military service of the Confederate States of America, or of the State of Arkansas, to desert such service, whether such desertion he effected or not, shall be deemed guilty of a felony.

"SEC. III. That any person or persons within this State who shall act as guide to the enemy, or any one or more of the army thereof, or who shall be engaged in giving or carrying any information, message or communication to the said enemy, the United States of America, or any officer or soldier belonging to the army thereof, or connected therewith, or any other person or persons adhering to the said United States, about any matter or thing concerning the conduct of the existing war, with the intent to aid or assist, in any wise, the said enemy, shall be deemed guilty of a felony.

"SEC. IV. That any and every person or persons within this State, who shall sell or deliver to the said enemy, or any one or more of them, whether by name known or unknown, any cotton, corn, grain, forage, meat, or provisions of any kind whatever, or shall place any such cotton or article or other thing, by any sale, assignment or transfer or removal thereof, in such manner, situation or place as will or shall better enable the said enemy, or any or them, to get the same, or who shall sell or deliver any cotton or other article, as aforesaid, to any person or persons whom such person or persons so selling or delivering may or should have reason to suspect or believe, will dispose of the same to, or place the same within the power of, the said enemy, or any one or more of them, or in any way suffer the said enemy, or any one of them, to have the use or benefit thereof, or any portion thereof, shall be deemed to have committed a high misdemeanor.

"SEC. V. Any person offending against any of the provisions of this act, shall be liable to indictment therefor in the Circuit Court of the county in which such offense may have been committed; or where any such offense may have been begun in one county and consummated in another county, such indictment may be preferred and tried in either of such counties, and every person convicted of offending against the first, second, and third sections of this act, shall suffer death, or punishment by confinement in the penitentiary of this State, for any term not less than five nor more than ten years, according to the discretion of the jury trying any such cause, or of the judge presiding at any such trial, when the jury returning a verdict of guilty shall fail to assess such punishment, and any person convicted of offending against the fourth section of this act, shall be fined in any sum not less than one thousand, nor more than ten thousand dollars, according as the jury trying such cause may assess the amount of such fine.

"Sec. VI. Any person or persons arrested under the provisions of this act, where, in the judgment of the examining court or magistrate, there may be reasonable or probable grounds for the detention of such person or persons, or where owing to the absence of, or difficulty of procuring witnesses, or material evidence on the part of the prosecution, because of such witnesses or witness, or evidence, being within the enemies lines, or where the country in which any such offense may have been committed may be, for the time being in possession or menaced by the enemy, so that a speedy examination or trial, as the case may be, of any such accusation cannot be had, any such person or persons shall not for any such cause he discharged for want of prosecution, but may be held in custody, or required to enter into recognizance with adequate security, according to the discretion of such court or magistrate, conditioned for the appearance of such person or persons, from time to time, and at such place as shall be specified in such recognizance, to answer such accusation.

"Sec. VII. This act shall take effect and be in force, from and after its passage.

"Approved Nov. 28, 1862."

We withhold comment. *The act was passed nine days before the battle of Prairie Grove.*

To revert to a peculiar phase of warfare in the south-west, where events are strongly suggestive of the old caution, that the devil must be fought with fire, we call up the "bush-whacker," or bush fighter. Except when a marauding expedition is agog, or individual license to be given, he rarely answers to his name. He may not, indeed, be far away, but he never spends time in acquiring the accomplishments of the regular soldier. In appearance, there was not, a year since, a more complete nondescript. Now, however, the outer man is familiar to those whom the fortune of war has thrown upon the frontier. A double-barreled shot-gun upon his shoulder, or swinging from his saddle horn; a horse all drowsiness in repose, but dashing through a thicket adding intelligence to speed; a slouched hat whose depressions in front and rear are peculiar to the south-west; a garb that vies with the soil in color and characteristics, and which, a short distance off, almost betrays one into the belief that a portion of mother earth has again assumed Adamic form and movement, and finally a countenance in which cunning and malice are strangely blended with stupidity, may serve, though imperfectly, to present him to the reader. Just at present he is well nigh ubiquitous. The leaves are beginning to appear, and the hiding places of the winter are abandoned for coverts by the highway, where the unsuspecting can easily be robbed and murdered.

The military telegraph now in operation to Fayetteville is frequently cut in the vicinity of Cross Hollows and at different points in the Sugar creek valley. The wire is scarcely put in order when communication is again broken, and exasperated details start simultaneously from Cassville in one direction and Fayettville the other. And here we will take occasion to say that the abandonment of the post at Elkhorn Tavern, whatever the cause that led to it, has operated disastrously upon the Union men in the vicinity, depriving them of protection and giving free scope to the "bushwhackers" of Benton county, who last autumn fell back to the White River Hills and were careful not to venture too near a military post. Occasionally these warriors *sui generis* have taken Federal soldiers prisoners and paroled them. The paroles themselves are models of everything that is *not* to be imitated in transactions of the kind, and invariably contain a clause binding the party to abstain from bearing arms against the Government of the Confederate States of America. It is puerile to say that these men are not in league with the rebels. Rare instances of inhumanity may, it is true, be frowned upon, but the system is not, and we have conversed with more than one soldier, who, taken prisoner by undoubted marauders, had been forwarded directly to the Arkansas river.

Not long since we received a communication from one James Ingram, the Captain of the most notorious of these bands that infest Benton county. The letter reached Fayetteville in a manner unknown to ordinary mail carrying, and was placed in our hands on the morning of the third of March. Why we should be the recipient of this missive we do not yet know, nor did the writer see fit to inform us. The letter was written in a bold hand, with red ink, or possibly a liquid more sanguineous, and as its chirography is another *argument* in favor of the intelligence of a class of men who so dread negro equality, we insert it *verbatim, punctualim, literatimque:*

"hed quarters
"White River hill to the molisha of Benton Madison and Washington co ark and all it ma consurn I am aposed to Burning and

Robing famileys of ther stuff and provisions and a Buse to women tha molisha is as well acquainted with the hill as I am and if tha can take the advantage of me and my men from the brush and kil ar take us prisnors we will But try to pa it Back and will not go and Burn nor plunder nor giv abuse but if you carey out the plan of Burning and Robing I shal Be compeled to paternise your plan But it is a plan that I abhor and I would Be glad you will drop the plan we dont want it sed that the suthern people Brot fameleys to suffer and turn out of Dores I Expect to fight you on all occasions and if men fal prisners in my hands tha will Be treeted as prisnors of wor tha will Be giv a triol and if tha ar not gilty of 4 crimes tha will not be hurt and that is Burning Robing women and childern of ther provisions house hole and abuse to fameleys and murdering men at home not in armes the molishy knows that I hav not robed nor Burnt and hav treeted prisnors with respect

"to Curnel Bishop Dont you no that the war is clost at a end and you should be carful for you hav giv orders to murder inosent unarm men and Burn if you dont mind you will not Be forgot after peace I think men women and children that had no hand in Bringing up the war shud not be hurt.

"Curnel Bishop post at fayetteville ark from Capt James Ingrum of the 6th provose co Benton Co Ark

"Feb 27 1863

"Capt JAMES INGRUN"

The *accomplished* Captain is to be commended for his abhorrence of "burning and robing," but he makes a great mistake when he assumes that we have "giv orders to murder inosent unarm men." His band is to-day the terror of Benton county, and the officer who catches him will deserve promotion.

The First Arkansas Cavalry are constantly scouring the country, but the necessity for frequent reports at head-quarters, and the limited time with which the present force at Fayetteville must necessarily hamper any particular scouting party, have rendered it impossible to give his case that lengthened attention that it so eminently deserves and will require. The species of warfare, however, in which he indulges cannot long endure. Take from it the sanction of the rebel authorities; let the marauder feel that there is no longer a refuge for him on the Arkansas river, when hard pressed in the hills and mountains, and "bushwhacking" in South-western Missouri and North-western Arkansas will cease. Its enterprises are even now unprofitable to engage in, notwithstanding certain sutlers and citizens, who thought they certainly could move about unmolested, have lately been most unmercifully robbed in the vicinity of Cross Hollows and Pea Ridge.

Since the falling back of the "Army of the Frontier" from Prairie Grove and Rhea's Mill to Missouri, the duty of dispersing these denizens of the woods has mainly devolved upon the First Arkansas Cavalry. To this regiment we have occasionally alluded, and as its organization and history are somewhat peculiar, it may not be inappropriate to refer to them. The battle of Pea Ridge over, the effect of this disaster to the rebel arms began to appear in scattered bands of lawless soldiery, and growing boldness in Union men. Prior to that event the loyal citizens of Arkansas were cowed and powerless. With difficulty they had avoided enlistment in the rebel army, and now that the reins of persecution began to slacken, they availed themselves of every opportunity to strike for the Federal lines. The Army of the South-west moved to Batesville, and Cassville, Barry county, Missouri, became the out-post of the frontier, with Lieutenant-Colonel C. B. Holland, of "Phelps' Missouri Volunteers," as commander of the post, and M. La Rue Harrison, then of the Thirty-sixth Illinois Infantry Volunteers, as Quartermaster and Commissary of Subsistence. Cassville was also at this time the seat of a general hospital, and in other respects a position important to hold.

On the tenth of May, 1862, there came to its pickets a band of eleven Arkansians, led by Thomas J. Gilstrap and Furiben Elkins,[42] of Crawford County. Listening to their story of suffering and wrong, and learning that others still were toiling their way northward, the idea occurred to Harrison of applying for authority to raise a regiment of loyal Arkansians, for the cavalry arm of the service.

Believing that

> "The flighty purpose never is o'ertook
> Unless the deed go with it,"

the necessary application was made at the earliest feasible moment.

On the sixteenth of June, 1862, a special order of the War Department was issued, authorizing the raising of the regiment, and Colonel Harrison, with unceasing zeal, now bent his energies to the task. Meantime, other fugitives had crossed the Missouri line. On the fourteenth of May there came into Cassville a band of thirty, led by Thomas Wilhite, of Washington County, men of nerve and activity, whose undesirable life on the Boston Mountains had, nevertheless, fitted them admirably for the wild-wood skirmishing in which they were destined to act a conspicuous part.

On the twentieth of June there arrived another detachment of the yeomanry of Washington County, one hundred and fifteen strong, under the leadership of Thomas J Hunt. Jesse M. Gilstrap, of Crawford County, and others whose loyalty rose with their danger, were likewise successful as recruiting officers, and on the tenth of July the first battalion was formally organized, with James J. Johnson, of the 36th Illinois Infantry Volunteers, and who had heartily co-operated with Colonel Harrison from the incipiency of his project, as Major. On the seventh of August the Colonel was mustered, and early in October a maximum regiment was in the field.

In June it rendezvoused at Springfield, and as rapidly as men were enlisted, they were placed on post duty. The hardships of their lot had but poorly prepared them for the active labors in which they were engaged, and it has always been regretted that the regiment could not have been permitted, even for a month, the life and discipline of a camp of instruction. However, the grand object was to raise a regiment of loyal men from a *seceded* State, and Colonel Harrison succeeded. There are officers in the army who knowingly shook their heads at the project, and prophesied nothing but failure.

Generals Commanding gave the idea encouragement, especially Brigadier General E. B. Brown,[43] then in charge or the South-western Division of the District of Missouri, but others of lesser rank, influence and calibre, derided what they could not appreciate.

To those who are familiar with the political history of Arkansas, since its secession, nothing can suggest itself as more important than to nurture the Union sentiment, and the discernment and energy of Colonel Harrison have resulted not only in raising the First Arkansas Cavalry, but a regiment of infantry and a battery of artillery. Nay, more, while we write, a second regiment of infantry is forming under his supervision, and, looking beyond fact to moral influence, we do not hesitate to say, that events and successes of this description are more to be relied upon than the victories of strange troops in a strange country.[44]

Let us not be understood though as insinuating even, that the latter are to be disparaged, but as the army of the Union marches triumphantly Southward, conviction must follow possession, and nothing can be more gratifying to the loyal men of North-western

Arkansas than to witness the present indications of the evident upris-
ing of their brethren on the farther side of the Arkansas river.

"Wild Bill," of the Magazine Mountain,[45] spurning the overtures
of General Cabell,[46] has appeared at Fayetteville, and the influence of
his name in Yell and adjoining counties, is felt in the constant dripping
of the waters of persecution into the great ocean of human freedom.

The poor whites of the South, when their attention is drawn to
the real nature and object of this war, do no fail to perceive that they
have nothing in common with those who rule at Richmond. They are
not apprehensive that their *status* will be shaken by adherence to the
old Union, and many of them are now clearly seeing that for a long
series of years they have been made the victims of delusion, hypocrisy
and cant.

"The old Union is good enough for them" they say, and this simple
yet pregnant sentence is shaping for the yeomanry of the South, a new
epoch and a new destiny.

FAYETTEVILLE, ARK.,
March, 1863.

ADDENDUM.

SINCE THE FOREGOING pages were written, events of such importance to North-western Arkansas have transpired, that we cannot forbear allusion to them, and to notice, also, the policy of the Government toward Arkansas in general, or perhaps, it were better to say, its apparent absence of all policy. After the battle of Prairie Grove, and the gradual retrogression of the Army of the Frontier into Missouri, Fayetteville was still held as a military post, and those of us who remained there were given to understand that the place would not be abandoned. The commanding officer, therefore, went to work in good faith and with marked success to tranquilize the country. For months matters prospered well. The demoralized enemy had fallen back to Little Rock, with the exception of weak nomadic forces that, like Stygian ghosts, wandered up and down the Arkansas from Dardanelle to Fort Smith, and nothing was now needed but belief in the permanent occupancy of the section. Public meetings were held in Fayetteville and Huntsville. The people were addressed as in civil times, and a general desire manifested to have North-western Arkansas represented in the Federal Congress. Further than this, a petition, praying for the adoption of the necessary preliminary measures, was very generally signed by prominent citizens of Benton, Madison, Washington, and other counties, and forwarded first for departmental aid. But the idea received no encouragement from head-quarters, and was necessarily abandoned.

Twelve counties asked the privilege of showing cause why they should be taken out of the President's Proclamation of January 1st, 1863, and by their own acts proven *not* to be in rebellion. The measure was at that time feasible. The Army of the Frontier was wending its sluggish way to Rolla, and could easily have parted with sufficient detachments to secure tranquility at the polls and a fair expression of opinion. It is true that the President's Proclamation of September 22, 1862, had ceased to become operative; nevertheless, had the proper representations been made at Washington, it is not at all improbable that another proclamation would have been issued to meet the exigencies of the case. Prior to the battle of Prairie Grove (December 7,

1862), an election under the proclamation of September could not have been held. After that event it could.

It was no fault of the loyal people of northwestern Arkansas that Hindman's men were overrunning their country until they were so signally defeated in December. For months and months loyal men had lifted up their hands for aid, and they were not strong enough without it to attempt an election. Nor is there sufficient reason to believe that their military Governor, the Hon. John S. Phelps of Missouri,[1] was not properly alive to their interests. He was not *"imperium in imperio."* A ministerial agent after all, he could not inaugurate, much less carry into effect, a policy of his own. He might indeed advise and recommend, but if the authorities at Washington saw fit to disregard his suggestions, that was the end of the matter.

The power to raise the First Arkansas Cavalry was procured with the greatest difficulty, and to Governor Phelps' persistent labors this result is attributable, still, the military Governorship of Arkansas has been more or less a myth to very many of her citizens. Whoever is censurable, there has been a lamentable oversight in the management of its affairs. The loyal people of the State have exercised themselves like "Rachel weeping for her children," and are to-day in almost profound ignorance of the advantages of a military Governorship.

Lately the office has been abolished, as a corollary, we suppose, to the capitulation of Vicksburg, for it would seem that the War Department now imagine that the restoration of civil law in Arkansas is speedily to take place; that senators and representatives will soon appear as of yore in congressional halls, and that the State, so rashly taken out of the Union, will return to its allegiance all the more willingly from the disastrous suspension of its laws. If this is not the anticipation, then the State should again have a military Governor, and *now* one of its own citizens. Earnest and able men call be found, and the thousand and one embarrassments that chill the ardor and weaken the loyalty of Arkansians will disappear. Perhaps, however, it is expected that the Commander of the Department of the Missouri will discharge the duties of two offices.

General Schofield doubtless possesses superior administrative ability, and perchance will prove himself equal to a position that possibly he may yet fill.[2] Should he avoid the rocks upon which his predecessor split, and remember that the bureau is subordinate to the field; that military vigor cometh first and reconstruction afterwards; that Little Rock is not simply a good strategic point for the concentration of department clerks and the ominous records of orders, general and special, that wind their sinuous way through the details of military life; but a grand centre of strength, a nucleus of power, from which can be made to radiate influences that will remould a State, substitute order for confusion, law for anarchy, and loyalty for treason, assistance will not be wanting, although many of the prominent citizens of the State are sunk so in the cess pool of rebellion that human power cannot extricate them, and there is no probability that the divine fiat will ever be interposed in their behalf.

While the Army of the Frontier was slowly moving on Rolla, and Generals were quarreling for command, the rebels were recovering from the disaster at Prairie Grove, and as spring drew nigh, began to threaten Fayetteville, the extreme south-western outpost of the department. It seemed strange to Arkansians that the "Army of the Frontier" should be marched so far away, and that Arkansas should be left, as it were, to take care of itself. Fayetteville was the exposed and prominent point, and the only troops detailed to hold it were the First Arkansas Cavalry and one battalion of the Tenth Illinois Cavalry, and the latter were withdrawn in March.

Col. W. A. Phillips commanding the eighth and ninth districts of the Department of the Missouri, was the immediate director of affairs, but engaged principally in the management of the Indian interest, he paid very slight attention to Arkansas. Hovering on the borders of the Cherokee Nation, he visited Fayetteville but once, we believe, during the winter and spring. Practically he had but little intercourse with Arkansians, and his measures for their relief were as scanty, as his presence was infrequent. The authorities at Fayetteville, however, and loyal citizens of the South, especially Dr. J. M. Johnson and E. D. Ham, Esq., of Huntsville, afterwards respectively Colonel and Major of the First Arkansas Infantry, went vigorously to work to strengthen and direct the growing loyalty of the section. The results of their labors were encouraging in a high degree.

A temporary militia was organized, out of which sprang, in part, the First Arkansas Infantry. A battery of Artillery was recruited, and other organizations were projected, and to some extent proceeded with. Knowledge of the intended permanent occupancy of Fayetteville was soon widely diffused, and Union men of cotton planting counties south of the Arkansas, secretly left their homes for this political Mecca. Hempstead, in particular, reported its delegation of patriots, conspicuous among whom was James Boren, of Mine Creek township, a hale, hearty old man, of three score years and ten, who had lived and intended to die beneath the aegis of the "Old Constitution." William J. Heffington, of Yell county, well known in Arkansas as "Wild Bill," a cool, daring, intelligent woodsman, who, unwillingly in the rebel service, had remained there long enough to become disgusted with it, and then betaking himself to his home near the Magazine Mountains, had rallied the bold spirits of the neighborhood, appeared with a band of followers, loyal all to the Stripes and Stars.

Others, also, shook off the bondage of an accursed usurpation, and by the first of April the establishment of this single post, had become fruitful of exceedingly cheering results, to all who were really interested in the development of Arkansian loyalty. A strange shortsightedness seemed to possess the ruling powers at St. Louis. It was known that Sterling Price—magical name in rebeldom—had returned to Arkansas; that Brigadier General W. L. Cabell had assumed command of the north-western district of the State, and that exertions would soon be made to wrest that section from our grasp. It was also known that our force was feeble, far too feeble for the duties imposed upon it; that it was one hundred miles from any support, and *that* the precarious aid that Springfield could render; that forage was scarce and guerrillas plentiful, and that the difficulty of communicating with Headquarters was daily becoming greater; still, we were to work away, holding the delusive chalice to the lips of suffering loyalty. *The post was not to be abandoned.* With rebels in our midst, it was to be supposed that the "grape-vine" telegraph was kept in active operation, and the expectation of attack was constant. We needed no large re-inforcements, but assuredly the commander of the Department should have foreseen the disastrous consequences of an evacuation of the country, and provided against such a contingency.

Meanwhile the rebels were daily growing bolder. "Bush-whacking," unfolding with the leaves, seemed suddenly to become the favorite avocation alike of farmers and artisans. Farther down in Dixie, troops began to bustle about, and as in the days of the Hindman dynasty, Clarksville and Ozark on the Arkansas river were instinct with martial life. The following proclamation by General Cabell appearing in March, was not without effect, though many ostensible secessionists neglected its counsels and disbelieved its prophesies:

"TO THE PEOPLE OF NORTH AND WEST ARKANSAS.

"In obedience to special orders from Headquarters Trans-Mississippi District, I this day assume command of all the troops, of whatever kind, in North-West Arkansas. In doing so, I hope to be able in a short time, to rid that section of the State of the presence of an insolent and unscrupulous abolition invader. To do this, I must have the hearty coöperation and sympathy of the citizens, and the united and determined effort of the soldier. I bring with me to the task, the lifetime experiences of a soldier, coupled with the zeal of a citizen. Arkansas is the home of my adoption, and that part of it in which I am assigned to command is my favorite locality.

"The soldiers of Arkansas have, in the present struggle for independence, distinguished themselves on every battle-field. The record they have made on the bloody plains of Virginia, Missouri, Tennessee and Mississippi, have shed a halo of glory around their name, and I know that in defending their homes and families they will maintain the character they have made in other States. I therefore ask every man in North-West Arkansas, capable of bearing arms, to rally to the defence of their homes and their firesides. Every man who knows he owes his country service, should come forward at once, and enroll themselves beneath their Country's flag, to protect their rights and their liberties. Come at once! In war, moments are precious.

"Those who betake themselves to arms are expected to do their whole duty;—those who remain at home should do theirs. The soldiers must be fed and clothed. I hope that a spirit of industry will pervade all classes; that farms will be cultivated with care; that the hum of the busy wheel will be heard in every household, and that the women of Arkansas will emulate the mothers and daughters of the Revolution. We are engaged in a war with a bitter, unscrupulous and mercenary enemy—our success alone can terminate it. The motto of our enemy is: subjugation and spoliation;—ours is: peace and independence. We must conquer it. The enemy must be driven from the soil of Arkansas, and beyond the borders of Missouri. The war has now assumed such vast proportions, and is being prosecuted with so much vigor, that it cannot, in the nature of things, be of long duration. One united and vigorous effort on the part of the soldiers in Arkansas will expel the invader. He will not return.

"W. L. CABELL,
"Brigadier General, Commanding North-West Arkansas."[3]

Thus spoke the over-confidant General: as a conquering hero, he has not yet appeared. Circumstances, we regret to say, have nevertheless partially favored the cause of his espousal, but their re-action is already to be felt, and, if we are not sadly mistaken in the signs of the times, the "enemy" speedily to be "driven from the soil of Arkansas" will be the deluded followers of his own standard. On the afternoon of the sixteenth of April, 1863, he left Ozark with a force reasonably estimated at twelve hundred men, for the purpose of surprising and, of course, capturing or routing the troops at Fayetteville. Cavalry and artillery were to do the work, and the principal officers and commands in Western Arkansas were to share the honor of the undertaking.

Colonel Monroe, a brave and gallant officer, was an especial reliance, and General Hindman's provost guards, *alias* bushwhackers, were not forgotten in organizing the triumphal procession—*that was to be.*

Early on the morning of the 18th of April, the cavalcade appeared before the doomed (?) town, defended by a portion of the First Arkansas Cavalry dismounted, and the First Arkansas Infantry, an incomplete regiment only partially armed, and that with the debris of Prairie Grove. We saw the approaching column, and let it suffice to say, that at 10 o'clock A.M. it was a broken, disordered aggregation of galloping humanity, fleeing, John Gilpin like, for the Arkansas river.[4] This was Gen. Cabell's first exploit as commander of the district of northwestern Arkansas. He must have had a copy of Hudibras in his pocket and bethought himself in time of the familiar reflection:

> "He that fights and runs away,
> May live to fight another day."

On the other hand, the Federal forces were really weak, and should have been strengthened long before the battle took place. The men, however, were brave and determined, and would have moved out to repel a second attack with even *greater* confidence and alacrity. They expected in fact the re-appearance of General Cabell, and representing the complainant in the case of Arkansas loyal *versus* Arkansas disloyal, were prepared to try conclusions on the question of jurisdiction. About this time, unfortunately, came an order for the evacuation of the place. Why it was issued we shall not assume to say. By the most of us it was very reluctantly obeyed, and personally we thought the measure most unwise and calamitous; an opinion which we have since seen no reason to change. It was but a moment's work for Gen.Curtis

to say "Fall back by forced marches on Springfield," but obedience to
the order involved consequences that we are loth to believe were com-
prehended at Department headquarters, or if they were, *then everlast-
ing shame upon the authors of a policy that directs the occupation of
seceded territory, and then unnecessarily abandons it.*

On the afternoon of the 25th of April the dreaded evacuation
began. At Mt. Comfort, three miles away, was a large camp of
refugees, who, hearing of the intended movement, came thronging
into town, and in almost every conceivable kind of vehicle filed into
an irregular line in front of the camp of the First Arkansas Cavalry.
Citizens of the place also, whose loyalty was not born of fear or policy, hastily gathered together a few of their more valuable effects and
prepared for the sorrowful journey. Some could not depart, and sorrowfully awaited the occupation of the town by the rebels, an event
that was certain to follow. At three o'clock the motley assemblage
began to move; the First Arkansas Cavalry, dismounted, (for their
horses had been worn out in the service,) and with transportation
altogether insufficient; the First Arkansas Infantry *with no transportation at all;* and in their rear, preceding a rear guard, a citizen
train bearing and accompanied by nearly two thousand people. This
last feature was particularly distressing. Family after family moved
despondingly out; the father careworn and dejected; the mother anxious, yet patient, and the children with a curious mixture of wonder
and excitement that served to buoy up rather than depress. All were
in the greatest destitution. The rude cart pulled wearily along by half
famished oxen, or the rough wagon with its tattered covering, contained all the worldly effects that they had the means of rescuing from
plundering rebels. Their houses had been burned; their cattle stolen;
their farms devastated, and now in the middle of the nineteenth century, and in the very heart of a continent consecrated to freedom of
thought, action and purpose, were exiles from the homes of a lifetime.
They had done no wrong. They were in fact what a King is in theory,
and believing it to be right to adhere to the Union, notwithstanding
the secession of the State, had spoken and acted accordingly. Many of
them had fathers, husbands or sons in the Federal army, and were
now bearing northward the mute testimonials of their sacrifices and
their devotion.

But enough. A brighter day will dawn for Arkansas. The fall of
Vicksburg foreshadows it; the repulse at Helena hastens it,[5] and to-
day the air of the southwest is instinct with the hum of earnest voices,

clamoring for, not only, but congratulating each other upon, the speedy occupation of that State.

Let us hope that imbecility or neglect will be followed now by wise and energetic measures, and that a State, a majority of whose citizens are at heart loyal, is at last to receive that aid, the withholding of which for so long a time has aggravated the strife and intensified the miseries of the Border.

SPRINGFIELD, MO.,
July, 1863.

APPENDIX.

APPENDIX.

WE APPEND THE official report of the Battle of Fayetteville, and the documents that accompanied its publication. This engagement, though of minor importance as compared with the contests of the Army of the Potomac, or the struggles that have recently culminated in the capitulation at Vicksburg, is not without its significance. It was the first battle of the war in which the loyal men of Arkansas were alone opposed to the organized treason of the State, and gave a very decided reproof to the rebel slander, that the Union men of Arkansas will not fight:[1]

"HEAD-QUARTERS POST,
"FAYETTEVILLE, ARK., APRIL 19, 1863.

"*Major-General* S. E. CURTIS,

"*Commanding Department of the Missouri:*

"GENERAL: The following report of the battle of yesterday at Fayetteville is respectfully submitted, in addition to the telegraphic dispatches of last evening. On Friday, 17th inst., a scout under command of Lieutenant Robb, First Arkansas Cavalry, returned from the direction of Ozark, and reported no apparent preparations of the enemy to move in this direction. Having no fresh horses I ordered Lieutenant Robb to take his command to quarters, expecting to be able to send a small scout again on the next day. On Saturday morning, 18th inst., at a few minutes after sunrise, the enemy having made a forced march from the Boston Mountains during the night, surprised and captured our dismounted picket on the Frog Bayou road, and approached the town with wild and deafening shouts. Their cavalry charged up a deep ravine on the east side of the city, and attacked my Head-quarters (the Colonel Tibbett's place). The firing of the picket had alarmed the command, and by the time the enemy had reached town the First Arkansas Infantry had formed on their parade ground under command of Lieutenant-Colonel E. J. Searle, assisted by Major E. D. Ham, and slowly retired, by my orders, toward the cavalry, then formed, dismounted, at their camp. Fearing that, not being uniformed, they might be mistaken for the enemy, and be fired upon by the cavalry, I ordered Lieutenant-Colonel Searle to post seven companies as a reserve in a sheltered position in our rear, two of which were afterward ordered to support the left wing. The remaining three companies of the First Infantry, together with four companies of the First Cavalry, formed the centre of our line, under my own immediate command. The right wing was composed of the Third Battalion, First Cavalry, under command of Major Ezra Fitch and the left wing, Second Battalion, (First Arkansas Cavalry), commanded by Lieutenant-Colonel A W. Bishop, assisted by Major T. J. Hunt. Head-Quarters was made the "bone of contention," and was repeatedly charged by the rebels, who were gallantly repulsed by our men. In less than thirty minutes after the first attack, the enemy planted two pieces of artillery—one a twelve-pounder, and one a six-pounder—upon the hill-side east of town, near Colonel Gunter's place, and opened a sharp fire of cannister and shell upon the camp of the First Arkansas Cavalry, doing some damage to tents and horses, but killing no men. At 8 A.M. our center had advanced and occupied the house, yard, out-buildings and hedges at my Head-Quarters; the right wing had advanced to the arsenal, and the left occupied the open field north-east of town, while the enemy had possession of the whole hill-side east, the Davis place, opposite to, and the grove south of Head-Quarters. This grove was formerly occupied by the buildings of the Arkansas College. At about 9 A.M., or a little before, Colonel Monroe led a gallant and desperate cavalry charge upon our right wing, which was met by a galling cross-fire from our right and center, piling rebel men and horses in heaps in front of our ordnance office, and causing the enemy to retreat in disorder to the woods. During this charge, Captains Parker and Smith, of the First Infantry, while bravely cheering their men, were both wounded in the head, though not dangerously. At about the same time, by my order, two companies of the First Cavalry, led by the gallant Lieutenant Robb, advanced within rifle range of the enemy's artillery, and guided by the blaze of its discharges, fired several volleys into the midst of the artillerists, which effectually silenced their battery and caused its precipitate withdrawal from the field. The enemy's center, occupying the Davis Place, made a desperate resistance for nearly an hour after both wings had partially given away, and skirmishing continued at intervals for some time with pickets, reconnoitering parties and stragglers. At 12 M. their whole force was in full retreat for Ozark. Having only a very few horses, and those already on duty with picketing and reconnoitering parties,

I was utterly unable to pursue them. During the whole action the enemy occupied ground covered with timber and brush, while my command were in the streets and open fields.

"Since the battle I have ascertained the following particulars: General Cabell and staff, with about 2,000 men and two pieces of artillery, left Ozark on Friday morning with three days rations and a full supply of ammunition. They halted at the crossing of the mountains at a little past noon and rested until nearly sunset, afterwards marching rapidly towards Fayetteville. They were delayed by the darkness of the night and the incumbrance of their artillery so that they did not commence the attack as early by nearly two hours as they had intended. Colonel Monroe recommended a cavalry attack, to be supported by the artillery, but was overruled by Cabell, and a halt was made until the artillery could come up. Their force was made up as follows: Brigadier General W. L. Cabell, commanding, accompanied by staff and escort; Carroll's First Arkansas Cavalry Regiment, Colonel Scott, of Virginia, commanding, assisted by Lieutenant Colonel Thompson.

"Monroe's Second Arkansas Cavalry, Colonel Monroe commanding in person.

"First Battalion Parson's Texas Cavalry, Lieutenant Colonel Noble commanding.

"One section of Artillery, commanding officer not known; four companies of bushwhackers, commanded by Mankins, Palmer, Brown and others. The enemy left all their dead and wounded which they could not take away on their retreat, in our hands, leaving Surgeon Russell and Assistant Surgeon Holderness to take charge of them. Today Captain Alexander arrived at our picket with a flag of truce bringing a communication from General Cabell, a copy of which I enclose. The flag was immediately ordered back with my reply, a copy of which is also enclosed. The following is a list of casualties on our side:[2]

"FIRST ARKANSAS INFANTRY.

"KILLED.

"S. Cockerill, company A.

"WOUNDED.

"Captain Randall Smith, company A, head, slightly.
"Captain Wm. C. Parker, company H, head, slightly.

"Corporal John Woods, company A, slightly.

"James Shockley, company A, mortally.

"Niles Slater, company A, slightly.

"Daniel Rupe, company E, slightly.

"William Rockdey, company F, severely.

"—— Nolin, company H, slightly.

"FIRST ARKANSAS CAVALRY.

"KILLED.

"Privates H. Morris and J. D. Bell, Company I; R. B. Burrows, company A.

"WOUNDED.

"Captain W. S. Johnson, company M; right arm, dangerously.

"Sergeant Frederick Kise, company A, slightly.

"Sergeant John Asbill, company D, severely.

"First Sergeant W. M. Burrows, company E, severely.

"Commissary Sergeant, Ben. K. Graham, company L, slightly.

"Corporal Josiah Fears, company A, slightly.

"Corporal Henry C. Lewis, company D, slightly.

"Corporal George A. Morris, company G, slightly.

"Corporal Doctor B. Morris, company M, slightly.

"Farrier Wm. Wooten, company C, slightly.

"John Hays, company A, severely.

"James Jack, company A, severely.

"William J. Quinton, company D, slightly.

"Francis M. Temple, company D, slightly.

"John Grubb, company E, slightly,

"Jordan Taylor, company E, severely.

"Wm. F. Davis, company G, slightly.

"George Davis, company H, mortally.

"William J. York, company H, severely.

"Davis Chyle, company M, slightly.

"MISSING.—Thirty-five. Mostly stampeded towards Cassville during the engagement.

"PRISONERS—One Lieutenant and eight men, First Arkansas Cavalry, taken while absent without leave, at a dance nine miles from town. Also, one private, First Arkansas Infantry, and six privates from other commands, taken in town.

"Total Killed, 4; Wounded, 26; Prisoners, 16; Missing, 15.

"The enemy's loss is not accurately known.[3] At and about this post are not less than twenty killed and fifty wounded. Citizens report one Colonel and several men as having died on the retreat; also a large number of wounded still moving on with the command. We captured, during the engagement, Major Wilson, Gen. Cabell's commissary, wounded, and Captain Jefferson of Carroll's regiment; also four sergeants, three corporals and forty-six privates, a part of them wounded; also not less than fifty horses and one hundred stand of arms, mostly shot guns. Among their killed are Captain Hubbard of Carroll's regiment, and a Captain of bushwhackers. The enemy admit the loss of over two hundred horses, killed, taken and stampeded. Enclosed please find a rough sketch of the position of forces at 9 A.M., when the battle culminated.

"Every field and line officer, and nearly every enlisted man fought bravely, and I would not wish to be considered as disparaging any one when I can mention only a few of the many heroic men who sustained so nobly the honor of our flag. Lieutenant Colonel Searle and Major Ham, in command of the reserve, did good service in keeping their men in position and preventing them from being terrified by the artillery. Lieutenant Colonel Bishop and Majors Fitch and Hunt, of the First Cavalry, led their men coolly up in the face of the enemy's fire, and drove them from their position. Captain W. S. Johnson, Company M, First Cavalry, had his right arm shattered while leading his men forward under a galling fire. Lieutenant Roseman, Post Adjutant, and Lieutenant Frank Strong, Acting Adjutant First Cavalry, deserve much praise.

"I remain, General, your most obedient servant,

"M. LA RUE HARRISON,

"Colonel First Arkansas Cavalry, Commanding.

"P. S. We had actively engaged during the battle between three and four hundred men only. I should not neglect also to mention that S. D. Carpenter, Assistant Surgeon of Volunteers, assisted by Assistant Surgeons Cafee, Drake and Tefft were actively engaged during the contest in carrying the wounded from the field and attending to their wants.

"M. LA RUE HARRISON,

"Colonel First Arkansas Cavalry, Commanding.

CORRESPONDENCE.

"Headquarters Northwest Arkansas,⎱
                    "April 19, 1863.   ⎰

"Sir—The bearer of this letter, Captain Alexander, visits your post under a flag of truce to bury any of my command that may be left dead from the engagement of yesterday. I respectfully request that you will suffer him to get up the dead and wounded, and that you will extend to him such assistance as may be necessary to enable him to carry out his instructions.

"I am, sir, very respectfully, your obedient servant,

"W. L. CABELL,

"Brig. Gen. Commanding Northwest Arkansas.

"To Colonel M. La Rue Harrison,

"Commanding Post of Fayetteville.

———

"Headquarters Post   ⎱
"Fayetteville, Ark., April 19, 1863. ⎰

"*Brig Gen.* W. L. Cabell, *Commanding:*

"General—In reply to dispatches from you, by hand of Captain Alexander, bearing flag of truce, I would respectfully state that the dead of your command have all been decently buried in coffins. The wounded are in charge of Surgeons Russell and Holderness, having been removed to our general hospital by my order. They are receiving every attention that men can receive, abundance of medicines, surgical instruments and subsistence stores having been placed under the control of your surgeons.

"Rest assured, General, that your wounded shall receive the best of care, such as we would hope to have from you were we placed in a like situation.

"Under the circumstances, I consider it unnecessary to retain your flag, and therefore return it.

"Your prisoners shall be paroled, and as fast as the men whose names are mentioned in your list report to our lines, the exchanges will be made.

"I am, General, very truly yours,

"M. LA RUE HARRISON,

"Colonel Commanding."

"GENERAL ORDER, NO. 16.

"READ AT DIVINE SERVICE, FAYETTEVILLE, SUNDAY, APRIL 19, 1863.

"HEAD-QUARTERS POST, ⎫
"FAYETTEVILLE, ARK., April 19,1863. ⎭

"Comrades in arms:

"Let the 18th of April, 1863, be ever remembered. The 'Battle of Fayetteville' has been fought and won. To-day the brave and victorious sons of Arkansas stand proudly upon the soil which their blood and their bravery have rendered sacred to every true-hearted American, but doubly sacred to them. In the light of this holy Sabbath sun we are permitted, through God's mercy, to gather together in his name, and in the name of our common country, to offer up our heartfelt thanks to the 'Giver of every good and perfect gift,' for the triumphs of our arms, and for the blessings which we this day enjoy.

"When yesterday's sun rose upon us, the hostile hordes of a bitter and unprincipled foe were pouring their deadly fire among our ranks; the booming of his artillery was reëchoing from mountain to mountain, and the clattering hoofs of his cavalry were tramping in our streets.

"At meridian, General Cabell, with his scattered and panic stricken cohorts, was retreating precipitately through the passes of the Boston Mountains toward the Arkansas river, leaving his dead and wounded in our hands.

"Fellow Soldiers: It is to your honor and credit I say it; he could not have left them in better hands. Not one act of barbarity or even unkindness stains the laurels you so proudly wear. Such may your conduct ever be; brave and unflinching in battle; kind and generous to the vanquished. Abstain from all cruelty and excess. Respect the immunities of private property. Never insult or injure women and children, the aged, the sick, or a fallen foe.

"Let us show to our enemies that the Federal soldiers are as generous as they are brave and patriotic; let us prove to them the justice of our cause and the purity of our purposes, so that soon we may gather together, under the broad folds of our time-honored and victorious banner every true hearted son of Arkansas.

"Fellow soldiers: I congratulate you all upon the glorious victory you have won, by your cool and determined bravery, for that Union which our revolutionary sires established by their valor and sealed with their blood. More than all do I congratulate you that this battle was fought upon Arkansas soil, and this victory won by Arkansians alone; thereby testifying to our patriot brethren in arms from other States that we are not only willing but anxious to second their efforts in rescuing our State from the dominion of traitors. But in all our rejoicing, let us not neglect to shed the tear of regret over the graves of those heroic men who fell beside us, fighting bravely for the nation's honor.

"Green be their mossy graves;
Immortal be their name;
Above, their banner proudly waves,
While Heav'n records their fame.

"A just cause is ours. The Stars and Stripes float gallantly over us. God is on our side; who can be against us ?

"By order of Col. M. LA RUE HARRISON, commanding Post.

"JAMES ROSEMAN,
"Lieutenant and Post Adjutant."

ARKANSIAN BATTLE HYMN

Air—*"Marching on."*

Arkansians are rallying round the glorious Stripes and Stars,
We have sworn unceasing vengeance 'gainst the hated stars and bars,
We know no law but justice, tho' covered o'er with scars,
>   As we go marching on.

> CHORUS— Glory! glory! hallelujah,
>   Glory! glory! hallelujah,
>   Glory! glory! hallelujah,
>   As we go marching on.

We were driven from our homes, our wives and children dear,
Our native hills and valleys no longer gave us cheer,
But now, thank God! forever, we once again are here,
>   Where the war goes bravely on.

> CHORUS— Glory &c.

We remember David Walker who sought our votes of old,
And linked to ours his "destiny," in voice of utt'rance bold,
But southward drove his "contrabands," a bid for rebel gold,
>   As we came marching on.

> CHORUS— Glory &c.

We scorn deception ever, we scorn it most of all,
In the proud and haughty rebels who are seeking still our fall,
But soon they'll hear the shouting and the trumpet's gath'ring call,
>   As we go marching on.

> CHORUS— Glory &c.

We've fought, bled, and suffered, but gladly sprang to arms,
To trample out the treason that desolates our farms,
We'll bear aloft our banner, and to peace restore her charms,
>   As we go marching on.

> CHORUS— Glory &c.

Let the Union of the FATHERS, be the Union ever more,
Of the sons and the daughters of those who fought of yore,
And moving on the Arkansas, we'll strike the farther shore,
>   As we go marching on.

> CHORUS— Glory &c.

Then JUBILATE DEO! let the welkin ever ring,
With the joyous songs of freemen attendant now on Spring,
And hosannas loudly shout to God alone our King,
>   As we go marching on.

> CHORUS— Glory &c.

FAYETTEVILLE, ARK., *April,* 1863.

Notes

EDITOR'S INTRODUCTION.

1. Gerald F. Linderman, *Embattled Courage: The Experience of Combat in the American Civil War* (New York: Free Press, 1989), 266–97; James M. McPherson, *For Cause and Comrades: Why Men Fought in the Civil War* (New York: Oxford University Press, 1997), 10–11.

2. "Testimonial of Respect to A. W. Bishop, Esq.," *Buffalo Commercial Advertiser*, July 28, 1860. Other early information on Bishop's life has been gleaned from obituaries appearing in *Buffalo Daily Courier*, Dec. 1, 1901; *Buffalo Evening News*, Nov. 30, 1901; *Buffalo Enquirer*, Nov. 30, 1901; and *Buffalo Times*, Nov. 30, 1861. Bishop's wedding notice appears in *Buffalo Commercial Advertiser*, Sept. 17, 1857.

3. Maria W. Bishop, "Early Days and Ways," ca. 1940, Cortland County Historical Society, Cortland, N.Y., manuscript.

4. "A Useful Career Closed," *The Washington Post*, Oct. 30, 1890. After the war Harrison remained in northwest Arkansas, where he worked for the Post Office Department and also surveyed the Boone County town that today bears his name. He died in Washington, D.C., on October 27, 1890.

5. Albert Webb Bishop, Compiled Service Record, Records of the Adjutant General's Office, Record Group [RG] 94, National Archives and Records Administration, Washington, D.C. [NARA]; Albert Webb Bishop Pension File, Pension Application Files Based upon Service in the Civil War and Spanish-American War, Records of the Veterans Administration, RG 15.7.3, NARA.

6. Bishop, Compiled Service Record.

7. William L. Shea, ed., "The Aftermath of Prairie Grove: Union Letters from Fayetteville," *Arkansas Historical Quarterly* 47, no. 4 (winter 1988): 354.

8. Albert Webb Bishop, *An Oration Delivered at Fayetteville, Arkansas* (New York: Baker and Godwin, 1865), 20.

9. Albert Webb Bishop, *What Is the Situation Now? A Review of Political Affairs in the Southern States* (Buffalo: Matthews-Northrup, 1894), 18–19; U.S. Senate, *Report of the Adjutant General of the State of*

Arkansas: For the Period of the Late Rebellion, and to November 1, 1866, 39th Cong., 2d sess., 1867, S. Misc. Doc. 53.

10. Bishop's law partners can be identified by the stationery heading on the only fragments of his professional correspondence that have survived. Albert Webb Bishop Papers, 1866–73, MS B54, Special Collections Division, University of Arkansas Libraries, Fayetteville; "Albert Webb Bishop," corrected proof sheet, Reynolds/Thomas Research Papers, 1908–9, MC 770, ibid.; Albert Webb Bishop, pension questionnaire, June 4, 1898, Bishop Pension File.

11. John Hugh Reynolds, *History of the University of Arkansas* (Fayetteville: University of Arkansas, 1910), 96–97.

12. Robert Allen Leflar, *The First 100 Years: Centennial History of the University of Arkansas* (Fayetteville: University of Arkansas Foundation, 1972), 39; "The A.I.U. Inauguration of Gen. A. W. Bishop as President," *Arkansas Gazette,* July 15, 1874.

13. Leflar, *First 100 Years,* 40–41; "A Slanderer," *Arkansas Gazette,* Nov. 4, 1874; "The A.I.U.," *Arkansas Gazette,* Dec. 16, 1874.

14. Harrison Hale, *University of Arkansas, 1871–1948* (Fayetteville: University of Arkansas Alumni Association, 1948), 24–25.

15. "The New Deal," *Arkansas Gazette,* July 29, 1876; Marvin Frank Russell, "The Republican Party in Arkansas, 1874–1913" (Ph.D. diss., University of Arkansas, 1985), 33–34.

16. "Bishop at Conway," *Arkansas Gazette,* Aug. 22, 1876.

17. "How Gen. Bishop was 'Dunn' for at Forest City," *Arkansas Gazette,* Sept. 1, 1876; "W. R. Miller on the Stump," *Arkansas Gazette,* Sept. 5, 1876; "Literature in Life," *Arkansas Gazette,* Apr. 25, 1877.

18. "Gen. A. W. Bishop," *Arkansas Gazette,* Dec. 20, 1879.

19. "Letter from Gen. Bishop," *Arkansas Gazette,* Dec. 27, 1879.

20. "Gen. A. W. Bishop," *Arkansas Gazette,* Dec. 20, 1879; Bishop, pension questionnaire, June 4, 1898.

21. Albert Webb Bishop to the Commissioner of Pensions, July 26, 1892, Bishop Pension File.

22. Bishop, *What Is the Situation,* 7, 5.

23. The only extant copy is held by Yale University.

24. Mina joined the faculty of the Cortland Normal School in 1890 and taught there for fifteen years. She then continued her career at the Hampton Institute in Hampton, Virginia, until her retirement in 1925. Afterward, Mina returned to Cortland, where she died on October 27, 1943, at the age of eighty-three. "Miss Bishop, 83, Dies in Cortland," *Cortland Standard,* Oct. 27, 1943; Grace Carew Sheldon, "Buffalo of the Olden Time," *Buffalo Evening Times,* Dec. 3, 1909; "Gen. Bishop's Sudden Death," *Buffalo Sunday Courier,* Dec. 1, 1901.

25. Robert R. Mackey, "Bushwhackers, Provosts, and Tories: The Guerrilla War in Arkansas," in *Guerrillas, Unionists, and Violence on the*

Confederate Homefront, ed. Daniel E. Sutherland (Fayetteville: University of Arkansas Press; 1999): 173–74.

26. Walker survived the war, though he lost a son at the battle of Jenkins' Ferry. He also returned to the Arkansas Supreme Court before his death in a buggy accident in 1879. Robert Childers, "The Secession Crisis and Civil War in Arkansas through the Eyes of Judge David Walker, Conditional Southern Unionist from Fayetteville" (master's thesis, University of Arkansas, 1995), 8–13; Walter L. Lemke, ed., *The Walker Family Letters* (Fayetteville: Washington County Historical Society, 1957), introduction.

27. James M. Woods, *Rebellion and Realignment: Arkansas's Road to Secession* (Fayetteville: University of Arkansas Press, 1987), 167–68.

PREFACE.

1. In an 1861 report to the secretary of war, Union major general Benjamin Butler referred to runaway slaves seeking refuge within Union lines as "contraband of war," and by 1863 the term had entered the slang of most Northern soldiers in reference to all Southern blacks. Mark Mayo Boatner III, *The Civil War Dictionary* (New York: David McKay, 1959), 172.

2. On September 22, 1862, Pres. Abraham Lincoln issued a formal proclamation regarding the status of slavery in the South. The Emancipation Proclamation declared that persons held in bondage within the borders of states in rebellion against the U.S. government would be free on January 1, 1863. Intended to draw its legal force as a war measure, Lincoln's declaration excluded specifically named counties in Louisiana and Virginia from its enforcement, essentially giving Federal protection to slavery in those areas the Union army controlled. Bishop's contention in this paragraph is that had northwestern Arkansas been under the control of the Union army when the proclamation had first been issued, elections reestablishing U.S. allegiance could have been held prior to January 1, 1863, and the state's slaveholders secured in their human property. James M. McPherson, *Battle Cry of Freedom: The Civil War Era* (New York: Ballantine, 1989), 557–60; William E. Gienapp, ed., *The Civil War and Reconstruction: A Documentary Collection* (New York: W. W. Norton, 2001), 165–70.

3. Following the battle of Pea Ridge, Arkansas, in early March 1862, Union major general Samuel Ryan Curtis marched his Army of the Southwest eastward across southern Missouri and crossed the border into Arkansas on April 29. The Federals' advance followed the course of the White River throughout the following summer, and Confederate major general Thomas Carmichael Hindman assembled a force to oppose them. After Curtis's army occupied Batesville, some of the first Arkansas Union

volunteers joined his army and participated in the unsuccessful drive to capture Little Rock. William L. Shea, "1862: A Continual Thunder," in *Rugged and Sublime: The Civil War in Arkansas,* ed. Mark K. Christ (Fayetteville: University of Arkansas Press, 1994), 41.

4. At least two Texas Confederate units deserted en mass during the Civil War, but Bishop was most likely referring to a company commanded by Martin D. Hart (1821?-63). Hart, a Texas state senator originally from Indiana, moved with his family to Texas around 1833. Martin and his brother, Hardin, established a law office in 1849 in Hunt County, where they prospered in the years prior to the war. In 1860 he voted for John Bell, the Constitutional Union presidential candidate, and publicly opposed secession. When Texas voted to join the Confederacy in 1861, Hart resigned from the senate and returned to Hunt County, where, in an apparent turnabout in political sympathies, he raised a mounted company and offered its services "in defense of Texas whenever she is invaded or threatened with invasion." Hart gained the trust of Confederate military authorities, who commissioned him and ordered him to northwest Arkansas. He promptly marched his men to southwest Missouri, where they enlisted in the Union army. Hart himself began leading a series of forays against the Rebel army in Arkansas and was "alleged to have murdered at least two prominent secessionists." He was captured by vengeful Confederate forces in Arkansas on January 18, 1863, and hanged at Fort Smith five days later. Cecil Harper Jr., "Hart, Martin D.," *Online Handbook of Texas,* Texas State Historical Association, Apr. 18, 2002 (accessed July 12, 2002), <http://www.tsha.utexas.edu/handbook/online/articles/view/HH/fhace.html>

INTRODUCTION.

1. The "absurd notion of negro equality" was exactly the possibility feared by Fayetteville, Arkansas, readers of the secessionist newspaper *The Arkansian.* Bishop likely had access to past issues of the sheet while residing in the town and had read the editor's 1861 "dire predictions of white men having to step aside while black men cast their votes." Woods, *Rebellion and Realignment,* 141.

2. Bishop is correct in his assertion that the "conditional Unionists" of the Upper South should have taken Lincoln's First Inaugural Address as a promise to do no more than seek a prevention of the spread of slavery into the territories. Gienapp, *Civil War and Reconstruction,* 57–68.

3. William Lloyd Garrison (1805–79) was one of the most famous voices from the abolitionist movement in the United States. He founded *The Liberator,* an influential antislavery newspaper, in 1831. In spite of his reputation among Southerners as a great threat to their security, he did not initially support Lincoln's war effort against the seceded states.

Stewart Sifakis, *Who Was Who in the Civil War* (New York: Facts on File, 1988), 240.

4. Unlike Garrison, Wendell Phillips (1811–84) advocated immediate emancipation, by force if necessary, and rejected all compromise on the issue of slavery. His numerous and well-publicized lectures during the prewar years could rightfully be seen by Southerners as representing a clear and present threat to their property. Ibid., 504.

5. Sterling Price (1809–67) was a Virginia native who moved to Missouri in 1831. He began his political career in the state legislature and was elected to the U.S. Congress in 1844. Resigning to fight in the Mexican War, Price became a general of volunteers and military governor of New Mexico. In 1853 he was elected governor of Missouri and served until 1857. Although initially opposed to secession, Price took command of the Missouri State Guard in May 1861. He led his troops throughout the war and, along with remnants of his command, entered Mexico following the fall of the Confederacy in 1865. Price returned the following year to Missouri, where he remained until his death. He enjoyed great popularity among those who served in the Missouri State Guard and who affectionately nicknamed him "Old Pap." Ezra J. Warner, *Generals in Gray* (1959; reprint, Baton Rouge: Louisiana State University Press, 1995), 246–47.

6. Claiborne Fox Jackson (1800–62) was elected governor of Missouri after serving in the state legislature. A dedicated secessionist, he authorized the organization of the Missouri State Guard under Sterling Price to resist Federal "coercion" and advocated that the state join the Confederacy. Union troops under the command of Brig. Gen. Nathaniel Lyon advanced on Jefferson City, the state capital, in the spring of 1861, and Jackson fled to the southwest portion of the state, where he attempted to establish a secessionist legislature in Neosho. This exiled state government failed to gain any effective support from the Confederacy despite Jackson's continuing efforts during the last year of his life. Sifakis, *Who Was Who,* 334.

7. Of the four guerillas mentioned here, scant information exists for only Isaac Bledsoe and Maj. Thomas R. Livingston. Most of Livingston's activities during the war took place in southwestern Missouri, but he is one of the few irregular cavalry commanders in the Trans-Mississippi to have left a written report in the *Official Records.* His company clashed with units of the First Arkansas Cavalry (U.S.) several times in 1863. U.S. War Department, *The War of the Rebellion: A Compilation of the Official Records of the Union and Confederate Armies,* 70 vols. in 128 pts. (Washington, D.C.: GPO, 1880–1901), ser. 1, 22(2):321 [hereafter referred to as *Official Records,* all references to series 1 unless otherwise stated]; Jay Anthony Prier, "Under the Black Flag: The Real War in Washington County, Arkansas, 1861–1865" (master's thesis, University

of Arkansas, 1992), 79. Bishop's portrait of Bledsoe, a Methodist minister, appears in a later chapter.

8. Union army commanders shared Bishop's condemnation of Keetsville, Missouri, as evidenced by numerous uncomplimentary references in the *Official Records*. The small hamlet was located on Washburn Prairie, eight miles southwest of Cassville. Burned to the ground sometime in 1863, Keetsville was rebuilt and later renamed Washburn. Bishop's footnote reference to "Joe Peevie" is somewhat misleading. Although Joseph G. Peevey did serve as a civil officer for the Confederacy, he apparently took his job seriously enough to administer justice impartially. Solomon Roberts, a Southerner who indiscriminately robbed Union sympathizers, was brought to justice by Peevey in 1862 for "breaking the rules of war" and subsequently executed. *History of Newton, Lawrence, Barry, and McDonald Counties, Missouri. From the Earliest Time to the Present* (Chicago: Goodspeed, 1888), 635.

ISAAC MURPHY.

1. Benjamin Johnson (1784–1849) was a Kentucky-born attorney who was first appointed as a superior court judge in Arkansas Territory by Pres. James Monroe in 1821. He held that position for fifteen years. Through marriage alliances and "sheer political sagacity," Johnson founded the Dynasty, a clique within the Democratic Party that dominated Arkansas politics until the eve of the Civil War. Benjamin Johnson eventually returned to Kentucky, where he died in 1849. Josiah Hazen Shinn, *Pioneers and Makers of Arkansas* (N.p.: Genealogical and Historical Publishing, 1908), 202–4; John Hallum, *Biographical and Pictorial History of Arkansas* (Albany, N.Y.: Weed, Parsons, 1887), 158–59.

2. Ambrose Hundley Sevier (1801–48) married Juliette E. Johnson, daughter of Judge Benjamin Johnson, in 1827. Originally from Tennessee, Sevier moved to Arkansas in 1820 and made his home with Henry Conway, his cousin and the territorial delegate to Congress. An able lawyer and effective politician, Sevier also served as the Arkansas territorial delegate in Congress and later as one of the state's first senators. His resignation from the Senate to serve as a peace commissioner in Mexico in 1848 proved his political undoing, and he died shortly after returning to Arkansas. Most historians seem to agree with the assessment that "he alone of all of Arkansas's pre–Civil War senators achieved any prominence" in Washington. Woods, *Rebellion and Realignment,* 38; James M. Woods, "Ambrose Hundley Sevier," in *Arkansas Biography: A Collection of Notable Lives,* ed. Nancy A. Williams (Fayetteville: University of Arkansas Press, 2000), 259–60; Brian Walton, "Ambrose Hundley Sevier in the United States Senate," *Arkansas Historical Quarterly* 32, no. 1 (spring 1973): 25–60.

3. Solon Borland (1809–63) was a Virginia-born physician who settled in Arkansas in 1843 to edit the *Arkansas Banner,* a Democratic Party newspaper. He served in Archibald Yell's regiment during the Mexican War and afterward was chosen by Gov. Thomas S. Drew to fill out the senatorial term of Ambrose Sevier when the latter resigned to serve as a peace commissioner to Mexico in 1848. Borland built a powerful political base in Arkansas and, during the subsequent election for a full Senate term, was able to defeat Sevier, the first major political setback for the Dynasty since statehood. In 1853 Borland also resigned his seat to serve as a diplomat (though his bellicose personality hardly seemed to qualify for such work), and his departure from the Senate allowed the Johnson family to reclaim the seat. Borland enlisted in the Confederate service at the outbreak of the war but resumed his medical practice in Little Rock shortly before his death. James M. Woods, "Solon Borland," in *Arkansas Biography: A Collection of Notable Lives,* ed. Nancy A. Williams (Fayetteville: University of Arkansas Press, 2000), 32–33; Woods, *Rebellion and Realignment,* 38; Fay Hempstead, *A Pictorial History of Arkansas : From Earliest Times to the Year 1890* (St. Louis: N. D. Thompson, 1890), 789.

4. Bishop's assessment of Sevier's political integrity was obviously colored by Isaac Murphy's admiration for the senator. During his tenure in office, Sevier managed to alienate the Arkansas legislature, which called him to account for financial irregularities regarding Arkansas Real Estate Bank bonds. Woods, "Ambrose Hundley Sevier," 259–60.

5. Robert Ward "Bob" Johnson (1814–79) was the eldest son of Benjamin Johnson and both a U.S. representative and senator from Arkansas. A Yale graduate, Johnson moved to Little Rock in 1835 to practice law. His political career began with a stint as Pulaski County attorney in 1840, and in 1846 he was elected to Congress. On July 6, 1853, he was appointed to the Senate when Solon Borland resigned, and he subsequently won election to a full term. A dedicated secessionist, he allied himself with Dynasty defector Thomas Carmichael Hindman on the eve of the Civil War to guide Arkansas into the Confederacy. He resigned from the U.S. Senate in 1861 and afterward served in the Confederate Congress. Following a failed attempt to regain his Senate seat in 1878, Johnson died in Little Rock. James M. Woods, "Robert Ward Johnson," in *Arkansas Biography: A Collection of Notable Lives,* ed. Nancy A. Williams (Fayetteville: University of Arkansas Press, 2000), 152–53.

6. Richard Henry Johnson (1826–89) was the first son of Benjamin Johnson born in Arkansas. His role in the Dynasty was that of a newspaper editor, having charge over the Little Rock *True Democrat* during the antebellum years. He was an unsuccessful candidate for governor in 1860, losing the election to Henry M. Rector. *Arkansas Gazette,* Sept. 8, 1889.

7. James Barnett Johnson (1828–62), the youngest son of Benjamin Johnson, enlisted in First Arkansas Infantry Battalion some time between May and August 1861. This unit was subsequently absorbed by the Eighteenth Arkansas Infantry the following December. On January 31, 1862, the Eighteenth Arkansas converted from a state organization to a Confederate regular-army unit and renamed the Third Confederate Infantry Regiment. Johnson became the unit's lieutenant colonel and was killed near Murfreesboro, Tennessee, in February 1862. Stewart Sifakis, *Compendium of the Confederate Armies,* vol. 2 (New York: Facts on File, 1992).

8. Thomas Carmichael Hindman (1828–68) had at first allied with the Dynasty and then defied the Johnson family in the Arkansas political arena. Born in Tennessee and raised in Mississippi, Hindman was a Mexican War veteran who later became a lawyer and moved to Helena, Arkansas, in 1856. He supported the state's Democratic Party as an able speaker and newspaper editor, gaining election to Congress in 1858. Hindman broke with the Johnsons to support the gubernatorial candidacy of Henry Massey Rector in 1860 but afterward cooperated with Sen. Robert W. Johnson to actively support secession. When the war broke out, Hindman served in the Confederate army, first being named colonel of the Second Arkansas Infantry and later being promoted to the rank of major general. He commanded the Trans-Mississippi Department in 1862, vigorously enforcing the Conscription Act and foiling Union attempts to take Little Rock that year. When Lt. Gen. Theophilus Hunter Holmes was sent by Richmond to replace him, Hindman was placed in charge of the District of Arkansas, leading Southern troops at the battle of Prairie Grove on December 7, 1862. He asked to be assigned to the Army of Tennessee in 1863, commanding a division until receiving a wound at the battle of Kennesaw Mountain on June 27, 1864, that left him partially blind. After the war Hindman went to Mexico, but he returned to Arkansas in 1867 and tried to resume his peaceful residence in Helena. He was assassinated the following year. Carl H. Moneyhon, "Thomas Carmichael Hindman," in *Arkansas Biography: A Collection of Notable Lives,* ed. Nancy A. Williams (Fayetteville: University of Arkansas Press, 2000), 142–43.

9. Henry Massie Rector (1816–99) became governor of Arkansas in 1860 on the eve of the Civil War. A native Kentuckian, Rector came to Arkansas in 1835 after his father had died and left him title to several tracts of land, including property around Hot Springs, where the U.S. government disputed his ownership claims. In 1841 he settled on a plantation in Collegeville, Arkansas, where he studied law. His political career began the following year when he received an appointment as a U.S. marshal. In 1854 he moved to Little Rock, where he continued to farm and stay active in politics, eventually serving on the Arkansas Supreme Court.

In 1860 Rector, with the backing of Thomas Hindman, ran for governor against the Dynasty candidate, Richard H. Johnson, and defeated him. A reluctant secessionist, Rector showed little enthusiasm for leading the state out of the Union, but he did refuse to furnish troops for the Lincoln government when asked and helped mobilize the state during the first few months of the war. He resigned as governor on November 3, 1862, and spent the remainder of his life operating cotton plantations in southern Arkansas. Jeannie M. Whayne, "Henry Massie Rector," in ibid., 234–35.

10. Albert Rust (1818–70) was born in Virginia and moved to Union County, Arkansas, in 1837. He became a lawyer and was elected to the state legislature for several terms, beginning in 1842. Rust served in Congress for two separate terms, in 1854 and 1858, but he resigned when the war broke out to join the Confederate army, first as colonel of the Third Arkansas Infantry, then in 1862 gaining promotion to brigadier general. He returned to Arkansas after the war and moved to the Little Rock area, where he farmed until his death. Warner, *Generals in Gray*, 266–67.

11. The Knights of the Golden Circle was a secret order of Southern sympathizers in the North. Dr. George W. L. Bickley organized the first "castle," or local branch, in Cincinnati in 1854 and soon took the order to the South, where it was enthusiastically received. Its principal object was to provide a force to colonize the northern part of Mexico and thus extend proslavery interests. But secession and the outbreak of the Civil War prompted a shift in the organization's aims from filibustering in Mexico to support of the new Confederate government. Whether or not they were active in Arkansas during the secession movement, as Bishop claims, would be difficult to prove. Boatner, *Civil War Dictionary*, 466.

12. Bishop's assessment of Walker's lack of moral courage does not display a complete understanding of the true political situation in Arkansas after Fort Sumter. As one historian has remarked, "It would now be almost impossible for a Unionist to oppose secession without appearing to be either a traitor to the slaveholding South or the hapless agent of Northern abolitionists." Woods, *Rebellion and Realignment*, 158.

13. The four delegates who changed their votes were H. H. Bolinger (Madison County), John Campbell (Searcy County), Thomas Montague Gunter (Washington County), and Samuel Kelly (Pike County), all from the mountainous regions of the state. Woods, *Rebellion and Realignment*, 159 n 35.

14. As dramatic as Bishop's tale of Murphy's vote may seem, it does not tell the whole story. Once Murphy had given his vote, Mrs. Frederick Trapnall threw a bouquet of roses to the floor of the gallery, demonstrating that not everyone present found his vote outrageous. Murphy may have been, in the words of one witness, "the only delegate who could have taken such a stand and not been mobbed," but Bishop's contention

that Murphy's life was in danger is probably overstated. The convention was in session for weeks after the vote was taken, and Murphy stayed until it adjourned on June 3, 1861, participating actively in its deliberations. Woods, *Rebellion and Realignment,* 160.

15. James M. Johnson (1832–?) was a native of Tennessee who moved to Madison County, Arkansas, with his parents prior in 1836. He attended the Ozark Institute at Mount Comfort and Arkansas College at Fayetteville. After spending his early years as a farmer, Johnson began to study the medical profession in Fayetteville and in 1857 attended the St. Louis Medical College. He returned to Arkansas in 1858 and began to practice medicine in Huntsville. In 1862 he went with Isaac Murphy to the Union army in Missouri, and he offered his services as a mail agent. In the spring of 1863, James Johnson was authorized to enlist soldiers from among loyal Arkansas men and became colonel of the First Arkansas Infantry (U.S.). After the end of the war, he received a brevet promotion to brigadier general. Although he was elected to Congress from Arkansas's Third District in 1864 and 1866, he never took his seat. In 1867 he became lieutenant governor of Arkansas and afterward served as secretary of state. James Johnson was active in the establishment of the Arkansas Industrial University, later the University of Arkansas, as a member of the board of trustees.

Francis M. "Frank" Johnson (1842–?) was a half-brother to James M. Johnson and an Arkansas native. He attended school in Madison County prior to the war, serving from the spring of 1862 as a scout and spy for the Union army. Taken prisoner in July 1862, he narrowly escaped execution, first by an administrative delay from Richmond authorities, then by a successful break for freedom by swimming the Arkansas River back to Union lines. He received a commission as first lieutenant in Company B, First Arkansas Infantry (U.S.), and by 1864 had gained the rank of major. He survived the war and returned to Madison County, where he was briefly the county treasurer. *History of Benton, Washington, Carroll, Madison, Crawford, Franklin, and Sebastian Counties, Arkansas: From the Earliest Time to the Present, Including a Department Devoted to the Preservation of Sundry Personal, Business, Professional, and Private Records; besides a Valuable Fund of Notes, Original Observations, Etc., Etc.* (Chicago: Goodspeed, 1889), 1098–99.

JOHN I. WORTHINGTON.

1. In the decades preceding the Civil War, a brisk river traffic operated on the waters of the White River to bring passengers and supplies to Arkansas's interior from ports such as New Orleans and Memphis. The river was treacherous, however, with snags and sandbars that often scuttled steamboats heavily laden with goods. The vessels were also subject to

NOTES TO PAGES 29–34

boiler explosions and related fires, such as the one that claimed the134-foot-long *Caroline* on March 26, 1854. The death toll of approximately forty-five people made it the worst accident along the White River during the mid–nineteenth century. Jim Pouge, "Divers Search for Remains of Wrecked Steamboats," *Engineer Update* (U.S. Army Corps of Engineers) 25, no. 11 (Nov. 2001): 12.

2. The county seat of Carroll County was moved from Carrollton to Berryville in 1869. *History of Benton, Washington, Carroll, Madison, Crawford, Franklin, and Sebastian Counties,* 390–91.

3. In May 1856 Samuel Lee was indicted for murder, and his trial was held in the Green County, Missouri, courtroom of Judge Charles S. Yancey. Appearing as witnesses were W. G. Townsend, W. E. Vines, James M. McNabb, William Duggan, and William Smith. *History of Newton, Lawrence, Barry, and McDonald Counties,* 628.

4. Most likely Bishop is either referring to either gambling with dominos or "chuck-a-luck," a popular dice game of the time.

5. When the Missouri state convention met on February 28, 1861, at Jefferson City, the first order of business was an adjournment to St. Louis, where Unionist sentiment remained strong. Fifty-three of the ninety-nine members were originally from Virginia or Kentucky, and all but seventeen of the delegates had been born in Southern states. Despite these numbers, the Conditional Unionists managed to prevent the passage of an ordinance of secession. John C. Moore, *Missouri,* vol. 9 of *Confederate Military History,* ed. Clement A. Evans (Atlanta: Confederate Publishing 1899), 33–34.

6. Waldo Porter Johnson (1817–85) was a Virginia attorney who moved to Missouri in 1842. Elected to the Senate in 1860, Johnson only served two years before he was expelled for his support of the Confederacy. He then joined the Southern army, was wounded at Pea Ridge, and in 1863 was appointed to the Confederate Senate. Johnson became a personal advisor to Pres. Jefferson Davis and fled to Canada at the war's end. He returned to Missouri in 1867 and practiced law there until his death. Jon L. Wakelyn, *Biographical Dictionary of the Confederacy* (Westport, Conn.: Greenwood, 1977), 257–58.

7. Brig. Gen. James S. Rains commanded the Eighth Division of the Missouri State Guard under Maj. Gen. Sterling Price. Bishop probably had him confused with Brig. Gen. James Edward Rains, a Tennessean who was killed at the battle of Murfreesboro, December 31, 1862. Warner, *Generals in Gray,* 250–51.

8. "Men in buckram" is sometimes proverbially used for nonexistent persons, an allusion to John Falstaff's "four rogues in buckram" from Shakespeare's *King Henry IV, Part One,* act 2.

9. Franz Sigel (1824–1902) was a German revolutionary who immigrated to the United States in 1852. He taught school at New York and

St. Louis and was appointed brigadier general in the Union army by the Lincoln administration in order to solidify the pro-Union German population of Missouri. Although he won promotion to major general in 1862, his military record was lackluster at best. After the war he served as a pension agent in New York City. Ezra J. Warner, *Generals in Blue* (1964; reprint, Baton Rouge, Louisiana State University Press, 1995), 447–48.

10. Mosby Monroe Parsons (1822–65) was another Virginian who came to Missouri. An attorney, Parsons served in the state legislature and was a Mexican War veteran. He was an ardent secessionist and assisted Sterling Price in organizing the Missouri State Guard at the outbreak of the war. Promoted to brigadier general in November 1862, he survived the conflict but refused to surrender, choosing instead to join the Mexican imperialist forces opposing Maximilian. He was killed near China, Mexico, while so engaged. Wakelyn, *Biographical Dictionary of the Confederacy,* 338–39.

11. Most likely 1st Lt. John Still, Missouri State Guard.

12. Nicholas Bartlett Pearce (1828–94) was a West Point graduate and brigadier general in the Army of Arkansas, as pro-Southern troops from the state were known prior to their formal induction into the Confederate army following the battle of Wilson's Creek. Pearce survived the war and, like Bishop, joined the faculty of the Arkansas Industrial University in Fayetteville. Nicholas B. Pearce, "Reminisces of N. D. [*sic*] Pearce, Late Brig. Genl. Commanding 1st Division, Army of Arkansas, C.S.A." 1892, Kie Oldham Collection, Arkansas History Commission, Little Rock.

13. William T. Jones, Company G, Fifth Arkansas Infantry. Jones was later cited for gallantry at the battle of Chickamauga. Desmond Walls Allen, *Index to Arkansas Confederate Soldiers,* 3 vols. (Conway: Arkansas Research, 1990), 2:78; Jon Walter, *Capsule Histories of Arkansas Military Units* [Middle Village, N.Y.: J. F. Walter, 1977], 211.

14. The animosity between the Arkansas and Texas Confederate troops and the Missouri State Guard has been well documented, generally cast in terms of Brig. Gen. Benjamin McCulloch's disagreement with Sterling Price over the deployment of Southern forces in Missouri. Obviously the feeling of betrayal held by Missouri soldiers against the Arkansas troops was widespread throughout the command structure. See William L. Shea and Earl J. Hess, *Pea Ridge: Civil War Campaign in the West* (Chapel Hill: University of North Carolina Press, 1992), 16–19.

15. John Charles Frémont (1813–90) was born in Georgia and attended college in Charleston, South Carolina. Expelled before graduating, he first became a mathematics teacher and then an officer with the U.S. Army Topographical Engineers in 1828. Frémont gained fame as an explorer and helped gain California for the United States in the Mexican War; he served as one of California's first senators. In 1856 "the Pathfinder" became the first presidential candidate of the Republican

Party. At the beginning of the Civil War, Lincoln appointed him a major general and gave him command of the Department of the West. From his headquarters in St. Louis, Frémont issued a proclamation ending slavery in Missouri, embarrassing the Lincoln administration and eventually causing his untimely removal from command (as Bishop describes). Frémont resigned his commission on June 4, 1864, after a particularly lackluster performance in the eastern theater. After the war he held a position as territorial governor in Arizona from 1878 to 1887. Warner, *Generals in Blue,* 160–61.

16. David Hunter (1802–86) was a West Point graduate whose early Civil War career encompassed activity in Kansas. A radical abolitionist, Hunter gained notoriety as the war progressed as an enthusiastic destroyer of secessionist property. He presided over the trial and execution of the Lincoln conspirators in 1865 and afterward lived out his life in retirement in Washington, D.C. Warner. *Generals in Blue,* 243–44.

17. William R. Judson (1810–?) was born in New York and was a saddle and harness maker in early life. A Mexican War veteran, Judson moved to Kansas during the 1850s and held several government positions prior to the outbreak of the war. He was given command of the Sixth Kansas Cavalry on September 10, 1861, and won a brevet rank as brigadier general by war's end. Two of his sons also served in his regiment. After the war he became a real estate dealer in New York, Kansas, and Michigan. H. B. Pierce, *History of Tioga, Chemung, Tompkins and Schuyler Counties, New York.* (Philadelphia: Everts and Ensign, 1879), 234.

18. Stand Waite (1806–71) was a Cherokee planter who had supported the removal treaty when his tribe was forced from Georgia to present-day Oklahoma in 1836. When the war broke out, he raised the First Cherokee Mounted Rifles, a volunteer regiment for the Confederate service. His promotion to brigadier general did not occur until 1864, and he has been identified as the last Southern general to surrender in 1865. After the war he returned to his farm along Honey Creek, Indian Territory. Warner, *Generals in Gray,* 327–28.

19. Dr. Charles R. Jennison (1834–88) was a New York native who first practiced medicine in Wisconsin before settling in Kansas in 1857. When the war broke out, Jennison received a commission as lieutenant colonel of the Seventh Kansas Cavalry. The unit quickly became known as "Jennison's Jayhawkers" and gained a reputation for brutal treatment of Southern sympathizers and guerrillas. Jennison survived the war and became a state legislator from Leavenworth County. William E. Connelley, *A Standard History of Kansas and Kansans* (Chicago: Lewis, 1918), transcribed by Tom Ward and Carolyn Ward, Oct. 1997 (accessed Sept. 2, 2002) <http://169.147.169.151/genweb/archives/1918ks/bioj/jenniscr.html>.

20. Col. George W. Dietzler, First Kansas Infantry.

21. Powell Clayton (1833–1915) came to Kansas from Pennsylvania in 1855 as an engineer. In 1861 he received a commission as captain in the First Kansas Infantry and was promoted to colonel of the Fifth Kansas Cavalry in March 1862. His wartime service included the successful defense of Pine Bluff, Arkansas, in 1863, when his outnumbered command, fighting behind breastworks of cotton bales hastily erected, defeated a superior attacking force of Confederates. Gaining promotion to brigadier general, Clayton remained in Arkansas after the war and became the state's governor in 1868. He also was instrumental in the development of Eureka Springs, Arkansas, and served as ambassador to Mexico at the turn of the century. Cathy Kunzinger Urwin, "Powell Clayton," in *Arkansas Biography: A Collection of Notable Lives,* ed. Nancy A. Williams (Fayetteville: University of Arkansas Press, 2000), 66–67.

22. The full report on this action, which actually took place on May 31, 1862, can be found in *Official Records,* 13:89–93.

23. The Whitney rifle was a .577-caliber muzzle-loading firearm similar to the Springfield and Enfield rifles and had a reputation for accuracy and reliability. These weapons were manufactured by an arms company founded by Eli Whitney in Whitneyville, Connecticut. Wayne Van Zwoll, *Americas Great Gun Makers* (South Hackensack, N.J.: Stoger, 1992), 137.

24. Thomas J. Hunt (1839–?) a native of Washington County, Arkansas, first served as captain of Company B, First Arkansas Cavalry (U.S.). On April 29, 1865, he became the regiment's lieutenant colonel. After the war he served as a state senator and, like Bishop himself, adjutant general of Arkansas. He also became a tax assessor and postmaster at Fayetteville. Wendell P. Beall, "Wildwood Skirmishers: The First Federal Arkansas Cavalry" (master's thesis, University of Arkansas, 1988), 309.

25. James M. Ingram (1826–70) was born in Illinois and likely farmed in Benton County prior to the outbreak of the war. He organized an irregular cavalry company in the months preceding the battle of Pea Ridge. After the defeat of March 8, 1862, most of the Confederate army retreated east of the Mississippi River, but Ingram and his men stayed in the region. An effective raider, Ingram led his guerillas on many forays against the First Arkansas Cavalry (U.S.) and was never captured. He survived the war, but not its violence. While attempting to go to church on September 4, 1870, Ingram was shot and killed by John Stone, the son of a man killed by Ingram's band in 1864. Prier, "Under the Black Flag," 47–54.

26. The only corroborating evidence that this skirmish actually took place comes from a brief mention in a letter written by Bishop himself. See *Official Records,* 13:800.

27. Worthington's "avenging arm" almost survived the war. After his promotion to major, he was killed in action on March 11, 1865, just a month before the Confederate surrender. Ibid., 48(1):1185.

THIRTY DAYS AT ELKHORN TAVERN.

1. Bishop's version is the sole known account on this skirmish; it appears nowhere in the *Official Records*. But a report written in December 1862 confirms that the women of the Murphy family were at home in Huntsville shortly before Christmas. *Official Records*, 22(1):165.

2. Bishop's report on this scout confirms that he too was convinced a large force lingered in the Huntsville area. Ibid., 13:805–6.

3. Sidney Drake Jackman (1826–86) had been born in Kentucky and moved to Missouri as a child. A farmer and Baptist preacher, Jackman headed up a home-guard unit in Bates County during the Kansas-Missouri border strife of the late 1850s. At the outbreak of the Civil War, he recruited another unit for Confederate service and gained a reputation for particular brutality against soldiers and civilians alike. Among his more notorious wartime exploits were the torture of some Federals who fell into his hands and the summary execution of others who surrendered. After the war Jackman moved to Texas, where he served in the state legislature and received an appointment as a U.S. marshal. Prier, "Under the Black Flag," 63–71.

4. Most likely John M. Bell (1829–?), a native of Indian Territory who operated a mercantile business in Bentonville, Arkansas in 1857. He enlisted in Company K, Thirty-Fourth Arkansas Infantry, a regiment raised primarily from Washington County in 1862, and eventually achieved the rank of orderly sergeant. After the war he became a farmer in Washington County and was a census taker in 1880. *History of Benton, Washington, Carroll, Madison, Crawford, Franklin, and Sebastian Counties*, 914.

5. Probably Harriette Vestal, listed in the 1860 census as the wife of Bentonville tavern-keeper William R. Vestal. U.S. Bureau of the Census, "Arkansas, 1860: Population" (Washington D.C.: National Archives and Records Administration). There are no reports of her detainment in the *Official Records*, series 2, which concerns the arrest and confinement of disloyal persons.

6. The battle of Cane Hill was a tactical victory for the Union since Confederate cavalry under Brig. Gen. John Sappington Marmaduke was driven over eleven miles into the mountains south of the town. Out of a force of approximately two thousand, the Confederates reported five killed, twenty-eight wounded, and six missing. Union forces officially accounted eight killed and thirty-six wounded out of approximately five thousand men who accompanied the expedition. But the fight can also be

viewed as a strategic victory for the Confederates since Marmaduke managed to escape with all of his artillery and accomplished Maj. Gen. Thomas Hindman's objective of holding Brig. Gen. James Blunt in place while the Southern infantry made its advance northward along the Cove Creek Road. Kim Allen Scott and Stephen Burgess, "Pursuing an Elusive Quarry: The Battle of Cane Hill, Arkansas," *Arkansas Historical Quarterly* 56, no. 1 (spring 1997): 26–55.

7. Although the text of this order does not appear in the *Official Records,* Bishop confirmed in a letter to Brig. Gen. Francis Herron that he received it on November 22, 1862. *Official Records,* 22(1):787.

8. First Lt. Robert N. Thompson, promoted to captain of Company F on October 20, 1862, resigned from the service on January 30, 1864. Beall, "Wildwood Skirmishers," 400.

9. Capt. Richard H. Wimpy was promoted from first sergeant, Company F, on August 11, 1862, and then promoted to major on May 1, 1865. Ibid., 408.

10. Lt. Col. Dudley Wickersham.

11. Col. Daniel R. Huston.

12. Generals Herron and Blunt were both arrested and charged with disobedience of orders in early 1863, for Maj. Gen. John M. Schofield, their superior, was angry at the two division commanders having forced a major engagement without his approval. The charges were dismissed after a hearing, and both Herron and Blunt were promoted to major general. *Official Records,* 22(2):6.

13. Marmaduke's forces held the summit of Reed's Mountain, blocking the route to the Cove Creek Road, on December 5 and 6. There would have been no way for Blunt's men to "watch the road," as Bishop suggests, though Blunt realized something was afoot along the road beyond the screening force. His mistake lay in his determination that the Confederate attack would come against him from the direction of Reed's Mountain. Ibid., 22(1):60–61.

14. Bishop is quite charitable in his brief description of the First Arkansas Cavalry's record at Prairie Grove. In the early morning hours of December 7, General Herron sent a cavalry force from his division forward toward Prairie Grove. What happened next is best told in the general's own words: "[Herron's cavalry detachment] encamped with the First Arkansas, this regiment having been ordered forward by General Blunt. Just at daylight they were attacked by a heavy cavalry force, under Marmaduke, and after several rounds were stampeded. They came back on me 6 miles south of Fayetteville, at 7:00 A.M., closely pursued by at least 3,000 cavalry. It was with the very greatest difficulty that we got them checked, and prevented a general stampede of the battery horses; but after some hard talking, and my finally shooting one cowardly whelp off his horse, they halted." Ibid., 102–3.

15. Bishop's assessment of Hindman's actions during the battle of Prairie Grove is partly accurate. That the Confederate commander lost his "self possession" is probably too strong a judgment, but it is true that Hindman seemed incapable of making a decision to assume the tactical offensive once the troops had engaged, merely holding his position on the high ground. As one historian has explained it, "Perhaps Hindman had an opportunity during the morning to mull over how his plans had gone awry." William L. Shea, *The War in the West: Pea Ridge and Prairie Grove* (Fort Worth: Ryan Place, 1996), 93.

16. First Lt. Crittenden C. Wells, First Arkansas Infantry Volunteers (U.S.). Wells would later desert his post during the battle of Fayetteville on April 18, 1863, for which he was successfully court-martialed. Kim Allen Scott, "The Civil War in a Bottle: Battle of Fayetteville, Arkansas," *Arkansas Historical Quarterly* 54, no. 3 (autumn 1995): 239–68.

17. Battery F, First Missouri Light Artillery.

CHARLES GALLOWAY.

1. Capt. Samuel A. Boak commanded Company G. Among the members of that unit were Jesse Galloway, Charles's cousin, and James Galloway, another relative. Jonathan Fairbanks and Clyde Edwin Tuck, *Past and Present of Greene County, Missouri: Early and Recent History and Genealogical Records of Many of the Representative Citizens* (Indianapolis: A.W. Bowen, 1915), 238.

2. In the presidential election of 1848, the Democratic candidate, Lewis Cass, lost to the Whig nominee, Zachary Taylor. Cass did, however, carry Missouri.

3. Probably Col. James M. McIntosh, Second Arkansas Mounted Rifles, who, while leading Brig. Gen. Benjamin McCulloch's Confederate cavalry brigade in Missouri, commanded several Texas regiments.

4. Col. John T. Coffee commanded the Sixth Cavalry Regiment, Eighth Division, Missouri State Guard. Organized in the fall of 1861, the unit officially disbanded in the spring of 1862, after which Coffee led a band of irregulars. Sifakis, *Compendium of the Confederate Armies*, 2:152.

5. On August 15, 1862, Maj. Emory S. Foster, Seventh Cavalry, Missouri State Militia, led an eight-hundred-man combined force from Lexington, Missouri. Upon reaching the Lone Jack area, he attacked Coffee's camp and dispersed the Confederate force of about fifteen hundred troops. But the next day the reinforced Rebels counterattacked, causing Foster to retreat to Lexington. Although technically a Confederate victory, Coffee still had to evacuate the area soon afterward, causing what Bishop refers to as his "discomfiture." *Official Records*, 13:238–39.

6. Although the raid on Cassville is mentioned in the list of actions taking place in Missouri, the *Official Records* contain no other corroboration of Bishop's colorful story.

7. Stephen Bess Enyart (?–1862) had served in Archibald Yell's regiment during the Mexican War. When the Civil War began, he received a commission as captain of Company G, Seventeenth Arkansas Infantry. Following the battle of Pea Ridge, the Seventeenth Arkansas was disbanded, and Enyart raised a company of irregulars in Washington County, probably including some veterans from his old command. As Bishop describes, Enyart was killed on December 1, 1862. Prier, "Under the Black Flag," 76–79.

8. This raid is not mentioned in the list of actions in the *Official Records*.

9. Peter "Old Pete" Mankins Jr. (1813–99) was born in Kentucky and in 1833 moved to Washington County, Arkansas, where he sold livestock. In 1849 he participated in the California gold rush and eventually returned to Arkansas with a "small fortune." Using his own money in the spring of 1861, he purchased the equipment to outfit a company of Arkansas State Troops that he recruited from the Middle Fork region of Washington County, but by the year's end, he turned the command over to others in order to resume his business activities. The arrest of his elderly father by Union troops sometime before the battle of Pea Ridge helped convince Mankins to return to the war, this time commanding a company of irregulars. His numerous clashes with the First Arkansas Cavalry (U.S.) made him a particular target of its troopers, but he evaded capture and survived the conflict to become "one of the old and highly renowned citizens of the county." Prier, "Under the Black Flag," 54–63.

10. Col. M. LaRue Harrison mentioned forwarding Galloway's report to Maj. Gen. John Schofield as an enclosure, but the report itself was not included in the *Official Records*. Apparently, Harrison's summary of the action was either all that was available when the *Official Records* were being compiled or it was deemed sufficient by the editors. See *Official Records*, 22(1):222.

11. Commanded by Col. Caleb Dorsey, this unit was assigned to Cabell's Cavalry Brigade, Steele's Division.

12. Lt. Col. James Stuart, Tenth Illinois Cavalry, commanded the expedition that returned to the ferry and destroyed the blockhouse on February 5, 1863. *Official Records*, 22(1):228–29.

13. Although Bishop's admiration for Galloway was not eroded by the death of Captain Travis, Colonel Harrison was not as charitable in his assessment. In his official report on the raid, sent to General Schofield, Harrison wrote: "Captain G. [Galloway] disobeyed my orders in two particulars: First, he went to Ozark before going to the canebrake, at [the] mouth of Mulberry; second, he did not surround the canebrake, but took

his command toward Fayetteville, allowing Captain [R. E.] Travis, a junior captain, to make the attack, unsupported, on 30 rebels at Therilkyl's Ferry. Captain Galloway's reputation as a commander of scouts; his thoroughness as a soldier and a man, and his success (in the main) on this and other scouts, have induced me not to place him under arrest, but to reprimand him in the place of it. If Captain G. had followed my instructions implicitly, the whole Mankins gang could and would have been taken in." Ibid., 222. Galloway was promoted to major on March 2, 1864, and resigned from the regiment on March 1, 1865. Beall, "Wildwood Skirmishers," 347.

THOMAS WILHITE.

1. Thomas Montague Gunter (1826–1904) was a Tennessee native and graduate of Irving College. He moved to Fayetteville to practice law in 1853. He served as colonel of the Thirteenth Arkansas Volunteer Infantry during the war and afterward as a prosecuting attorney for the Fourth Judicial Circuit. In 1874 he was elected to Congress, and in 1882 he resumed the private practice of law in Fayetteville. Joel D. Treese, *Biographical Directory of the American Congress, 1774–1996* (Alexandria, Va.: CQ Staff Directories,1997), 1134.

2. Wilburn D. Reagan was a Tennessee attorney who came to Arkansas in 1830. He first settled in Carroll County, where he studied law and taught school. In 1835 he began the practice of law and was twice elected to the state legislature. Apparently a better debater than legal scholar, he had a reputation of being a particularly aggressive barrister. Oscar Eugene Williams, *The Bench and Bar of Washington County, Arkansas, 1830–1960*, Washington County Historical Society Bulletin 39 (Fayetteville, Ark.: Washington County Historical Society, 1961), 9; Hallum, *Biographical and Pictorial History of Arkansas*, 255.

3. In mid-June 1862 three expeditions were sent into Arkansas from Cassville by Brig. Gen. Egbert Benson Brown. Commanding two of the columns were Maj. William H. Miller, Second Wisconsin Cavalry, and Maj. J. M. Hubbard, First Missouri Cavalry. During their foray, they captured a number of Confederate army officers, twenty privates, sixty stands of arms, twelve teams, and twenty-five thousand pounds of lead and powder. Although in his report dated June 27, 1862, Brown mentioned the capture of Judge David Walker, Gunter was not listed among the soldiers taken by Federal forces. *Official Records*, 13:451–52.

4. John P. A. Parks (1808–92) came from Tennessee to Washington County, Arkansas, in 1853. He farmed land near Hogeye along the Butterfield Overland Mail route. In 1861 he was elected to the Arkansas Secession Convention as a Unionist, but like many others he changed his vote when the convention met again after Fort Sumter. He survived

assassination attempts by vengeful Union sympathizers during the war and afterward returned to farming. Joseph C. Neal, *History of Washington County Arkansas* (Springdale, Ark.: Shiloh Museum, 1989), 1265–66.

5. Of all these men Bishop names here, positive information can be established for only two. Alfred Douglas Strickler (1838–1913) was born in Washington County to parents who had come from Tennessee. Their home became the center of a community along the Old Wire Road known as Strickler, and Alfred's father, Benjamin Strickler, served as postmaster in 1860. In the spring of 1862, Alfred enlisted in the Thirty-Fourth Arkansas Infantry but was captured before the war's end and held prisoner for ten months at Rock Island, Illinois. William David Sharp (?–1865) had moved from Missouri to Washington County sometime during the 1830s. He established a farm southeast of Prairie Grove, but the war eventually drove him from the area. He died in Texas. Ibid., 1393–94.

6. Tandy K. Kidd (1810–1862) was a prominent Cane Hill businessman. Born in Virginia, Kidd came to Arkansas sometime in 1840 with his family and slaves. He had the money to purchase various tracts of land in Washington County, especially those with access to running water. In addition to operating a mercantile operation and a tavern, Kidd established a prosperous mill along Jordan Creek, about three miles south of Boonsboro (Cane Hill). It was at this location the incident described by Bishop took place, and it was also likely the site of Kidd's murder on August 19, 1862. Kidd had attempted to placate partisans of both sides during the first two years of the war, but he gained a reputation as hostile to any payment in Confederate money. An altercation over a business deal gone sour with Joel Perry Parks resulted in Parks shooting Kidd in the stomach with a double-barreled shotgun. Parks was reported to have said afterward that he had settled a score with "one damn old union son-of-a-bitch." Forrest Dutton Poorman, "Tandy Key/Kee Kidd 13 November 1810–19 August 1862: His Life, His Family, and His Death," [1999], Genealogy Collection, Washington County Public Library, Fayetteville, Ark., photocopy.

7. William Zinnamon was a thirty-five-year-old farmer from Kentucky with property valued at two hundred dollars in Cove Creek Township. He became a farrier for Company A, First Arkansas Cavalry (U.S.). Bureau of the Census, "Arkansas, 1860: Population"; Beall, "Wildwood Skirmishers," 410.

8. For Hindman's infamous order, see *Official Records*, 13: 835. Rebels and Yankees alike shared Bishop's disgust at the ramifications of this directive. Confederate brigadier general Albert Pike complained that it "deprived me of my command by attempting to make these staff officers wholly independent of me," while Union colonel Graham H. Finch,

in a letter to Hindman, declared the order "an encouragement to rapine and murder upon the part of those in this State, if there be such, so lost to all sense of honor as to avail themselves of your permission to commit such depredations." Ibid., 109, 850.

9. Sutton F. Cotterill is listed as a forty-six-year-old merchant living in Van Buren, born in Alabama, with real estate valued at $2,000 and $5,400 of personal property. Bureau of the Census, "Arkansas, 1860: Population."

10. A Frank Oliver is listed as a thirty-seven-year-old farmer born in Tennessee and living in Lees Creek Township, Crawford County, with real estate valued at $2,000 and personal property at $598. From a partially reconstructed roster of men who rode with the Oliver band of irregulars in northwest Arkansas, six bear the surname Oliver. Frank Oliver apparently had three sons who were captured by a Union guerilla band led by Jess Morton and tortured for information on the whereabouts of their father. Ibid, 732; Prier, "Under the Black Flag," 163, 231.

11. Similar to the expression "catch a tiger by the tail," meaning to get hold of something that cannot be subdued.

12. No corroborating evidence can be found of this encounter in the *Official Records*.

13. Unfortunately for Wilhite, the war had no happy ending. Dismissed from the First Arkansas Cavalry (U.S.) on January 7, 1864, for reasons that have yet to be positively established, Wilhite attempted to return to his home in southwestern Washington County. Shortly thereafter, Rebel guerillas captured him and his father, Hiram, and hanged both men. Prier, "Under the Black Flag," 148–50.

A PROVOST MARSHALSHIP.

1. Bishop's assessment of his duties as a provost marshal predate the official establishment of the Arkansas provost-marshal system in September 1863 by the occupying Union army under Maj. Gen. Frederick Steele. The duties itemized by Bishop are essentially the same, however.

2. Bishop is humorously referring to a popular book of the time by Sir Edward Shepherd Creasy, *The Fifteen Decisive Battles of the World, from Marathon to Waterloo* (New York: A. L. Burt, 1851).

3. The identification of Pin Indians by Bishop is essentially correct. A secret society of Cherokees called the Keetoowahs had formed on April 15, 1859, ostensibly to perpetuate tribal traditions but also to oppose slavery and secession. Whether or not a safeguard issued by a Union provost marshal in Arkansas would have protected citizens from attacks by the Keetoowahs is debatable. Cherokee Nation Cultural Resource Center, "Civil War—A War within a War," *The Cherokee Nation*

(accessed May 20, 2002) <http://www.cherokee.org/Culture/History
Page.asp?ID=15>.

4. William A. Phillips (1824–93) was born in Scotland came with his
parents to a farm in Randolph County, Illinois, at the age of fifteen. He first
worked as a newspaper editor and later became a lawyer, moving to
Kansas in 1855. Shortly after the outbreak of the war, Phillips was commissioned major of the First Indian Regiment. He eventually achieved the rank
of colonel in the Third Indian Regiment and commanded the Union Indian
Brigade from January 1863 to the end of the war. After the war he returned
to Kansas, where, among other clients, he represented the Cherokee
Indians. In 1872 Phillips was elected to Congress. Wiley Britton, "Some
Reminiscences of the Cherokee People," *Chronicles of Oklahoma* 5, no. 2
(June 1927): 180; Connelley, *Standard History of Kansas and Kansans.*

DEWITT C. HOPKINS.

1. Narciso Lopez was a Venezuelan-born Spanish general who led
four filibustering expeditions into Cuba from 1849 to 1851, with the goal
of liberating the island from Spain and preserving slavery. Most of his
forces were paid mercenaries from the United States. In August 1851
Lopez landed at Bahja Honda with a party of 435 men. Two days later
his small army was defeated by the Spanish in the village of Las Pozas.
The survivors from the expedition were executed by a firing squad on
August 16, 1851, and Lopez himself was shot in Havana on September 1.
William Walker (1824–60) was another filibuster. His expeditions began
with an invasion of Lower California in 1853 and culminated in a temporary conquest of Nicaragua in 1856. He made a final, abortive attempt to
conquer Central America in 1860, but after being forced to surrender to
the British navy, he was turned over to Honduran authorities and also
executed by a firing squad. Tom Chaffin, "'Sons of Washington': Narciso
Lopez, Filibustering, and U.S. Nationalism, 1848–1851," *Journal of the
Early Republic* 15, no. 1 (spring 1995): 79.

2. This tale, while colorful in the extreme, is also highly questionable.
Had Hopkins really accompanied Lopez on his final expedition to Cuba
in the summer of 1851, the boy would have been only ten years old. The
details of the expedition are also fictional, for Lopez only entered Havana
after he had been captured.

3. The Union commander of the Neosho garrison was Capt. Joseph
Conrad, Company B, Third Missouri Infantry (U.S.). After their surrender
on July 5, Conrad and his men were paroled by the Confederates and
allowed to return to Springfield. *Official Records,* ser. 2, 3:23.

4. Originally members of the Iroquois Confederation of the New
York State area, the Senecas joined with several other northeastern tribes
in Ohio during the latter part of the eighteenth century. Pressure from

white settlers in Ohio caused the tribes to sign treaties in 1831 that stipulated their removal west of the Mississippi to the Indian Territory on land adjoining neighboring Missouri and Kansas. One community was located at Tiff City along Buffalo Creek and was likely the location of "acting chief" Small Cloud Spicer's home. "The form of the Seneca's political organization in 1860 is unknown, although it seems that the hereditary chief's titles of the Iroquois Confederacy were not represented in any of these western Iroquois." William C. Sturtevant, "Oklahoma Seneca-Cayuga," *Handbook of North American Indians,* 20 vols. (Washington, D.C.: Smithsonian Institution, 1978), 15:537–43.

5. The Pulaski Light Artillery Battery, commanded by Capt. William E. Woodruff Jr. was known by a variety of different names as the war progressed. Among the alternate designations were Totten Artillery Battery, the Third Arkansas Field Artillery Battery, and Marshall's Artillery Battery. See William W. Woodruff Jr., *With the Light Guns in '61–'65* (Little Rock: Central Printing, 1903).

6. Brig. Gen. Benjamin McCulloch gave Montgomery high praise for acting as his aide during the battle of Wilson's Creek. *Official Records,* 3:107. Ironically, the U.S. Army officer who served as quartermaster at Fort Smith prior to its abandonment in 1861 was named Alexander Montgomery. Ibid, 1:656–57.

7. Bishop's superiors were inclined to agree with his assessment of Hopkins's value as a scout. Brig. Gen. John McNeil specifically requested Hopkins services upon his assumption of command in the District of the Frontier on November 2, 1863. Ibid., 22(2):692.

JOHN W. MORRIS.

1. John Campbell (1806–79) was born in Warren County, Tennessee, and moved to Searcy County, Arkansas, in 1837. Although a prosperous farmer and miller, he also taught school and interested himself in politics. He began his political career when he was elected county surveyor in 1838 and also held office as a state legislator and county judge. Campbell served in the Arkansas volunteers during the Mexican War and in 1861 was elected to the secession convention as a Unionist. With the outbreak of war, he enlisted in the Confederate army, first as a lieutenant in the Fourteenth Arkansas Infantry and later attaining the rank of lieutenant colonel in the Niter and Mining Bureau. After the war he returned to Searcy County and served two terms in the state senate before his death. F. Dwight Campbell, "The Honorable John Campbell and his Descendants," n.d., Searcy County Library, Marshall, Ark.

2. John Campbell was one of the five delegates who initially voted against the secession ordinance in May 1861, but he fell prey to the pressure to change his ballot, thereby earning Bishop's contempt.

3. The Arkansas Peace Society was a secret organization of men who wished to avoid service in the Confederate army and to protect their homes and families from marauders. Almost Masonic in its rituals and passwords, the movement was concentrated in Searcy, Marion, Carroll, Izard, Fulton, and Van Buren Counties and could have had a membership exceeding seventeen hundred. Ted R. Worley, "The Arkansas Peace Society of 1861: A Study in Mountain Unionism," *Journal of Southern History* 24, no. 4 (1958): 445–56.

4. These men have been identified as members of the Forty-Fifth Arkansas Militia, part of the Army of Arkansas mobilized by Governor Rector in the early months of the war. Unit members either left the service or were reorganized in the Arkansas volunteers within the Confederate army. James J. Johnston, "Searcy County, Arkansas, during the Civil War," ca. 1963, Special Collections Division, University of Arkansas Libraries, Fayetteville, 14.

5. Morris was appointed third sergeant of Company I, Eighteenth Arkansas Infantry, otherwise known as Marmaduke's Infantry. By the time they had transferred east of the Mississippi, this regiment had been redesignated the Third Confederate Infantry. Johnston, "Searcy County," 168.

6. The Lazzaroni of Naples were the underclass of that Sicilian city, notorious for a brutish lifestyle and easily prone to criminal activity and mob violence.

7. John Wortman Morris did not remain in the Union army to "strike for family and fireside" beyond a few months. Appointed first lieutenant of Company H on July 23, 1862, he resigned his commission on February 2, 1863. He returned to civilian life and died in Searcy County on August 14, 1919, after his eighty-fifth birthday. Shortly before Morris's death, his daughter Margaret published a book on his life, which heavily paraphrases much of Bishop's version. See Margaret Lavina Morris Bromley, *Biography of John W. Morris* (Marshall, Ark., 1916).

PARIS G. STRICKLAND.

1. John Holmes apparently later joined the Confederate army, but his regiment is unknown. Holmes and the unidentified Garrison reported their suspicions about the Peace Organization to authorities in Van Buren County. Johnston, "Searcy County," 14.

2. Lorenzo D. Jameson, first sergeant, Company H, First Arkansas Cavalry (U.S.). Jameson was discharged from the army for disability. Beall, "Wildwood Skirmishers," 359.

3. These men have all been identified as residents of Bear Creek Township. Thornton was listed as a private in Borland's Regiment, Arkansas Militia, and Griffen as a private in the Forty-Fifth Militia. Johnston, "Searcy County," 31.

4. Mark P. Hogan, James D. Shaw, Gibson Parks, and J. J. Dawson were all residents of Bear Creek Township; Terrill Young, Campbell Township; Martin Blair, Sulphur Spring Township; and John L. Russell, Mountain Township. Ibid., 32.

5. John W. McDaniel, sergeant, Company H, First Arkansas Cavalry (U.S.). Beall, "Wildwood Skirmishers," 373.

NORTH-WESTERN ARKANSAS.

1. Sophia Sawyer (1792–1854) was born in Fitchburg, Massachusetts, and had joined the American Board of Missions to serve as a missionary in the Cherokee Nation in the early 1830s. She went with the Ridge family, a faction of the tribe that had supported the removal treaty, to their new home in Indian Territory in 1835. After John Ridge was assassinated on June 22, 1839, Sawyer and Ridge's widow moved to Fayetteville, where they established their home and, in 1841, a school for other refugee girls, the Fayetteville Female Seminary (on land donated by Judge David Walker). Originally established for Cherokee girls, the school eventually accepted white students as well and was an influential institution in the frontier community. Neal, *History of Washington County,* 127–28; *History of Benton, Washington, Carroll, Madison, Crawford, Franklin and Sebastian Counties, Arkansas,* 290–91; William S. Campbell, *One Hundred Years of Fayetteville, 1828–1928* (Fayetteville, Ark.: Washington County Historical Society, 1977), 54.

2. First established as the Far West Seminary by Cephas Washburn in 1842, the Ozark Institute was organized by Robert W. Mecklin after a fire destroyed the original building sometime around 1845. The school, located near the small community of Mount Comfort, "was in existence from 1845 to 1857 and was the second school chartered in Washington County and the twelfth by the Arkansas General Assembly." Neal, *History of Washington County,* 748.

3. Arkansas College was established in Fayetteville in 1852 on land donated by William McGarrah. Robert Graham (1822–1901) was a Christian Church minister from Liverpool, England, who had come to Pittsburgh, Pennsylvania, when he was nine years old. He made his living as a carpenter in his youth, but after working on the original building of Bethany College, an institution founded by evangelist Alexander Campbell, he eventually attended classes and became a preacher. Graham came to Washington County in 1848 and commenced studies at Arkansas College with twenty students who had followed him from Mecklin's school. The institution flourished in the years immediately preceding the war, with an attractive ten-acre campus, a large classroom building with a library, and nearby homes for Graham and his successor, William Baxter. The building was burned to the ground on February 20, 1862, during the Confederate

evacuation prior to the battle of Pea Ridge, and the campus would serve as a focal point for the battle of Fayetteville on April 18, 1862. Graham left Fayetteville in 1860 for Ohio, where he preached for a time, but then resumed his academic career, serving as president of Hocker Female College and the College of the Bible at Lexington, Kentucky. Dwight Eshelman Stevenson, *Lexington Theological Seminary, 1865–1965: The College of the Bible Century* (St. Louis: Bethany, 1964); Neal, *History of Washington County,* 131–32.

4. Often confused with Sophia Sawyer's Fayetteville Female Seminary, the Fayetteville Female Institute had been established by T. B. Van Horne in 1858. Like the seminary and Arkansas College, it was a victim of the conflagration of February 20, 1862. The ruins of its buildings' foundations provided cover for the defending Union troops during the battle of Fayetteville. Neal, *History of Washington County,* 134.

5. Bishop's prediction of flourishing vineyards came to pass. At the community of Tontitown, ten miles northwest of Fayetteville, an influx of Italian immigrants established a colony in 1898. Led by Father Pietro Bandini, the original thirty-five families had increased to seventy by 1909 and, despite local prejudices against their ethnicity, persisted and succeeded in the cultivation of highly abundant truck farms and vineyards. Ibid., 251–52.

6. There can be no doubt that Fayetteville suffered far worse at the hands of Confederate forces than Union during the war. The arson, looting, and pillaging of the town on February 20, 1862, was entirely the work of retreating Southern troops and a few civilians who got swept up in the chaos of the moment. Kim Allen Scott, "Witness for the Prosecution, The Civil War Letter of Lieutenant George Taylor," *Arkansas Historical Quarterly* 48, no. 3 (autumn 1989): 260–71.

7. Elias Cornelius Boudinot (1835–90) was the son of a prominent Cherokee leader and Stand Watie's nephew. Born near Rome, Georgia, he moved with his father's family to Indian Territory, where the elder Boudinot was assassinated for his support of the removal treaty. Elias studied engineering at Manchester, Vermont, and in 1856 moved to Fayetteville, where he studied law with attorney Alfred M. Wilson. He also founded a newspaper there, the *Arkansian,* which supported the Dynasty and secession. He was secretary during the secession convention and during the war attained the rank of lieutenant colonel in the Confederate army. After the war Boudinot tried a number of business schemes, including the construction of a tobacco factory in the Cherokee Nation, which he was convinced could be operated with a federal tax exemption. But white tobacco manufacturers from Missouri complained, and the factory was seized by U.S. authorities, resulting in years of legal wrangling in which Boudinot eventually prevailed. He died in Fort Smith, Arkansas. Edward Everett Dale, *Cherokee Cavaliers: Forty Years of*

Cherokee History as Told in the Correspondence of the Ridge-Watie-Boudinot Family (Norman: University of Oklahoma Press, 1939), 263–64; Campbell, *One Hundred Years of Fayetteville, 99.*

8. Albert Pike (1809–91) was one of the most famous of all nineteenth-century Arkansans. In turn a teacher, newspaper editor, poet, lawyer, soldier, and Masonic scholar, he was born in Boston and received formal training at an academy in Framingham, Massachusetts. He taught school in that state until early 1831 and pursued classical studies on his own, obtaining a reading knowledge of Hebrew, Greek, and Latin. After leaving Massachusetts for the West, he arrived at Fort Smith, Arkansas, in December 1832. Relocating to Little Rock the next year, Pike began a career as a newspaper editor. On October 10, 1834, he married Mary Ann Hamilton, and with her money Pike was eventually able to purchase the *Arkansas Advocate,* a newspaper he edited while studying law. In 1837 he sold the paper to practice his new profession full time. He later served as an officer with Archibald Yell's regiment during the Mexican War. Although Pike, as a conservative Whig, opposed the doctrine of secession, he nevertheless offered his services to the Confederacy once Arkansas had left the Union. Commissioned a brigadier general on November 22, 1861, he worked to build alliances with the tribes in Indian Territory. Pike also saw combat at the battle of Pea Ridge in March 1862, leading a brigade of Creeks, Choctaws, Chickasaws, and Cherokees. But during the following months, he quarreled constantly with generals Thomas Hindman and Theophilus Holmes over their failure to support the Confederacy's Indian allies and excesses in their suppression of civil liberties in Arkansas. The bitterness eventually resulted in Pike's arrest in 1863, and he was taken to Washington, Arkansas, to answer charges against the propriety of his actions. His resignation was eventually accepted, and he served as a justice of the Arkansas Supreme Court. After the war Pike practiced law and edited newspapers in Memphis and Washington D.C., devoting himself to the advancement of Freemasonry. See Walter Lee Brown, *A Life of Albert Pike* (Fayetteville: University of Arkansas Press, 1997).

9. Elbis, roughly analogous in Islam to Lucifer in Judeo-Christian traditions, once lived in Azazil, a heavenly kingdom closest to God. But after he rebelled when commanded to bow down to Adam, the first man, God punished Elbis by casting him out of Azazil and into hell. Lewis Spence, *An Encyclopedia of Occultism* (New York: Carol, 1996), 133.

10. Saint Peray was unofficially acknowledged as the patron of drink and wine, glorified in a poem by Thomas William Parsons. Thomas R. Lounsbury, ed., *Yale Book of American Verse* (New Haven: Yale University Press, 1912), 146.

11. Philip Barton Key was the grandson of Francis Scott Key, the composer of "The Star Spangled Banner." A notorious Washington, D.C.,

socialite, Key was gunned down by New York congressman Daniel Sickles on February 27, 1859, for having an affair with Sickles's wife. The sarcastic comparison to "Roman Tully" refers to Marcus Tullius Cicero (106–43 BC), a Roman orator, statesman, and man of letters. At the time Bishop wrote, Key was considered such a notorious character that the comparison to a classical historical figure seemed all the more ludicrous.

12. William Minor Quesenbury (1822–88) was born in Crawford County, Arkansas, and eventually graduated from St. Joseph's College in Bardstown, Kentucky. He made two journeys to California in the 1840s and served in Archibald Yell's regiment during the Mexican War. Quesenbury married Adaline Parks of Cane Hill in 1847, and during the early 1850s, the couple made their home in Fayetteville, where he edited a newspaper called the *Northwest Independent*. A scholarly, witty man and accomplished poet and artist, "Bill Cush" became well known to Arkansas readers through his own newspaper and others that reprinted his columns. During the Civil War, he served as an Indian commissioner for the Confederate government and as brigade quartermaster, with the rank of major, for General Pike. Sometime after the war he moved to Neosho, Missouri, where he died in 1888. Beulah Blake, "A Sketch of the Life of W. M. Quesenbury (Bill Cush) 1822–1888," *Arkansas Historical Quarterly* 4, no.3 (autumn 1945): 315–16; Pat Donat, "Adaline Quesenbury's Diary," *Flashback* 27, no. 4 (Nov. 1977): 37–46.

13. Warren Hastings (1732–1818) was the first governor-general of British India. He began his career in 1750 as a clerk for the East India Company in Calcutta. In 1773 he became governor-general and greatly expanded the power of the company. Hastings assumed much authority himself and used military force to prevent a French incursion in the Bengal Province, thereby saving India exclusively for the British. Yet Hastings's heavy-handed administration had alienated many of his fellow country-men, including Sir Phillip Francis, whom he had wounded during a duel. Resigning his position in 1784 and returning to England, Hastings had to face impeachment for his actions. His trial, pressed by Francis and other influential British politicians, lasted more than seven years before Hastings was acquitted. Melanie Perry, ed. *Chambers Biographical Dictionary*, 6th ed. (New York: Larousse, Kingfisher, Chambers, 1997), 847.

14. Cyrus G. Gilbreath (1808–80) was a native of North Carolina who came to Arkansas in 1833. Farming first in Independence County, Gilbreath moved to Washington County in 1835 and thereafter pros-pered. He also served as a justice of the peace and county court judge. Gilbreath's son, Stephen, serviced in the First Arkansas Cavalry (U.S.). *History of Benton, Washington, Carroll, Madison, Crawford, Franklin, and Sebastian Counties*, 942; Neal, *History of Washington County*, 1506.

15. Little is known of William R. Dye other than his membership in the West Fork Christian Church and marriage to Mary J. Peerson

(1839–98). W. D. Dye, another signer of this document, was obviously a relative but otherwise unidentifiable. Neal, *History of Washington County,* 1275.

16. John Calvin Stockburger (1829–?) was born in Stokes County, North Carolina, and came to Washington County in 1852. Stockburger homesteaded land on Round Mountain, about four miles northeast of West Fork, eventually expanding his holdings to 410 acres. He also practiced medicine and was a ruling elder in the Cumberland Presbyterian Church. *History of Benton, Washington, Carroll, Madison, Crawford, Franklin, and Sebastian Counties,* 1022; Neal, *History of Washington County,* 1163–64.

17. David Elbert Robinson, was born in Dickson County, Tennessee, and later moved first to Illinois, then to Arkansas. An U.S. Army veteran, he served one year in the Seminole War before wedding Mary Harrer in March 1841. He had been a Whig during the years preceding the Civil War and was an ardent Republican Party member for the remainder of his life. Robinson was also a member of the Christian Church. *History of Benton, Washington, Carroll, Madison, Crawford, Franklin, and Sebastian Counties,* 1012; Neal, *History of Washington County,* 1070.

18. Alexander W. Reed (1825–94) was born in Tennessee and moved to Richland County, Arkansas, in his youth. He worked as a blacksmith with his father until 1840, and in 1861 he married Elizabeth McGarrah, a former student of the Fayetteville Female Seminary and a daughter of William McGarrah, one of Fayetteville's earliest settlers. Reed was nearly killed during the war when bushwhackers raided his farm for food. *History of Benton, Washington, Carroll, Madison, Crawford, Franklin, and Sebastian Counties, Arkansas,* 1007–8; Neal, *History of Washington County,* 1108, 1238, 1303–4.

19. John A. Rutherford arrived in Washington County prior to 1830 and married Winifred Grigsby. One of their daughters, Julia, married William Hugh Campbell, who eventually enlisted in the Confederate army. Neal, *History of Washington County,* 896–97, 960.

20. Thomas McKnight (1823–?) was a Washington County farmer originally from Lawrence County, Arkansas. A Mexican War veteran, McKnight married Elizabeth Bloyd after his return home in 1848. In 1862 he enlisted in Company A, First Arkansas Cavalry (U.S.), but only served a year before receiving a discharge for disability. McKnight survived the war, including raids on his farm by bushwhackers, and is considered one of the founders of the town of West Fork. Like most of the other signers of this document, he was a member of the Christian Church. Ibid., 859; *History of Benton, Washington, Carroll, Madison, Crawford, Franklin, and Sebastian Counties,* 981.

21. Bishop is referring to a poem by Lydia Marie Child (1802–80), a Boston writer, poet, and abolitionist.

22. This is a quote from Virgil's *Aeneid,* Book 6, lines 126–29:

> The way down to Avernus (hell) is easy:
> night and day, the door of the dark god is open;
> but to go back and return to the upper air,
> this is a task, this is work.

23. Alfred McIlroy Wilson (1817–1907) came to Fayetteville from Tennessee in 1837 and practiced law. He served a term in the state legislature in 1848 and in 1852 was appointed U.S. district attorney for the Western District of Arkansas. He was a supporter of secession, and although his home was destroyed during the war, he personally survived. Wilson had a reputation for fairness and honesty that served him well in the postwar era, and Republican president Benjamin Harrison appointed the former secessionist to the Cherokee Commission in 1889. He quit the practice of law around 1894 and lived out his days peacefully in Fayetteville. Campbell, *One Hundred Years of Fayetteville,* 92; *Fayetteville Daily Democrat,* July 5, 1907.

24. A reference to Shakespeare's *Macbeth.* According to the prophecy of the witches in act 4, scene 1, Macbeth would only meet his doom when Birnam Wood came "marching" to Dunsinane, his residence.

25. "The health of the body is the most important thing when in trouble."

26. Capt. William C. Parker, Company I, First Arkansas Infantry (U.S.). Ironically, in addition to the bullet that cost Parker his eye (described by Bishop later in this chapter), the captain was again wounded in the head during the battle of Fayetteville, April 18, 1863.

27. Many members of the White family appear to have settled in Mount Magazine, Johnson (now in Logan) County, Arkansas, about 1857. Originally from Georgia, the family's several brothers included George A. White (1839–?) and Henry Harrison "Tip" White (1840–?), both of whom served in Company E, First Arkansas Cavalry (U.S.). Beall, "Wildwood Skirmishers," 405–6.

28. The Lee family had come from Tennessee before moving to Franklin County, Arkansas, around 1857. James H. Lee and Sir William Lee were privates in Company E, First Arkansas Cavalry (U.S.). James died on September 26, 1862, and Sir William was discharged for disability on February 1, 1863, dying shortly thereafter. Ibid., 366–67.

29. Levastus McKinney Lee (1843–ca. 1910) also served in Company E. He survived the war and later moved to Texas. U.S. Bureau of the Census, "Red River County, Texas, 1900: Population" (Washington D.C.: National Archives and Records Administration); U.S. Bureau of the Census, "Fannin County, Texas, 1910: Population." Other Lees in Company E were Landsden W. Lee and John S. Lee. Beall, "Wildwood Skirmishers," 366–67.

30. Bishop's assessment of Fayetteville merchant Stephen Bedford can be corroborated by at least two sources. That he had initially opposed

secession is evidenced by his outspoken opposition to the secession convention at a meeting on February 2, 1861, called to consider the matter, and his varied career background is confirmed in a letter dated January 17, 1863, by Fred Russell, who was the son of a surgeon at the post of Fayetteville. Russell's letter confirms that the Bedford family was opposed to taking the loyalty oath imposed by Provost Marshal Bishop, and it likely led to Stephen's arrest. *History of Benton, Washington, Carroll, Madison, Crawford, Franklin, and Sebastian Counties,* 204–5; Shea, "Aftermath of Prairie Grove," 345–61.

31. "Colonel" Henry Rieff (1823–74) was born in Wilson County, Tennessee, and was one of Fayetteville's successful merchants before the war. He is often confused for Americus V. Rieff, who served with Monroe/Fagan's Arkansas Cavalry and eventually rose to the rank of lieutenant colonel himself. Jonathon Kennon Smith, *Death Notices from the Christian Advocate, Nashville Tennessee, 1874–1876* (Jackson, Tenn.: J. K. T. Smith, 2000).

32. George W. M. Reed (1830–97) was born near Roseville in Franklin County, Arkansas. After moving to Washington County, Reed began a career as a merchant. He served for six years as clerk of the circuit court and was captain of Company D, First Arkansas Cavalry (U.S.). Afterward he made his home in Fayetteville, where he was postmaster, a land agent, and a pension agent for a number of years. An active Mason, Reed was also a member of the Travis Post, Grand Army of the Republic. *History of Benton, Washington, Carroll, Madison, Crawford, Franklin, and Sebastian Counties,* 1007–8; Campbell, *One Hundred Years of Fayetteville,* 101.

33. Jesse M. Gilstrap was a miller in the Narrows (present-day Mountainburg). Jesse and his three brothers were all Unionists, though their father did not share in their sentiments. Jesse raised one of the first companies for the First Arkansas Cavalry (U.S.), which became Company D under his captaincy. His brother Thomas John Gilstrap became first lieutenant of the company. Jesse was discharged from the service in 1863, but he survived the war to serve briefly in the state legislature before his death in 1866. Jesse was also the brother-in-law of Reuben Beele Burrows, a private of Company A, First Arkansas Cavalry (U.S.), who was killed in the battle of Fayetteville, April 18, 1863. Neal, *History of Washington County,* 891; Prier, "Under the Black Flag," 300.

34. Thomas John Gilstrap was the first lieutenant of Company D, First Arkansas Cavalry (U.S.), and died on November 1, 1862. His two younger brothers, Benjamin and Wesley, were also in the unit. Prier, "Under the Black Flag," 300.

35. Samuel P. Lane (1817–?) was from Tennessee and an early settler along Richland Creek, Madison County, Arkansas. Neal, *History of Washington County,* 1170.

36. Jacob E. Yoes (1839–1906) was a native of Washington County, Arkansas. He worked as a lead miner in Granby, Missouri, in 1856, but he returned to Washington County, where he married and started a farm near Signal Mountain. Yoes served in Company D, First Arkansas Cavalry (U.S.), and attained the rank of sergeant. After the battle of Prairie Grove, Yoes spent a great deal of his time on "detached duty," and he became notorious as a Union guerilla, rumored to have killed fifty men. He survived the war and became sheriff of Washington County, a state representative in 1868, and a successful businessman. Prier, "Under the Black Flag," 142–45.

37. Frank Crawford Armstrong (1835–1909) was the son of a U.S. Army officer and born in Indian Territory. He attended the Holy Cross Academy in Massachusetts and accepted a commissioned as a regular-army officer after graduation. Initially, Armstrong wore the blue uniform and saw action at the first battle of Bull Run, but he resigned his commission on August 13, 1861, and offered his services to the Confederacy. He served as a staff officer under Brig. Gen. Ben McCulloch at the battle of Pea Ridge and afterward became colonel of the Third Louisiana Infantry. He switched to the cavalry before the war's end and held commands under Gens. Sterling Price, Nathan Bedford Forrest, and Stephen D. Lee, attaining the rank of brigadier general on January 20, 1863. After the war he received appointments as U.S. Indian inspector and assistant commissioner of Indian affairs. Warner, *Generals in Gray*, 12–13.

38. James P. White could possibly have been the son of William H. White, a Washington County farmer who died at the hands of bushwhackers during the war. If so, he had two brothers in the Confederate army. Neal, *History of Washington County*, 1477–78.

39. James H. Stirman was a prominent Fayetteville attorney and merchant. He represented Washington County in the Arkansas Secession Convention, and his cousin Erasmus "Ras" Stirman became a colonel of his own regiment of sharpshooters. Ibid., 818; Pat Carr, *In Fine Spirits: The Civil War Letters of Ras Stirman* (Fayetteville, Ark.: Washington County Historical Society, 1986), 6–7.

40. Thomas J. Pollard was a physician from Kentucky and one of the founding members of the Fayetteville lodge of Royal Arch Masons. He married Mary W. Stirman in 1830, and the couple moved to Fayetteville in 1839. Mary Stirman Pollard obituary, *Fayetteville Democrat*, Dec. 3, 1886; Neal, *History of Washington County*, 792.

41. Washington Lafayette Wilson (1810–64) was a native New Yorker who likely came to Fayetteville in the early 1830s. One of the town's leading merchants, Wilson dealt in dry goods and operated a store on the north side of the town square. He represented Washington County in the Arkansas General Assembly in 1838 and later served in the Mexican War. It was his home that Col. M. Larue Harrison retired to after the battle of

Fayetteville to first compose his report of the action. Neal, *History of Washington County*, 857.

42. Furiben Elkins served as a private in Company A, First Arkansas Cavalry (U.S.). Beall, "Wildwood Skirmishers," 344.

43. Egbert Benson Brown (1816–1902) was born in New York and spent his youth as a sailor. In 1852 he moved to St. Louis, where he worked in the railroad business and supported efforts to keep Missouri from seceding. When he began his military career, Brown became lieutenant colonel of the Seventh Missouri Infantry (U.S.) but was appointed a brigadier general on November 29, 1862. His entire Civil War service was spent in Missouri. Afterward Brown farmed and became a pension agent in St. Louis. Warner, *Generals in Blue*, 47–48.

44. In all, nearly ten thousand loyal Arkansans served in the Federal army, composing four cavalry regiments, eight infantry regiments, and two light artillery batteries. All of these troops served inside the state, where their knowledge of the countryside and inhabitants made them particularly valuable in the type of counterinsurgency warfare Union forces had to wage. Mackey, "Bushwhackers, Provosts, and Tories," 180–81.

45. William J. Heffington (?–1863) was from Tennessee and raised by his unmarried mother, Lousia McBride, but as an adult he took the surname of the man rumored to be his father. He came to Arkansas with his mother's family 1842, and they settled in Yell County. Heffington first enlisted in 1861 with the Seventeenth Arkansas Confederate Infantry and eventually rose to the rank of second lieutenant. On May 20, 1862, he left the Confederate army and returned home, where he raised a band of independent rangers that seemed to prey on secessionists and Unionists alike. By March 1863 Heffington and some of his guerillas joined the Union army as members of the First Arkansas Infantry (U.S.), but after the battle of Fayetteville the following month and the regiment's abandonment of the town, Heffington stayed behind to resume his guerrilla operations. He was finally captured and hanged by the Confederates on August 15, 1863. Prier, "Under the Black Flag," 137–45.

46. William L. Cabell (1827–1911) was a native Virginian and an 1850 West Point graduate. He specialized in his military service as a quartermaster officer, and after he resigned from the U.S. Army in 1861, the Confederate army initially gave him similar duties. Appointed brigadier general on January 20, 1863, Cabell served in the Trans-Mississippi until his capture in October 1864 during the aftermath of General Price's raid into Missouri. He was released in August 1865 and, after settling in Fort Smith, Arkansas, became an attorney. He served four terms as mayor of Dallas, Texas, and also held a commission as a U.S. marshal. Toward the end of his life, he took an active role in the United Confederate Veterans. Cabell is buried in Dallas. Warner, *Generals in Gray*, 42.

ADDENDUM.

1. John S. Phelps (1814–86) was a native of Simsbury, Connecticut, who came to Missouri in 1837. Phelps had read law with his father and began his Missouri practice in Springfield, where he quickly achieved political prominence. In 1840 he was elected to the general assembly from Greene County, and in 1844 he was elected to Congress. When the Civil War broke out, he raised a regiment of volunteers and was commissioned its colonel. In July 1862 he was appointed military governor of Arkansas. At the time, however, the only territory in the state directly under Union control were outposts held in the northwestern corner of the state and the town of Helena along the Mississippi River. Phelps became ill while serving in Helena and soon retired from the army. After the war he was elected governor of Missouri in 1876. *Pictorial and Genealogical Record of Greene County, Missouri, Together with Bibliographies of Prominent Men of Other Portions of the State, Both Living and Dead* (Chicago: Goodspeed, 1893), 55–57.

2. John McAllister Schofield (1831–1906) was born in New York and graduated from West Point in 1853. He taught at the academy after graduating and also at Washington University in St. Louis. When the war began, he helped organize Missouri Union troops and received a commission as a brigadier general on November 21, 1861, commanding the state's militia force. Schofield's next assignment was the command of the Army of the Frontier in 1862, and he went on to become a corps commander in Tennessee. After the war he stayed in the army, though he held a brief appointment as secretary of war in Pres. Andrew Johnson's cabinet. In 1888, after the death of Gen. Philip Sheridan, Schofield became the commanding general of the army. Warner, *Generals in Blue*, 425–26.

3. This proclamation does not appear in the *Official Records*.

4. Bishop's assertion of a disorganized Confederate retreat is not sustained by Cabell's own report, and it hardly seems likely that a "Gilpin-like" retreat would have resulted in the Southern general's return to Fayetteville of a staff officer with a flag of truce to check on the disposition of the dead and wounded. The battle of Fayetteville has been the subject of two in-depth investigations that consider Bishop's account along with other primary sources. See Russell Mahan, *The Battle of Fayetteville, Arkansas* (Centerville, Utah: Historical Enterprises, 1996); and Scott, "Civil War in a Bottle."

5. On July 4, 1863, Lt. Gen. Theophilus C. Holmes led a Confederate force against the Union garrison at Helena, Arkansas, in an ill-advised attempt to divert troops from the ongoing operations against Vicksburg. The attack, launched the very day of Vicksburg's capitulation, was a botched series of badly timed assaults against fortified positions that, in all cases but one, were repulsed before they reached their objectives. The

Confederates lost 1,536 men killed, wounded, or missing from a total force of 7,646. Their defeat allowed Helena to remain a staging area for a successful drive on Little Rock the following September. Thomas A. DeBlack, "1863: We Must Stand or Fall Alone," in *Rugged and Sublime: The Civil War in Arkansas,* ed. Mark K. Christ (Fayetteville: University of Arkansas Press, 1994), 79–84.

APPENDIX

1. These reports appear virtually the same in the *Official Records,* 22(1):305–13.

2. A complete tabulation of all Union casualties can be found in Mahan, *The Battle of Fayetteville,* 47–48.

3. A complete tabulation of all Confederate casualties can be found in ibid., 45–46.

Bibliography

MANUSCRIPTS

Bishop, Albert Webb. Letters, 1866, 1873. MS B54. Special Collections Division, University of Arkansas Libraries, Fayetteville.

Bishop, Albert Webb. Papers, 1861–64. Buffalo–Erie County Historical Society, Buffalo, New York.

Compiled Service Records of Volunteer Union Soldiers Who Served in Organizations from the State of Arkansas. Records of the Adjutant General's Office, Record Group 94. National Archives and Records Administration, Washington, D.C.

Pension Application Files Based upon Service in the Civil War and Spanish-American War. Records of the Veterans Administration, Record Group 15.7.3. National Archives and Records Administration, Washington, D.C.

Reynolds/Thomas Research Papers, 1908–9. MC 770. Special Collections Division, University of Arkansas Libraries, Fayetteville.

Washington County Historical Society Collection, ca. 1833–1995. MC 1368. Special Collections Division, University of Arkansas Libraries, Fayetteville.

NEWSPAPERS

Arkansas Gazette
Buffalo Commercial Advertiser
Buffalo Daily Courier
Buffalo Enquirer
Buffalo Evening News
Buffalo Evening Times
Buffalo Sunday Courier
Buffalo Times
Cortland (N.Y.) Standard

PUBLISHED SOURCES

Allen, Desmond Walls. *Index to Arkansas Confederate Soldiers.* 3 vols. Conway: Arkansas Research, 1990.

Beall, Wendell P. "Wildwood Skirmishers: The First Federal Arkansas Cavalry." Master's thesis, University of Arkansas, 1988.

Biographical and Historical Memoirs of Pulaski, Jefferson, Lonoke,
    Faulkner, Grant, Saline, Perry, Garland, and Hot Spring Counties,
    Arkansas: Comprising a Condensed History of the State . . .
    Biographical Sketches of Their Prominent Citizens. Chicago:
    Goodspeed, 1889.

Bishop, Albert Webb. *An Oration Delivered at Fayetteville, Arkansas.*
    New York: Baker and Godwin, 1865.

———. *What is the Situation Now? A Review of Political Affairs in the*
    Southern States. Buffalo: Matthews-Northrup, 1894.

Blake, Beulah. "A Sketch of the Life f W. M. Quesenbury (Bill Cush),
    1822–1888." *Arkansas Historical Quarterly* 4, no. 3 (autumn 1945):
    315–16.

Boatner, Mark Mayo, III. *The Civil War Dictionary.* New York: David
    McKay, 1959.

Carr, Pat. *In Fine Spirits: The Civil War Letters of Ras Stirman.*
    Fayetteville, Ark.: Washington County Historical Society, 1986.

Campbell, William S. *One Hundred Years of Fayetteville, 1828–1928.*
    Fayetteville, Ark.: Washington County Historical Society, 1977.

Connelley, William E. *A Standard History of Kansas and Kansans.*
    Chicago: Lewis, 1918. Transcribed by Tom Ward and Carolyn Ward,
    Oct. 1997 (accessed Sept. 2, 2002), <http://169.147.169.151/gen-
    web/archives/1918ks/bioj/jenniscr.html>.

Dale, Edward Everett. *Cherokee Cavaliers; Forty Years of Cherokee*
    History as Told in the Correspondence of the Ridge-Watie-Boudinot
    Family. Norman: University of Oklahoma Press, 1939.

DeBlack, Thomas A. "1863: We Must Stand or Fall Alone." In *Rugged*
    and Sublime: The Civil War in Arkansas, edited by Mark K. Christ,
    59–103. Fayetteville: University of Arkansas Press, 1994.

Fairbanks, Jonathan, and Clyde Edwin Tuck. *Past and Present of Greene*
    County, Missouri: Early and Recent History and Genealogical
    Records of Many of the Representative Citizens. Indianapolis: A. W.
    Bowen, 1915.

Goodrich, Thomas. *Black Flag : Guerrilla Warfare on the Western*
    Border, 1861–1865. Bloomington : Indiana University Press, 1995.

Hale, Harrison. *University of Arkansas, 1871–1948.* Fayetteville:
    University of Arkansas Alumni Association, 1948.

Hallum, John. *Biographical and Pictorial History of Arkansas.* Albany,
    N.Y.: Weed, Parsons, 1887.

Hempstead, Fay. *A Pictorial History of Arkansas: From Earliest Times to*
    the Year 1890. St. Louis: N. D. Thompson, 1890.

Herbert, Hilary A. *Why the Solid South? or, Reconstruction and Its*
    Results. Baltimore: R. H. Woodward, 1890.

Hewett, Janet B., ed. *The Roster of Confederate Soldiers, 1861–1865.*
    Wilmington, N.C.: Broadfoot, 1995.

History of Benton, Washington, Carroll, Madison, Crawford, Franklin, and Sebastian Counties, Arkansas: From the Earliest Time to the Present, Including a Department Devoted to the Preservation of Sundry Personal, Business, Professional, and Private Records; besides a Valuable Fund of Notes, Original Observations, Etc., Etc. Chicago: Goodspeed, 1889.

History of Newton, Lawrence, Barry, and McDonald Counties, Missouri. From the Earliest Time to the Present. Chicago: Goodspeed, 1888.

Johnston, James J. "Searcy County, Arkansas, during the Civil War," ca. 1963. Special Collections Division, University of Arkansas Libraries, Fayetteville.

Leflar, Robert Allen. *The First 100 Years: Centennial History of the University of Arkansas.* Fayetteville: University of Arkansas Foundation, 1972.

Lounsbury, Thomas R., ed. *Yale Book of American Verse.* New Haven: Yale University Press, 1912.

Mackey, Robert R. "Bushwhackers, Provosts, and Tories: The Guerrilla War in Arkansas." In *Guerrillas, Unionists, and Violence on the Confederate Homefront,* edited by Daniel E. Sutherland, 171–85. Fayetteville: University of Arkansas Press, 1999.

McPherson, James M. *Battle Cry of Freedom: The Civil War Era.* New York: Ballantine, 1989.

———. *For Cause and Comrades: Why Men Fought in the Civil War.* New York: Oxford University Press, 1997.

Moore, John C. *Missouri in the Civil War.* Vol. 9 of *Confederate Military History,* edited by Clement A. Evans. Atlanta: Confederate Publishing, 1899.

Neal, Joseph C. *History of Washington County Arkansas.* Springdale, Ark.: Shiloh Museum, 1989.

Prier, Jay Anthony. "Under the Black Flag: The Real War in Washington County, Arkansas, 1861–1865." Master's thesis, University of Arkansas, 1998.

Pierce, H. B. *History of Tioga, Chemung, Tompkins, and Schuyler Counties, New York.* Philadelphia: Everts and Ensign, 1879.

Pompey, Sherman Lee. *Genealogical Notes on the 1st Missouri Cavalry, Union.* United States: s.n., 1990.

Reynolds, John Hugh. *History of the University of Arkansas.* Fayetteville: University of Arkansas, 1910.

Russell, Marvin Frank. "The Republican Party in Arkansas, 1874–1913." Ph.D. diss., University of Arkansas, 1985.

Scott, Kim Allen. "The Civil War in a Bottle: Battle of Fayetteville, Arkansas." *Arkansas Historical Quarterly* 54, no. 3 (autumn 1995): 239–68.

———. "The Preacher, the Lawyer, and the Spoils of War." In *Civil War Arkansas: Beyond Battles and Leaders,* edited by Anne J. Bailey and Daniel E. Sutherland, 101–15. Fayetteville: University of Arkansas Press, 1999.

Scott, Kim Allen, and Stephen Burgess. "Pursuing an Elusive Quarry: The Battle of Cane Hill, Arkansas." *Arkansas Historical Quarterly* 56, no. 1 (spring 1997): 26–55.

Shea, William L. "1862: A Continual Thunder." In *Rugged and Sublime: The Civil War in Arkansas,* edited by Mark K. Christ, 21–58. Fayetteville: University of Arkansas Press, 1994.

———. *The War in the West: Pea Ridge and Prairie Grove.* Fort Worth: Ryan Place, 1996.

———, ed. "The Aftermath of Prairie Grove: Union Letters from Fayetteville." *Arkansas Historical Quarterly* 47, no. 4 (winter 1988): 345–61.

Shea, William L., and Earl J. Hess. *Pea Ridge: Civil War Campaign in the West.* Chapel Hill: University of North Carolina Press, 1992.

Shinn, Josiah Hazen. *Pioneers and Makers of Arkansas.* N.p.: Genealogical and Historical Publishing, 1908.

Sifakis, Stewart. *Compendium of the Confederate Armies.* Vol. 2. New York: Facts on File, 1992.

———. *Who Was Who in the Civil War.* New York: Facts on File, 1988.

Stevenson, Dwight Eshelman. *Lexington Theological Seminary, 1865–1965: The College of the Bible Century.* St. Louis: Bethany, 1964.

Treese, Joel D. *Biographical Directory of the American Congress, 1774–1996.* Alexandria, Va.: CQ Staff Directories, 1997.

U.S. House. *Letter from A. W. Bishop, Adjutant General of Arkansas, Relative to the Treatment of Union Men in that State.* 39th Cong., 2d sess., 1866. H. Doc. 15.

U.S. Senate. *Report of the Adjutant General of the State of Arkansas: For the Period of the Late Rebellion, and to November 1, 1866.* 39th Cong., 2d sess., 1867. S. Misc. Doc. 53.

U.S. War Department. *The War of the Rebellion: A Compilation of the Official Records of the Union and Confederate Armies.* 70 vols. in 128 pts. Washington, D.C.: GPO, 1880–1901.

Wakelyn, Jon L. *Biographical Dictionary of the Confederacy.* Westport, Conn.: Greenwood, 1977.

Walter, John F. *Capsule Histories of Arkansas Military Units.* [Middle Village, N.Y.: J. F. Walter, 1977].

Warner, Ezra J. *Generals in Gray.* 1959. Reprint, Baton Rouge: Louisiana State University Press, 1995.

———. *Generals in Blue.* 1964. Reprint, Baton Rouge: Louisiana State University Press, 1995.

Williams, Nancy A. *Arkansas Biography: A Collection of Notable Lives.*
    Fayetteville: University of Arkansas Press, 2000.
Williams, Oscar Eugene. *The Bench and Bar of Washington County,*
    Arkansas, 1830–1960. Washington County Historical Society
    Bulletin 39. Fayetteville, Ark.: Washington County Historical Society,
    1961.
Woods, James M. *Rebellion and Realignment: Arkansas's Road to*
    Secession. Fayetteville: University of Arkansas Press, 1987.

Index

EDITOR'S NOTE: Unless otherwise indicated, all place names are in Arkansas.